Working with Short Stories

◆

Michael Kilduff

Ros Hamer

& Judith McCannon

◆

 CAMBRIDGE
UNIVERSITY PRESS

Published by the Press Syndicate of the University of Cambridge
The Pitt Building, Trumpington Street, Cambridge CB2 1RP
40 West 20th Street, New York, NY 10011–4211, USA
10 Stamford Road, Oakleigh, Victoria 3166, Australia

First published 1991
Reprinted 1991

Printed in Great Britain by Scotprint, Musselburgh, Scotland

British Library cataloguing in publication data
Kilduff, Michael
Working with short stories.
1. Short stories in English – Critical studies
I. Title II. Hamer, Ros III. McCannon, Judith
ISBN 0 521 377951

Text design by Pippa Martin at Design Section

Picture research by Callie Kendall

Contents

Introduction

In producing this book, our aims have been:
- to encourage the enjoyment of reading,
- to develop the ability to read attentively,
- to offer ideas for GCSE coursework in language and literature,
- to produce work suitable for timed assignments.

Our reasons for choosing these particular stories were:
- to stimulate discussion of important social issues,
- to encourage an awareness of aspects of human nature,
- to broaden understanding of different ways of life,
- to give opportunities for discussion and exploration of students' own experience,
- to provide examples of good writing in different styles and with a varying degree of difficulty,
- to introduce techniques which can be incorporated in students' own writing,
- to appeal to both sexes and all abilities.

The work on each story is carefully structured. Preliminary tasks, both oral and written, lead the student to a choice of assignments, some more demanding than others. We have included three very short stories with questions suitable for timed, controlled conditions assignments, believing that it is more satisfying to write about a whole text rather than an extract. The stories are arranged in sequence, with the most demanding at the end. While we have deliberately avoided a thematic approach, there is scope for the teacher to make connections between the stories or with popular novels, plays and poetry. The work lends itself to a variety of teaching methods, including supported self-study, and can bridge the gap between GCSE and A Level examination syllabuses which incorporate coursework.

MK/RH/JM

I

My Sad Face

The title of the story gives you a clue as to its mood. This short assignment before you read the story in full is to help you think about how authors achieve the mood or atmosphere that they want from the very opening of the story. Novelists have the space and the scope to develop their atmosphere, characters and plot. Writers of short stories do not have such scope. They must compress things.

● **Cloze exercise: atmosphere at the beginning of the story**

Below is the opening paragraph of the story. Some words have been missed out and it is your task to compile a suitable list of words to fill the spaces.

Discuss your choices and the reasons for them. Remember, you expect the atmosphere to be one of sadness, because of the title.

         While I was standing on the dock watching the seagulls, my

1   _____ face attracted the attention of a policeman on his

2,3,4   rounds. I was _____ _____ in the sight of the _____ birds

5   as they shot up and swooped down in a _____ search for

6   something edible: the harbour was _____, the water greenish

7   and thick with _____ oil, and on its crusty film floated all

8,9,10 kinds of _____ _____; not a vessel was to be _____,

11,12 the cranes had _____, the freight sheds _____; not even

13,14 _____ seemed to inhabit the _____ ruins along the wharf,

15   silence _____. It was years since all connection with the

16   _____ world had been cut off.

When you have completed this exercise, compare your words with those of the original story. Explain how Böll has created an atmosphere or a mood from the very first paragraph of his story.

Now read the complete story.

My Sad Face

Heinrich Böll

While I was standing on the dock watching the seagulls, my sad face attracted the attention of a policeman on his rounds. I was completely absorbed in the sight of the hovering birds as they shot up and swooped down in a vain search for something edible: the harbour was deserted, the water greenish and thick with foul oil, and on its crusty film floated all kinds of discarded junk; not a vessel was to be seen, the cranes had rusted, the freight sheds collapsed; not even rats seemed to inhabit the black ruins along the wharf, silence reigned. It was years since all connection with the outside world had been cut off.

I had my eye on one particular seagull and was observing its flight. Uneasy as a swallow sensing thunder in the air, it usually stayed hovering just above the surface of the water, occasionally, with a shrill cry, risking an upward sweep to unite with its circling fellows. Had I been free to express a wish, I would have chosen a loaf of bread to feed to the gulls, crumbling it to pieces to provide a white fixed point for the random flutterings, to set a goal at which the birds could aim, to tauten this shrill flurry of crisscross hovering and circling by hurling a piece of bread into the mesh as if to pull together a bunch of strings. But I was as hungry as they were, and tired, yet happy in spite of my sadness because it felt good to be standing there, my hands in my pockets, watching the gulls and drinking sadness.

Suddenly I felt an official hand on my shoulder, and a voice said, "Come along now!" The hand tugged at my shoulder, trying to pull me round, but I did not budge, shook it off, and said quietly, "You're nuts."

"Comrade," the still invisible one told me, "I'm warning you."

"Sir," I retorted.

"What d'you mean, 'Sir'?" he shouted angrily. "We're all comrades."

With that he stepped round beside me and looked at me, forcing me to bring back my contentedly roving gaze and direct it at his simple, honest face: he was as solemn as a buffalo that for twenty years has had nothing to eat but duty.

"On what grounds ..." I began.

"Sufficient grounds," he said. "Your sad face."

I laughed.

"Don't laugh!" His rage was genuine. I had first thought he was bored, with no unlicensed whore, no staggering sailor, no thief or fugitive to arrest, but now I saw he meant it: he intended to arrest me.

"Come along now!"

"Why?" I asked quietly.

Before I realized what was happening, I found my left wrist enclosed in a thin chain, and instantly I knew that once again I had had it. I turned towards the swerving gulls for a last look, glanced at the calm grey sky, and tried with a sudden twist to plunge into the water, for it seemed more desirable to drown alone in that scummy dishwater than to be strangled by the sergeants in a back yard or to be locked up again. But the policeman suddenly jerked me so close to him that all hope of wrenching myself free was gone.

"Why?" I asked again.

"There's a law that you have to be happy."

"I am happy!" I cried.

"Your sad face ..." he shook his head.

"But this law is new," I told him.

"It's thirty-six hours old, and I'm sure you know that every law comes into force twenty-four hours after it has been proclaimed."

"But I've never heard of it!"

"That won't save you. It was proclaimed yesterday, over all the loudspeakers, in all the papers, and anyone" – here he looked at me scornfully – "anyone who doesn't share in the blessings of press or radio was informed by leaflets scattered from the air over every street in the country. So we'll soon find out where you've been spending the last thirty-six hours, Comrade."

He dragged me away. For the first time I noticed that it was cold and I had no coat, for the first time I became really aware of my hunger growling at the entrance to my stomach, for the first time I realized that I was also dirty, unshaved, and in rags, and that there were laws demanding that every comrade be clean, shaved, happy, and well-fed. He pushed me in front of him like a scarecrow that has been found guilty of stealing and is compelled to abandon the place of its dreams at the edge of the field. The streets were empty, the police station was not far off, and, although I had known they would soon find a reason for arresting me, my heart was heavy, for he took me through the places of my childhood which I had intended to visit after looking at the harbour: public gardens that had been full of bushes, in glorious confusion, overgrown paths – all this was now levelled, orderly, neat, arranged in squares for the patriotic groups obliged to drill and march here on Mondays, Wednesdays, and Saturdays. Only the sky was as it used to be, the air the same as in the old days when my heart had been full of dreams.

Here and there as we walked along I saw the government sign displayed on the walls of a number of love-barracks, indicating whose turn it was to participate in these hygienic pleasures on Wednesdays; certain taverns also were evidently authorized to hang out the drinking sign, a beer glass cut out of tin and striped diagonally with the national colours: light brown, dark brown, light brown. Joy was doubtless already filling the hearts of those whose names appeared in the official list of Wednesday drinkers and who would thus partake of the Wednesday beer.

All the people we passed were stamped with the unmistakable mark of earnest zeal, encased in an aura of tireless activity probably intensified by the sight of the policeman. They all quickened their pace, assumed expressions of perfect devotion to duty, and the women coming out of the goods depots did their best to register that joy which was expected of them, for they were required to show joy and cheerful gaiety over the duties of the housewife, whose task it was to refresh the state worker every evening with a wholesome meal.

But all these people skilfully avoided us in such a way that no one was forced to cross our path directly; where there were signs of life on the street, they disappeared twenty paces ahead of us, each trying to dash into a goods depot or vanish round a corner, and quite a few may have slipped into a strange house and waited nervously behind the door until the sound of our footsteps had died away.

Only once, just as we were crossing an intersection, we came face to face with an elderly man, I just caught a glimpse of his schoolteacher's badge. There was no time for him to avoid us, and he strove, after first saluting the policeman in the prescribed manner (by slapping his own head three times with the flat of his hand as a sign of total abasement) – he strove, as I say, to do his duty by spitting three times into my face and bestowing upon me the compulsory epithet of 'filthy traitor'. His aim was good, but the day had been hot, his throat must have been dry, for I received only a few tiny, rather ineffectual flecks which – contrary to regulations – I tried involuntarily to wipe away with my sleeve, whereupon the policeman kicked me in the backside and struck me with his fist in the small of my back, adding in a flat voice, "Phase One," meaning: first and mildest form of punishment administerable by every policeman.

The schoolteacher had hurriedly gone on his way. Everyone else managed to avoid us; except for just one woman who happened to be taking the prescribed stroll in the fresh air in front of a love-barracks prior to the evening's pleasures, a pale, puffy blonde who blew me a furtive kiss, and I smiled gratefully while the policeman tried to pretend he hadn't noticed. They are required to permit these women liberties that for any other comrade would unquestionably result in severe punishment; for, since they contribute substantially to the general working morale, they are tacitly considered to be outside the law, a concession whose far-reaching consequences have been branded as a sign of incipient liberalization by Prof. Bleigoeth, Ph.D., D.Litt., the political philosopher, in the obligatory periodical for (political) philosophy. I had read this the previous day on my way to the capital when, in a farm outhouse, I came across a few sheets of the magazine that a student – probably the farmer's son – had embellished with some very witty comments.

Fortunately we now reached the police station, for at that moment the sirens sounded, a sign that the streets were about to be flooded with thousands of people wearing expressions of restrained joy (it being required at closing time to show restraint in one's expression of joy, otherwise it might look as though work were a burden; whereas rejoicing was to prevail when work began – rejoicing and singing), and all these thousands would have been compelled to spit at me. However, the siren indicated ten minutes before closing time, every worker being required to devote ten minutes to a thorough washing of his person, in accordance with the motto of the head of state: Joy and Soap.

The entrance to the local police station, a squat concrete box, was guarded by two sentries who, as I passed them, gave me the benefit of the customary 'physical punitive measures', striking me hard across the temple with their rifles and cracking the muzzles of their pistols down on my collarbone, in accordance with the preamble to State Law No. 1: 'Every police officer is required, when confronted by any apprehended person, to demonstrate violence *per se*, with the exception of the officer performing the arrest, the latter being privileged to participate in the pleasure of carrying out the necessary physical punitive measures during the interrogation.' The actual State Law No. 1 runs as follows: 'Every police officer *may* punish anyone: he *must* punish anyone who has committed a crime. For all comrades there is no such thing as exemption from punishment, only the possibility of exemption from punishment.'

We now proceeded down a long bare corridor provided with a great many large windows; then a door opened automatically, the sentries having already announced our arrival, and in those days, when everything was joy, obedience, and order and everyone did his best to use up the mandatory pound of soap a day, in those days the arrival of an apprehended comrade was naturally an event.

We entered an almost empty room containing nothing but a desk with a telephone and two chairs. I was required to remain standing in the middle of the room; the policeman took off his helmet and sat down.

At first there was silence, nothing happened. They always do it like that, that's the worst part. I could feel my face collapsing by degrees, I was tired and hungry, and by now even the last vestiges of that joy of sadness had vanished, for I knew I had had it.

After a few seconds a tall, pale-faced, silent man entered the room wearing the light-brown uniform of the preliminary interrogator. He sat down without a word and looked at me.

"Status?"

"Ordinary comrade."

"Date of birth?"

"1.1.1," I said.

"Last occupation?"

"Convict."

The two men exchanged glances.

"When and where discharged?"

"Yesterday, Building 12, Cell 13."

"Where to?"

"The capital."

"Certificate."

I produced the discharge certificate from my pocket and handed it to him. He clipped it to the green card on which he had begun to enter my particulars.

"Your former crime?"

"Happy face."

The two men exchanged glances.

"Explain," said the interrogator.

"At that time," I said, "my happy face attracted the attention of a police officer on a day when general mourning had been decreed. It was the anniversary of the Leader's death."

"Length of sentence?"

"Five."

"Conduct?"

"Bad."

"Reason?"

"Deficient in work-enthusiasm."

"That's all."

With that the preliminary interrogator rose, walked over to me, and neatly knocked out my three front centre teeth: a sign that I was to be branded as a lapsed criminal, an intensified measure I had not counted on. The preliminary interrogator then left the room, and a fat fellow in a dark-brown uniform came in: the interrogator.

I was beaten by all of them: by the interrogator, the chief interrogator, the supreme interrogator, the examiner, and the concluding examiner; in addition, the policeman carried out all the physical punitive measures demanded by law, and on account of my sad face they sentenced me to ten years, just as five years earlier they had sentenced me to five years on account of my happy face.

I must now try to make my face register nothing at all, if I can manage to survive the next ten years of Joy and Soap ...

● Close study of the text: the political and social situation

In this assignment, and in others in this section, you will be looking at the way of life shown in the country where this story is set.

Here are some definitions from *Chambers English Dictionary*. Study them as they will help you with this assignment.

sociology	The study of the structure and functioning of human society.
politics	The art or science of government; the management of a political party; political affairs or opinions.
political science	The science or study of government, as to its principles, aims, methods, etc.
degree	A mark of distinction conferred by universities, whether earned by examination or granted as a mark of honour.

Few tourists ever reach the country in this story. The government discourages them. Few students of Sociology or Politics ever gain permission to study the land and its people. You are a student of both these subjects, studying for a joint degree. Your professor asks you to study this story in order to extract from it as much knowledge as you can about life there.

Your first task is to examine the story and make a list of statements about what a visitor would notice on arrival in the city where it is set. Your title is 'The look of the place'.

Your statements are to be supported by evidence from the story. Set your work out like this:

The look of the place

Statement	Evidence
1. Docks and harbours are neglected.	No vessels, cranes rusted, etc.
2. Few public gardens for pleasure.	Large squares have been constructed for parades.
3. The place is generally colourless.	
4. The national insignia appear everywhere.	

Aim for as many statements as possible. Remember, the task only asks you to list things that a visitor would notice on arrival.

● Making notes and organising material for an essay

Your professor next wishes you to analyse the life of the country and write a paper for him to deliver at a conference he is to attend. He presents you with the following list of quotations to help you organise your ideas. Make notes on each one to help you draft your paper. It should be said that the professor is very busy and has not even put the quotations into any sort of order. You will need to organise your thoughts before writing the first draft.

1. 'it seemed more desirable to drown alone in that scummy dishwater than to be strangled by the sergeants in a backyard ...'
2. 'every law comes into force twenty-four hours after it has been proclaimed'
3. 'there were laws demanding every comrade be clean, shaved, happy, and well-fed'
4. 'patriotic groups obliged to drill'
5. 'all the people were stamped with the unmistakable mark of earnest zeal, encased in an aura of tireless activity probably intensified by the sight of the policeman'

6. 'women ... were required to show joy and cheerful gaiety over the duties of the housewife, whose task it was to refresh the state worker every evening with a wholesome meal'

7. 'it being required at closing time to show restraint in one's expression of joy'

Being a somewhat disorganised student, you lose the second page of quotations given you by the professor, so have to compile your own list in order to continue with your work.

Compile your list and make notes in similar fashion to those you made on the quotations above.

● Written assignment (language and literature): conference paper

When you have done this, write the paper for the professor.

The paper is a descriptive account of life as we see it in the land described in this story.

Your title is: 'Life in the Land of Joy and Soap'.

● Illustrating the conference paper

The paper you wrote for the professor pleased him so much he wishes to have it published in a learned periodical. He invites you to produce illustrations for the publication.

Here are his notes, suggesting things you might use:

> Some ideas for illustrations
>
> motto 'Joy and Soap'
>
> badges, e.g. schoolteacher, farmer, policeman
>
> national colours in flags and notices
>
> tavern signs, love-barracks, goods depot
>
> official lists of drinkers
>
> typical scenes, marches, arrests

Use his ideas and some of your own to illustrate his article.

● Spoken assignments: role play in pairs

In pairs, carry out one of the following assignments.

Either

1. When you have completed your illustrations you test their effect on a

fellow student. This student has not read either the story or the paper and has never heard of the country about which you write, so you have to spell out your ideas very clearly, showing how they match what is known of the country and its people.

Or

2. You show your illustrations to the professor, explaining them and justifying them under his stern questioning.

Your partner assumes the role of listener and questioner i.e. fellow student or professor. You may then reverse roles while your partner carries out the assignment.

Following these assignments, selected pupils may be allowed to enact the part of the professor, in front of the class, delivering the lecture, showing the illustrations and answering questions from members of the audience.

These assignments may be recorded on tape or video.

● Written assignment (language): letter writing

In this assignment you explain what you think about the régime.

Having done all this work for the professor, you are now regarded as an expert on the country and its laws and people. As a consequence, your fame becomes known in the country itself and you are mistakenly thought to be a supporter of the régime. You are invited to visit the country, all expenses paid, as a guest of the government. You are indignant! This misunderstanding could seriously injure your reputation as a scholar and prejudice your chances of employment when you graduate. You decide you must do something about it.

You think that a couple of letters will help in the first instance:

1. To a newspaper – probably *The Times*, but possibly another serious paper. Write, addressing your remarks to the editor. You explain your position, the misunderstanding and your opinion of the régime. Remember, the editor is unlikely to print a very long letter, so you must be concise and direct in your remarks.

2. To the government official who invited you. Write, addressing your remarks to the Foreign Minister or the Minister of the Interior. You make it quite clear, in the strongest terms, that you disapprove of the régime. You

give reasons for your position and you angrily refuse the invitation. You may write at length as there are no constraints as in the previous case.

Set the letters out as business letters, making up suitable addresses and dates.

● General assignments (language and literature)

You can stop being the student now and become yourself again!

Choose one of these to write about. Which one you choose, and how you write, will determine whether the piece is seen as language or as literature coursework, or even as both at the same time.

1. Write a story, 'My Sad Face', as you imagine it might continue.

2. Write a sequel, entitled 'My Sad Face – Ten Years Later'.

3. Write a completely different story set in the country, true to the facts as you know them.

4. Write a story set in another country where things have been taken to extremes in a similar way.

5. Forge a document. You create a document that appears to be several pages taken from the police and interrogator's manual, setting out clearly what they must do when arresting, escorting and questioning a person. Use facts and phrases from the story.

6. What have you appreciated and enjoyed in this story? Back up your ideas by reference to the text.

7. Writers can alert us to dangers we face in society. Do you agree? Use this story, and any others you have read, as a basis for expressing your views.

Where a title is not given, choose a suitable one for your work.

2

A Sound of Thunder

The work on this story is intended to develop your skills in language and literature. Topics covered include the setting of the story, the writing of advertising copy, tasks on descriptive language and verbs. You also look at the idea that change in the past would have had an effect on the language we now speak. You are invited to write questions in the form of worksheets. You also look at language and how it has changed, as well as the language of the story.

A Sound of Thunder

Ray Bradbury

The sign on the wall seemed to quaver under a film of sliding warm water. Eckels felt his eyelids blink over his stare, and the sign burned in this momentary darkness:

TIME SAFARI, INC.

SAFARIS TO ANY YEAR IN THE PAST.

YOU NAME THE ANIMAL.

WE TAKE YOU THERE.

YOU SHOOT IT.

A warm phlegm gathered in Eckel's throat; he swallowed and pushed it down. The muscles around his mouth formed a smile as he put his hand slowly out upon the air, and in that hand waved a cheque for ten thousand dollars to the man behind the desk.

"Does this safari guarantee I come back alive?"

"We guarantee nothing," said the official, "except the dinosaurs." He turned. "This is Mr Travis, your Safari Guide in the Past. He'll tell you what and where to shoot. If he says no shooting, no shooting. If you disobey instructions, there's a stiff penalty of another ten thousand dollars, plus possible government action, on your return."

Eckels glanced across the vast office at a mass and tangle, a snaking and humming of wires and steel boxes, at an aurora that flickered now orange, now silver, now blue. There was a sound like a gigantic bonfire burning all of Time, all the years and all the parchment calendars, all the hours piled high and set aflame.

A touch of the hand and this burning would, on the instant, beautifully reverse itself. Eckels remembered the wording in the advertisements to the letter. Out of chars and ashes, out of dust and coals, like golden salamanders, the old years, the green years, might leap; roses sweeten the air, white hair turn Irish-black, wrinkles vanish; all, everything fly back to seed, flee death, rush down to their beginnings, suns rise in western skies and set in glorious easts, moons eat themselves opposite to the custom, all and everything cupping one in another like Chinese boxes, rabbits into hats, all and everything returning to the fresh death, the seed death, the green death, to the time before the beginning. A touch of a hand might do it, the merest touch of a hand.

"Hell and damn," Eckels breathed, the light of the Machine on his thin face. "A real Time Machine." He shook his head. "Makes you think. If the election had gone badly yesterday, I might be here now running away from the results. Thank God Keith won. He'll make a fine President of the United States."

"Yes," said the man behind the desk. "We're lucky. If Deustcher had gotten in, we'd have the worst kind of dictatorship. There's an anti-everything man for you, a militarist, anti-Christ, anti-human, anti-intellectual. People called us up, you know, joking but not joking. Said if Deutscher became President they wanted to go live in 1492. Of course it's not our business to conduct Escapes, but to form Safaris. Anyway, Keith's President now. All you got to worry about is
…"

"Shooting my dinosaur," Eckels finished it for him.

"A *Tyrannosaurus rex*. The Thunder Lizard, the damnedest monster in history. Sign this release. Anything happens to you, we're not responsible. Those dinosaurs are hungry."

Eckels flushed angrily. "Trying to scare me!"

"Frankly, yes. We don't want anyone going who'll panic at the first shot. Six Safari leaders were killed last year, and a dozen hunters. We're here to give you the damnedest thrill a *real* hunter ever asked for. Travelling you back sixty million years to bag the biggest damned game in all Time. Your personal cheque's still there. Tear it up."

Mr Eckels looked at the cheque for a long time. His fingers twitched.

"Good luck," said the man behind the desk. "Mr Travis, he's all yours."

They moved silently across the room, taking their guns with them, toward the Machine, toward the silver metal and the roaring light.

First a day and then a night and then a day and then a night, then it was day-night-day-night-day. A week, a month, a year, a decade! A.D. 2055. A.D. 2019. 1999! 1957! Gone! The Machine roared.

They put on their oxygen helmets and tested the intercoms.

Eckels swayed on the padded seat, his face pale, his jaw stiff. He felt the trembling in his arms and he looked down and found his hands tight on the new rifle. There were four other men in the Machine. Travis, the Safari Leader, his assistant, Lesperance, and two other hunters, Billings and Kramer. They sat looking at each other, and the years blazed around them.

"Can these guns get a dinosaur cold?" Eckels felt his mouth saying.

"If you hit them right," said Travis on the helmet radio. "Some dinosaurs have two brains, one in the head, another far down the spinal column. We stay away from those. That's stretching luck. Put your first two shots into the eyes, if you can, blind them, and go back into the brain."

The Machine howled. Time was a film run backward. Suns fled and ten million moons fled after them. "Good God," said Eckels. "Every hunter that ever lived would envy us today. This makes Africa seem like Illinois."

The Machine slowed; its scream fell to a murmur. The Machine stopped.

The sun stopped in the sky.

The fog that had enveloped the Machine blew away and they were in an old time, a very old time indeed, three hunters and two Safari Heads with their blue metal guns across their knees.

"Christ isn't born yet," said Travis. "Moses has not gone to the mountain to talk with God. The Pyramids are still in the earth, waiting to be cut out and put up. *Remember* that. Alexander, Caesar, Napoleon, Hitler – none of them exists."

The men nodded.

"That" – Mr Travis pointed – "is the jungle of sixty million two thousand and fifty-five years before President Keith."

He indicated a metal path that struck off into green wilderness, over steaming swamp, among giant ferns and palms.

"And that," he said, "is the Path, laid by Time Safari for your use. It floats six inches above the earth. Doesn't touch so much as one grass blade, flower, or tree. It's an anti-gravity metal. Its purpose is to keep you from touching this world of the past in any way. Stay on the Path. Don't go off it. I repeat. *Don't go off.* For *any* reason! If you fall off, there's a penalty. And don't shoot any animal we don't okay."

"Why?" asked Eckels.

They sat in the ancient wilderness. Far birds' cries blew on a wind, and the smell of tar and an old salt sea, moist grasses, and flowers the colour of blood.

"We don't want to change the Future. We don't belong here in the Past. The government doesn't *like* us here. We have to pay big graft to keep our franchise. A Time Machine is damn finicky business. Not knowing it, we might kill an important animal, a small bird, a roach, a flower even, thus destroying an important link in a growing species."

"That's not clear," said Eckels.

"All right," Travis continued, "say we accidentally kill one mouse here. That means all the future families of this one particular mouse are destroyed, right?"

"Right."

"And all the families of the families of the families of that one mouse! With a stamp of your foot, you annihilate first one, then a dozen, then a thousand, a million, a *billion* possible mice!"

"So they're dead," said Eckels. "So what?"

"So what?" Travis snorted quietly. "Well, what about the foxes that'll need those mice to survive? For want of ten mice, a fox dies. For want of ten foxes, a lion starves. For want of a lion, all manner of insects, vultures, infinite billions of life forms are thrown into chaos and destruction. Eventually it all boils down to this: fifty-nine million years later, a cave man, one of a dozen on the *entire world*, goes hunting wild boar or sabre-tooth tiger for food. But you, friend, have *stepped* on all the tigers in that region. By stepping on *one* single mouse. So the cave man starves. And the cave man, please note, is not just *any* expendable man, no! He is an *entire future nation*. From his loins would have sprung ten sons. From *their* loins one hundred sons, and thus onward to a civilization. Destroy this one man, and you destroy a race, a people, an entire history of life. It is comparable to slaying some of Adam's grandchildren. The stomp of your foot, on one mouse, could start an earthquake, the effects of which could shake our earth and destinies down through Time, to their very foundations. With the death of that one cave man, a billion others yet unborn are throttled in the womb. Perhaps Rome never rises on its seven hills. Perhaps Europe is forever a dark forest, and only Asia waxes healthy and teeming. Step on a mouse and you crush the Pyramids. Step on

a mouse and you leave your print, like a Grand Canyon, across Eternity. Queen Elizabeth might never be born, Washington might not cross the Delaware, there might never be a United States at all. So be careful. Stay on the Path. *Never* step off!"

"I see," said Eckels. "Then it wouldn't pay for us even to touch the *grass*?"

"Correct. Crushing certain plants could add up infinitesimally. A little error here would multiply in sixty million years, all out of proportion. Of course maybe our theory is wrong. Maybe Time *can't* be changed by us. Or maybe it can be changed only in little subtle ways. A dead mouse here makes an insect imbalance there, a population disproportion later, a bad harvest further on, a depression, mass starvation, and, finally, a change in *social* temperament in far-flung countries. Something much more subtle, like that. Perhaps only a soft breath, a whisper, a hair, pollen on the air, such a slight, slight change that unless you looked close you wouldn't see it. Who knows? Who really can say he knows? We don't know. We're guessing. But until we do know for certain whether our messing around in Time *can* make a big roar or a little rustle in history, we're being damned careful. This Machine, this Path, your clothing and bodies, were sterilised, as you know, before the journey. We wear these oxygen helmets so we can't introduce our bacteria into an ancient atmosphere."

"How do we know which animals to shoot?"

"They're marked with red paint," said Travis. "Today, before our journey, we sent Lesperance here back with the Machine. He came to this particular era and followed certain animals."

"Studying them?"

"Right," said Lesperance. "I track them through their entire existence, noting which of them lives longest. Very few. How many times they mate. Not often. Life's short. When I find one that's going to die when a tree falls on him, or one that drowns in a tar pit, I note the exact hour, minute, and second. I shoot a paint bomb. It leaves a red patch on his side. We can't miss it. Then I correlate our arrival in the Past so that we meet the Monster not more than two minutes before he would have died anyway. This way, we kill only animals with no future, that are never going to mate again. You see how *careful* we are?"

"But if you came back this morning in Time," said Eckels eagerly, "you must've bumped into *us*, our Safari! How did it turn out? Was it successful? Did all of us get through – alive?"

Travis and Lesperance gave each other a look.

"That'd be a paradox," said the latter. "Time doesn't permit that sort of mess – a man meeting himself. When such occasions threaten, Time steps aside. Like an airplane hitting an air pocket. You felt the Machine jump just before we stopped? That was us passing ourselves on the way back to the Future. We saw nothing. There's no way of telling *if* this expedition was a success, *if we* got our monster, or whether all of us – meaning *you*, Mr Eckels – got out alive."

Eckels smiled palely.

"Cut that," said Travis sharply. "Everyone on his feet!"

They were ready to leave the Machine.

The jungle was high and the jungle was broad and the jungle was the entire world forever and forever. Sounds like music and sounds like flying tents filled the sky, and those were pterodactyls soaring with cavernous grey wings, gigantic bats out of delirium and a night fever. Eckels, balanced on the narrow Path, aimed his rifle playfully.

"Stop that!" said Travis. "Don't even aim for fun, damn it! If your guns should go off ..."

Eckels flushed. "Where's our *Tyrannosaurus?*"

Lesperance checked his wrist watch. "Up ahead. We'll bisect his trail in sixty seconds. Look for the red paint, for Christ's sake. Don't shoot till we give the word. Stay on the Path. *Stay on the Path!*"

They moved forward in the wind of morning.

"Strange," murmured Eckels. "Up ahead, sixty million years, Election Day over. Keith made President. Everyone celebrating. And here we are, a million years lost, and they don't exist. The things we worried about for months, a lifetime, not even born or thought about yet."

"Safety catches off, everyone!" ordered Travis. "You, first shot, Eckels. Second, Billings. Third, Kramer."

"I've hunted tiger, wild boar, buffalo, elephant, but Jesus, this is *it*," said Eckels. "I'm shaking like a kid."

"Ah," said Travis.

Everyone stopped.

Travis raised his hand. "Ahead," he whispered. "In the mist. There he is. There's His Royal Majesty now."

The jungle was wide and full of twitterings, rustlings, murmurs, and sighs.

Suddenly it all ceased, as if someone had shut a door.

Silence.

A sound of thunder.

Out of the mist, one hundred yards away, came *Tyrannosaurus rex*.

"Jesus God," whispered Eckels.

"Sh!"

It came on great oiled, resilient, striding legs. It towered thirty feet above half of the trees, a great evil god, folding its delicate watchmaker's claws close to its oily reptilian chest. Each lower leg was a piston, a thousand pounds of white bone, sunk in thick ropes of muscle, sheathed over in a gleam of pebbled skin like the mail of a terrible warrior. Each thigh was a ton of meat, ivory, and steel mesh. And from the great breathing cage of the upper body those two delicate arms dangled out front, arms with hands which might pick up and examine men like toys, while the snake neck coiled. And the head itself, a ton of sculptured stone, lifted easily upon the sky. Its mouth gaped, exposing a fence of teeth like daggers. Its eyes rolled, ostrich eggs, empty of all expression save hunger. It closed its mouth in a death grin. It ran, its pelvic bones crushing aside trees and bushes, its taloned feet clawing damp earth, leaving prints six inches deep wherever it set-tled its weight. It ran with a gliding ballet step, far too poised and balanced for its ten tons. It moved into a sunlit arena warily, its beautifully reptile hands feeling the air.

"My God!" Eckels twitched his mouth. "It could reach up and grab the moon."

"Sh!" Travis jerked angrily. "He hasn't seen us yet."

"It can't be killed." Eckels pronounced this verdict quietly, as if there could be no argument. He had weighed the evidence and this was his considered opinion. The rifle in his hands seemed a cap gun. "We were fools to come. This is impossible."

"Shut up!" hissed Travis.

"Nightmare."

"Turn around," commanded Travis. "Walk quietly to the Machine. We'll remit one half your fee."

"I didn't realise it would be this *big*," said Eckels. "I miscalculated, that's all. And now I want out."

"It *sees* us!"

"There's the red paint on its chest!"

The Thunder Lizard raised itself. Its armoured flesh glittered like a thousand green coins. The coins, crusted with slime, steamed. In the slime, tiny insects wriggled, so that the entire body seemed to twitch and undulate, even while the monster itself did not move. It exhaled. The stink of raw flesh blew down the wilderness.

"Get me out of here," said Eckels. "It was never like this before. I was always sure I'd come through alive. I had good guides, good safaris, and safety. This time, I figured wrong. I've met my match and admit it. This is too much for me to get hold of."

"Don't run," said Lesperance. "Turn around. Hide in the Machine."

"Yes," Eckels seemed to be numb. He looked at his feet as if trying to make them move. He gave a grunt of helplessness.

"Eckels!"

He took a few steps, blinking, shuffling.

"Not *that* way!"

The Monster, at the first motion, lunged forward with a terrible scream. It covered one hundred yards in four seconds. The rifles jerked up and blazed fire. A windstorm from the beast's mouth engulfed them in the stench of slime and old blood. The Monster roared, teeth glittering with sun.

Eckels, not looking back, walked blindly to the edge of the Path, his gun limp in his arms, stepped off the Path, and walked, not knowing it, in the jungle. His feet sank into green moss. His legs moved him, and he felt alone and remote from the events behind.

The rifles cracked again. Their sound was lost in shriek and lizard thunder. The great lever of the reptile's tail swung up, lashed sideways. Trees exploded in clouds of leaf and branch. The Monster twitched its jeweller's hands down to fondle at the men, to twist them in half, to crush them like berries, to cram them into its teeth and its screaming throat. Its boulder-stone eyes levelled with the men. They saw themselves mirrored. They fired at the metallic eyelids and the blazing black iris.

Like a stone idol, like a mountain avalanche, *Tyrannosaurus* fell. Thundering, it clutched trees, pulled them with it. It wrenched and tore the metal Path. The men flung themselves back and away. The body hit, ten tons of cold flesh and stone. The guns fired. The Monster lashed its armoured tail, twitched its snake jaws, and lay still. A fount of blood spurted from its throat. Somewhere inside, a sac of fluids burst. Sickening gushes drenched the hunters. They stood, red and glistening.

The thunder faded.

The jungle was silent. After the avalanche, a green peace. After the nightmare, morning.

Billings and Kramer sat on the pathway and threw up. Travis and Lesperance stood with smoking rifles, cursing steadily.

In the Time Machine, on his face, Eckels lay shivering. He had found his way back to the Path, climbed into the Machine.

Travis came walking, glanced at Eckels, took cotton gauze from a metal box, and returned to the others, who were sitting on the Path.

"Clean up."

They wiped the blood from their helmets. They began to curse too. The Monster lay, a hill of solid flesh. Within, you could hear the sighs and murmurs as the furthest chambers of it died, the organs malfunctioning, liquids running a final instant from pocket to sac to spleen, everything shutting off, closing up forever. It was like standing by a wrecked locomotive or a steam shovel at quitting time, all valves being released or levered tight. Bones cracked; the tonnage of its own flesh, off balance, dead weight, snapped the delicate forearms, caught underneath. The meat settled, quivering.

Another cracking sound. Overhead, a gigantic tree branch broke from its heavy mooring, fell. It crashed upon the dead beast with finality.

"There." Lesperance checked his watch. "Right on time. That's the giant tree that was scheduled to fall and kill this animal originally." He glanced at the two hunters. "You want the trophy picture?"

"What?"

"We can't take a trophy back to the Future. The body has to stay right here where it would have died originally, so the insects, birds, and bacteria can get at it, as they were intended to. Everything in balance. The body stays. But we *can* take a picture of you standing near it."

The two men tried to think, but gave up, shaking their heads.

They let themselves be led along the metal Path. They sank wearily into the Machine cushions. They gazed back at the ruined Monster, the stagnating mound, where already strange reptilian birds and golden insects were busy at the steaming armour.

A sound on the floor of the Time Machine stiffened them. Eckels sat there, shivering.

"I'm sorry," he said at last.

"Get up!" cried Travis.

Eckels got up.

"Go out on that Path alone," said Travis. He had his rifle pointed. "You're not coming back in the Machine. We're leaving you here!"

Lesperance seized Travis's arm. "Wait ..."

"Stay out of this!" Travis shook his hand away. "This son of a bitch nearly killed us. But it isn't *that* so much. Hell, no. It's his *shoes*! Look at them! He ran off the Path. My God, that *ruins* us! Christ knows how much we'll forfeit! Tens of thousands of dollars of insurance! We guarantee no one leaves the Path. He left it. Oh, the damn fool! I'll have to report to the government. They might revoke our licence to travel. God knows *what* he's done to Time, to History!"

"Take it easy, all he did was kick up some dirt."

"How do we *know*?" cried Travis. "We don't know anything! It's a damn mystery! Get out here, Eckels!"

Eckels fumbled his shirt. "I'll pay anything. A hundred thousand dollars!"

Travis glared at Eckels' cheque book and spat. "Go out there. The Monster's next to the Path. Stick your arms up to your elbows in his mouth. Then you can come back with us."

"That's unreasonable!"

"The Monster's dead, you yellow bastard. The bullets! The bullets can't be left behind. They don't belong in the Past; they might change something. Here's my knife. Dig them out!"

The jungle was alive again, full of the old tremorings and bird cries. Eckels turned slowly to regard that primeval garbage dump, that hill of nightmares and terror. After a long time, like a sleepwalker, he shuffled out along the Path.

He returned, shuddering, five minutes later, his arms soaked and red to the elbows. He held out his hands. Each held a number of steel bullets. Then he fell. He lay where he fell, not moving.

"You didn't have to make him do that," said Lesperance.

"Didn't I? It's too early to tell." Travis nudged the still body. "He'll live. Next time he won't go hunting game like this. Okay." He jerked his thumb wearily at Lesperance. "Switch on. Let's go home."

1492. 1776. 1812.

They cleaned their hands and faces. They changed their caking shirts and pants. Eckels was up and around again, not speaking. Travis glared at him for a full ten minutes.

"Don't look at me," cried Eckels. "I haven't done anything."

"Who can tell?"

"Just ran off the Path, that's all, a little mud on my shoes – what do you want me to do – get down and pray?"

"We might need it. I'm warning you, Eckels, I might kill you yet. I've got my gun ready."

"I'm innocent. I've done nothing!"

1999. 2000. 2055.

The Machine stopped.

"Get out," said Travis.

The room was there as they had left it. But not the same as they had left it. The same man sat behind the same desk. But the same man did not quite sit behind the same desk.

Travis looked around swiftly. "Everything okay here?" he snapped.

"Fine! Welcome home!"

Travis did not relax. He seemed to be looking at the very atoms of the air itself, at the way the sun poured through the one high window.

"Okay, Eckels, get out. Don't ever come back."

Eckels could not move.

"You heard me," said Travis. "What're you *staring* at?"

Eckels stood smelling of the air, and there was a thing to the air, a chemical taint so subtle, so slight, that only a faint cry of his sublimal senses warned him it was there. The colours, white, grey, blue, orange, in the wall, in the furniture, in the sky beyond the window, were ... were ... And there was a *feel*. His flesh twitched. His hands twitched. He stood drinking the oddness with the pores of his body. Somewhere, someone must have been screaming one of those whistles that only a dog can hear. His body screamed silence in return. Beyond this room, beyond this wall, beyond this man who was not quite the same man seated at this desk that was not quite the same desk ... lay an entire world of streets and people. What sort of world it was now, there was no telling. He could feel them moving there, beyond the walls, almost, like so many chess pieces blown in a dry wind...

But the immediate thing was the sign painted on the office wall, the same sign he had read earlier today on first entering.

Somehow, the sign had changed:

TYME SEFARI INC.

SEFARIS TU ANY YEER EN THE PAST.

YU NAIM THE ANIMALL.

WEE TAEK YU THAIR.

YU SHOOT ITT.

Eckels felt himself fall into a chair. He fumbled crazily at the thick slime on his boots. He held up a clod of dirt, trembling. "No, it *can't* be. Not a *little* thing like that. No!"

Embedded in the mud, glistening green and gold and black, was a butterfly, very beautiful, and very dead.

"Not a little thing like *that* ! Not a butterfly!" cried Eckels.

It fell to the floor, an exquisite thing, a small thing that could upset balances and knock down a line of small dominoes and then big dominoes and then gigantic dominoes, all down the years across Time. Eckels' mind whirled. It *couldn't* change things. Killing one butterfly couldn't be *that* important! Could it?

His face was cold. His mouth trembled, asking: "Who – who won the presidential election yesterday?"

The man behind the desk laughed. "You joking? You know damn well. Deutscher, of course! Who else? Not that damn weakling Keith. We got an iron man now, a man with guts, by God!" The official stopped. "What's wrong?"

Eckels moaned. He dropped to his knees. He scrabbled at the golden butterfly with shaking fingers. "Can't we," he pleaded to the world, to himself, to the officials, to the Machine, "can't we take it *back*, can't we *make* it alive again? Can't we start over? Can't we ..."

He did not move. Eyes shut, he waited, shivering. He heard Travis breathe loud in the room; he heard Travis shift his rifle, click the safety catch, and raise the weapon.

There was a sound of thunder.

The assignments that follow can be done in pairs or groups, although part of each task should be done individually.

- ## Devising a questionnaire: the situation at the beginning of the story

Stories are set in time, and writers make them realistic by the way in which they imagine the events in the story.

Make a list of ten questions, where the answers would tell you the location, time, characters and political situation at the beginning of the story.

Set your questions out as a questionnaire, with space for someone to write in the answers. Your questions will be satisfactory only if the answers are the ones you wanted to get. Any question that is not clear, or produces an ambiguous response, should be re-written.

If you are working in pairs, work alone on your list. If you are working in a group of four, work in pairs. The idea is to have someone else to try your questions out on.

Set it out like this:

Questionnaire

Set by .... Answered by .... Checked by ....

Question 1   Answer 1
In which country is the story set?   ....

Question 2   Answer 2
....

Question 3   Answer 3
....

Question 4   Answer 4
....

Question 5   Answer 5
....

Question 6   Answer 6
....

Question 7   Answer 7
....

Question 8   Answer 8
....

Question 9   Answer 9
....

Question 10   Answer 10

....

Comment on the effectiveness of my questions: ....

....

....

....

● Preparing publicity material

You work for the advertising agency that prepares all the publicity for Time Safari, Inc.

Using words, phrases and ideas from the story, illustrations and pictures cut out from magazines, and drawings and slogans of your own, prepare materials for an advertising campaign.

The materials will include: a poster, a brochure, a newspaper advertisement, and a luggage label.

Remember, in writing your copy, you are appealing chiefly to hunters, but must attract them with things other than just animals to shoot.

Before Time Safari, Inc. allow people to travel, they check very carefully that they are fit, and they ensure that customers know the strict rules and conditions laid down before bookings are made.

Design a form that customers must sign making clear all the rules and conditions under which bookings are made. Leave plenty of space for customers to answer your questions and to sign that they accept all conditions imposed upon them.

When you have finished this assignment you should have a dossier containing the following items:

> a poster advertising Time Safari, Inc.,
>
> a brochure giving full details,
>
> a newspaper advertisement,
>
> a luggage label,
>
> a booking form.

- ## Spoken assignment: Role play in pairs

Explain to your partner, the chief executive of Time Safari, Inc., the ideas behind the advertising materials you have prepared for his/her company. Be prepared to answer stiff questions. No-one is going to pay for advertising materials if they are unlikely to appeal to the public. You need good logos, slogans, illustrations and, above all, good copy.

When you have completed your explanation, change roles to use your partner's material.

This assignment may be recorded on tape or video.

- ## Close study of the text: descriptive writing

Work in groups or pairs in preparation for a written assignment.

Re-read the description of Tyrannosaurus rex, from the part of the story that starts 'It came on great oiled, resilient, striding legs.' to 'It moved into a sunlit arena warily, its beautifully reptile hands feeling the air.'

What ideas do you get from the following phrases?
Make brief notes on the ideas that are discussed:

(a) 'a great evil god',

(b) 'its delicate watchmaker's claws',

(c) 'each lower leg was a piston',

(d) 'thick ropes of muscle',

(e) 'each thigh was a ton of meat, ivory and steel mesh',

(f) 'the head itself, a ton of sculptured stone',

(g) 'eyes rolled, ostrich eggs',

(h) 'it closed its mouth, a death grin'.

In the description of Tyrannosaurus rex, the writer uses *similes* to make clear to us what is happening. Here are some:

- 'a gleam of pebbled skin like the mail of a terrible warrior',
- 'hands which might pick up and examine men like toys',
- 'a fence of teeth like daggers'.

Explain to each other what ideas you get from them. If necessary, draw sketches to show what you see in your mind's eye.

● Written assignment (language): descriptive writing

Using ideas gained during this discussion, write a description of your own monster, using images and similes to create a powerful impression.

Give your monster an impressive and royal-sounding name. (Remember that 'rex' means 'king' in Latin.)

You could make comparisons between your monster and some of the following objects and ideas:

- a huge steam engine,
- a black thunder cloud,
- a volcano about to erupt,
- a moving mountain,
- polished marble or shining gold,
- razor-sharp weapons,
- a graceful dancer.

Describe the smaller, more delicate features of your monster as Bradbury did in his story. Make your monster move.

If there is time, illustrate your description with a drawing or sketch.

Your title is: 'Description of my Monster'.

● Descriptive writing: a study of verbs

Ray Bradbury uses verbs which are appropriate to the circumstances. Early in the story he writes:

> 'Eckels remembered the wording in the advertisements to the letter. Out of chars and ashes, out of dust and coals, like golden salamanders, the old years, the green years, might *leap*; roses sweeten the air, white hair turn Irish-black, wrinkles *vanish*; all, everything *fly* back to seed, *flee* death, *rush* down to their beginnings, suns rise in western skies and set in glorious easts, moons eat themselves opposite to the custom, all and everything cupping one in another like Chinese boxes, rabbits into hats, all and everything returning to the fresh death, the seed death, the green death, to the time before the beginning. A touch of a hand might do it, the merest touch of a hand.'

The verbs in italics in this passage all indicate the speed with which things can happen. Discuss each one and show why it is appropriate to the circumstance. Writing them out in a list might help you to see the sequence more clearly:

Verb   **Why it is appropriate**

leap

vanish

fly

flee

rush

Ray Bradbury uses very carefully-chosen words to enable us to appreciate movement.

Below are some examples. Identify where they come from in the story and explain carefully the different sorts of movement these particular words evoke.

Re-arrange the order of the six examples so that the verb with the least violent movement is top of the list and the one with the most violent at the bottom.

Be prepared to mime the different movements to the class or the members of your group:
- clawing damp earth,
- gliding ballet step,
- tiny insects wriggled,
- he took a few steps, blinking, shuffling,
- the monster lashed its armoured tail,
- the monster lunged forward.

● Written assignment (language): descriptive writing

Describe a playground at break, a storm at sea, a wind in a forest, a wedding group after a ceremony.

Concentrate on strong, carefully chosen words. As movement increases, so your words should convey greater strength. Use sequences of verbs like the 'leap ... rush' list you discussed above.

Remember your previous attempt at descriptive writing.

Your title is: 'Descriptions with Movement'.

● Close study of the text: predicting the outcome of the story

This story moves to a climax and a decisive ending but what happens at the end seems inevitable to those who detected warning signs.

Pick out three sentences which warn us that Eckels is probably going to step off the path and bring about disaster. Discuss your choice of sentences.

● Written assignment (language): report writing

Either

1. Write Travis's report on why he shot Eckels. Set it out as you think it might be done on company notepaper. Use any logos you designed previously to make the report look like an authentic document.

Or

2. Draw a diagram or a chart starting with the dead butterfly, and try to show how its death changed the world. Use Travis's advice on the death of a mouse as a guide.

Write a report, to accompany your diagram, explaining the change. Ensure that the events you plot slowly increase in magnitude or importance. In other words, there should be some kind of climax achieved in your report as you record change.

● Devising a questionnaire: the situation at the end of the story

In an earlier assignment you made up a list of ten questions, the answers to which established the location, time, characters and political situation at the beginning of the story.

Do the same now for the situation as it exists at the end of the story. As before, set your questions out in the form of a questionnaire, with space for someone to write in the answers. Any question which is not clear, or which produces an ambiguous response, should be re-written.

Ask yourself how Ray Bradbury has brought us through the change.

● Written assignment (literature): appreciation

Either

1. Using the ideas you have discussed, the notes you have made, and all the things you have learned from the tasks set, write an appreciation of the story, saying what you think of the story and the author's way of writing.

Or

2. Imagine you are speaking to the pupils of another class who have not read this story. Write the text of your speech saying what lies in store for that class. But do not give away the ending!

● Study of language change

The tasks set here explore the idea that changes in the past, small or large, could have had an effect on the language we now speak.

Discuss and answer the questions that follow, bearing in mind that the focus of your interest has been directed by reading *A Sound of Thunder*.

1. The first language spoken in Britain was probably Celtic. The Celts were driven to the remote western parts of these islands by invaders from the east. It is in these areas that words from Celtic and the Celtic language itself live on.

Explain why you think three-quarters of the place names in Cornwall are of Celtic origin, while only about 2% of place names in Suffolk are Celtic. A small sketch map of the British Isles might help you to explain clearly.

2. Consider the following:

Over the 8th, 9th and 10th centuries there was a series of invasions by people we refer to as the Vikings. They did not all speak the same language. Some settled in the north of these islands, others in the midlands and the south. A common language started to evolve.

'Synonyms' are pairs of words with the same or very similar meanings. The modern English language is rich in them. Suggest a reason why we have in English pairs of synonyms such as *hide/skin* and *sick/ill*. Surely one word is enough? Discuss how the growth of synonyms might have come about.

3. In 1066 the Normans, under William the Conqueror, invaded Britain successfully. Their language, French, existed alongside the language spoken by the people of Britain.

The following list contains words from both French and Old English. Discuss the slightly different meanings and uses of the words and suggest which word from each pair might not exist in our language if the Battle of Hastings had been won by Harold or if it had never taken place.

meet/assemble	odour/smell	lord/sire
old/ancient	meal/repast	loving/amorous

4. Some of the synonyms below might originally have had exactly the same meaning. Now they have slightly different meanings or applications. Explain why this is so. It may help to put yourself in the position of a poor farmer at the time of the Norman Conquest.

ask/demand	house/mansion	tell/count

5. You could visit the library for evidence and information to help you with the following questions:

    (a)   If Britain had not had an Empire how might the English language be poorer?

            (For example, we might not have words like *polo*, *loot* and *bungalow*.)

    (b)   How has American influence on the language changed it?

    (c)   Where do recently created words such as the following come from?

            drip-dry, *NATO*, *hi-fi*, *lay-by*, *sit-in*

● General assignments (language and literature)

Choose one of the following to write about. Which one you choose, and how you write, will determine whether the piece is seen as language or as literature coursework.

1. If time were a dimension in which we could freely travel, where in the past

would you like to go? Imagine your journey there, and a day spent in the location of your choice.

2. Eckels killed a butterfly and changed history. Write about an event which you think could have changed history if it had taken a different course.

3. Imagine you could send a time machine back into the past to make a minor adjustment which could make life better now. Describe the passengers, the events and the benefits enjoyed.

4. What do you like about this story or any other science fiction book you have read?

5. Write a science fiction story of your own. Before you start to write, work out the sort of society you are creating, the heroes or heroines you need, and what they feel about that society.

3

The Landlady

● **Prediction exercise: the elements of the story**

In groups, look carefully at the list of ingredients below and decide how they can be combined in such a way as to make a good story. For example, the handsome youth may be the owner of the parrot and he might also keep a boarding house.

Ingredients

Handsome youth	*Kind, middle-aged lady*
Missing persons	*Taxidermist*
Cold night	*Boarding house*
Cup of tea	*Parrot*
Dachshund	*Smell of almonds*
Warm, cosy fire	*Journey by train*

Draft an outline of the story. One person from each group reports to the class on the plan and the links to be made between the items in the list of ingredients.

Read the story and then compare the way Roald Dahl has used the items on the list with the way you suggested using them.

The Landlady

Roald Dahl

Billy Weaver had travelled down from London on the slow afternoon train, with a change at Swindon on the way, and by the time he got to Bath it was about nine o'clock in the evening and the moon was coming up out of a clear starry sky over the houses opposite the station entrance. But the air was deadly cold and the wind was like a flat blade of ice on his cheeks.

"Excuse me," he said, "but is there a fairly cheap hotel not too far away from here?"

"Try The Bell and Dragon," the porter answered, pointing down the road.

"They might take you in. It's about a quarter of a mile along on the other side."

Billy thanked him and picked up his suitcase and set out to walk the quarter-mile to The Bell and Dragon. He had never been to Bath before. He didn't know anyone who lived there. But Mr Greenslade at the Head Office in London had told him it was a splendid city. "Find your own lodgings," he had said, "and then go along and report to the Branch Manager as soon as you've got yourself settled."

Billy was seventeen years old. He was wearing a new navy-blue overcoat, a new brown trilby hat, and a new brown suit, and he was feeling fine. He walked briskly down the street. He was trying to do everything briskly these days. Briskness, he had decided, was *the* one common characteristic of all successful businessmen. The big shots up at Head Office were absolutely fantastically brisk all the time. They were amazing.

There were no shops on this wide street that he was walking along, only a line of tall houses on each side, all of them identical. They had porches and pillars and four or five steps going up to their front doors, and it was obvious that once upon a time they had been very swanky residences. But now, even in the darkness, he could see that the paint was peeling from the woodwork on their doors and windows, and that the handsome white façades were cracked and blotchy from neglect.

Suddenly, in a downstairs window that was brilliantly illuminated by a street-lamp not six yards away, Billy caught sight of a printed notice propped up against the glass in one of the upper panes. It said BED AND BREAKFAST. There was a vase of pussywillows, tall and beautiful, standing just underneath the notice.

He stopped walking. He moved a bit closer. Green curtains (some sort of velvety material) were hanging down on either side of the window. The pussywillows looked wonderful beside them. He went right up and peered through the glass into the room, and the first thing he saw was a bright fire burning in the hearth. On the carpet in front of the fire, a pretty little dachshund was curled up asleep with its nose tucked into its belly. The room itself, so far as he could see in the half-darkness, was filled with pleasant furniture. There was a baby-grand piano and a big sofa and several plump armchairs; and in one corner he spotted a large parrot in a cage. Animals were usually a good sign in a place like this, Billy told himself; and all in all, it looked to him as though it would be a pretty decent house to stay in. Certainly it would be more comfortable than The Bell and Dragon.

On the other hand, a pub would be more congenial than a boarding-house. There would be beer and darts in the evenings, and lots of people to talk to, and it would probably be a good bit cheaper, too. He had stayed a couple of nights in a pub once before and he had liked it. He had never stayed in any boarding-houses, and, to be perfectly honest, he was a tiny bit frightened of them. The name itself conjured up images of watery cabbage, rapacious landladies, and a powerful smell of kippers in the living-room.

After dithering about like this in the cold for two or three minutes, Billy decided that he would walk on and take a look at The Bell and Dragon before making up his mind. He turned to go.

And now a queer thing happened to him. He was in the act of stepping back and turning away from the window when all at once his eye was caught and held in the most peculiar manner by the small notice that was there. BED AND BREAKFAST, it said. BED AND BREAKFAST, BED AND BREAKFAST, BED AND BREAKFAST. Each word was like a large black eye staring at him through the glass, holding him, compelling him, forcing him to stay where he was and not to walk away from that house, and the next thing he knew, he was actually moving across from the window to the front door of the house, climbing the steps that led up to it, and reaching for the bell.

He pressed the bell. Far away in a back room he heard it ringing, and then *at once* – it must have been at once because he hadn't even had time to take his finger from the bell-button – the door swung open and a woman was standing there.

Normally you ring the bell and you have at least a half-minute's wait before the door opens. But this dame was like a jack-in-the-box. He pressed the bell – and out she popped! It made him jump.

She was about forty-five or fifty years old, and the moment she saw him, she gave him a warm welcoming smile.

"*Please* come in," she said pleasantly. She stepped aside, holding the door wide open, and Billy found himself automatically starting forward into the house. The compulsion or, more accurately, the desire to follow after her into that house was extraordinarily strong.

"I saw the notice in the window," he said, holding himself back.

"Yes, I know."

"I was wondering about a room."

"It's *all* ready for you, my dear," she said. She had a round pink face and

very gentle blue eyes.

"I was on my way to The Bell and Dragon," Billy told her. "But the notice in your window just happened to catch my eye."

"My dear boy," she said, "why don't you come in out of the cold?"

"How much do you charge?"

"Five and sixpence a night, including breakfast."

It was fantastically cheap. It was less than half of what he had been willing to pay.

"If that is too much," she added, "then perhaps I can reduce it just a tiny bit. Do you desire an egg for breakfast? Eggs are expensive at the moment. It would be sixpence less without the egg."

"Five and sixpence is fine," he answered. "I should like very much to stay here."

"I knew you would. Do come in."

She seemed terribly nice. She looked exactly like the mother of one's best school-friend welcoming one into the house to stay for the Christmas holidays. Billy took off his hat, and stepped over the threshold.

"Just hang it there," she said, "and let me help you with your coat."

There were no other hats or coats in the hall. There were no umbrellas, no walking-sticks – nothing.

"We have it *all* to ourselves," she said, smiling at him over her shoulder as she led the way upstairs. "You see, it isn't very often I have the pleasure of taking a visitor into my little nest."

The old girl is slightly dotty, Billy told himself. But at five and sixpence a night, who gives a damn about that? "I should've thought you'd be simply swamped with applicants," he said politely.

"Oh, I am, my dear, I am, of course I am. But the trouble is that I'm inclined to be just a teeny weeny bit choosy and particular – if you see what I mean."

"Ah, yes."

"But I'm always ready. Everything is always ready day and night in this house just on the off-chance that an acceptable young gentleman will come along. And it is such a pleasure, my dear, such a very great pleasure when now and again I open the door and I see someone standing there who is just *exactly* right." She was half-way up the stairs, and she paused with one hand on the stair-rail, turning her head and smiling down at him with pale lips. "Like you," she added, and her blue eyes travelled slowly all the way down the length of Billy's body, to his feet, and then up again.

On the first-floor landing she said to him, "This floor is mine."

They climbed up a second flight. "And this one is *all* yours," she said. "Here's your room. I do hope you'll like it." She took him into a small but charming front bedroom, switching on the light as she went in.

"The morning sun comes right in the window, Mr Perkins. It *is* Mr Perkins, isn't it?"

"No," he said. "It's Weaver."

"Mr Weaver. How nice. I've put a water-bottle between the sheets to air them out, Mr Weaver. It's such a comfort to have a hot water-bottle in a strange bed with clean sheets, don't you agree? And you may light the gas fire at any time if you feel chilly."

"Thank you," Billy said. "Thank you ever so much." He noticed that the bedspread had been taken off the bed, and that the bedclothes had been neatly turned back on one side, all ready for someone to get in.

"I'm so glad you appeared," she said, looking earnestly into his face. "I was beginning to get worried."

"That's all right," Billy answered brightly. "You mustn't worry about me." He put his suitcase on the chair and started to open it.

"And what about supper, my dear? Did you manage to get anything to eat before you came here?"

"I'm not a bit hungry, thank you," he said. "I think I'll just go to bed as soon as possible because tomorrow I've got to get up rather early and report to the office."

"Very well, then. I'll leave you now so that you can unpack. But before you go to bed, would you be kind enough to pop into the sitting-room on the ground floor and sign the book? Everyone has to do that because it's the law of the land, and we don't want to go breaking any laws at *this* stage in the proceedings, do we?" She gave him a little wave of the hand and went quickly out of the room and closed the door.

Now, the fact that his landlady appeared to be slightly off her rocker didn't worry Billy in the least. After all, she was not only harmless – there was no question about that – but she was also quite obviously a kind and generous soul. He guessed that she had probably lost a son in the war, or something like that, and had never got over it.

So a few minutes later, after unpacking his suitcase and washing his hands, he trotted downstairs to the ground floor and entered the living-room. His land-lady wasn't there, but the fire was glowing in the hearth, and the little dachshund was still sleeping in front of it. The room was wonderfully warm and cosy. I'm a lucky fellow, he thought, rubbing his hands. This is a bit of all right.

He found the guest-book lying open on the piano, so he took out his pen and wrote down his name and address. There were only two other entries above his on the page, and, as one always does with guest-books, he started to read them. One was a Christopher Mulholland from Cardiff. The other was Gregory W. Temple from Bristol.

That's funny, he thought suddenly. Christopher Mulholland. It rings a bell. Now where on earth had he heard that rather unusual name before?

Was he a boy at school? No. Was it one of his sister's numerous young men, perhaps, or a friend of his father's? No, no, it wasn't any of those. He glanced down again at the book.

> Christopher Mulholland   23 Cathedral Road, Cardiff
> Gregory W. Temple   27 Sycamore Drive, Bristol

As a matter of fact, now he came to think of it, he wasn't at all sure that the second name didn't have almost as much of a familiar ring about it as the first.

"Gregory Temple?" he said aloud, searching his memory. "Christopher Mulholland? ..."

"Such charming boys," a voice behind him answered, and he turned and saw his landlady sailing into the room with a large silver tea-tray in her hands. She was holding it well out in front of her, and rather high up, as though the tray were a pair of reins on a frisky horse.

"They sound somehow familiar," he said.

"They do? How interesting."

"I'm almost positive I've heard those names before somewhere. Isn't that queer? Maybe it was in the newspapers. They weren't famous in any way, were they? I mean famous cricketers or footballers or something like that?"

"Famous," she said, setting the tea-tray down on the low table in front of the sofa. "Oh no, I don't think they were famous. But they were extraordinarily handsome, both of them, I can promise you that. They were tall and young and handsome, my dear, just exactly like you."

Once more, Billy glanced down at the book. "Look here," he said, noticing the dates. "This last entry is over two years old."

"It is?"

"Yes, indeed. And Christopher Mulholland's is nearly a year before that – more than *three years* ago."

"Dear me," she said, shaking her head and heaving a dainty little sigh. "I would never have thought it. How time does fly away from us all, doesn't it, Mr Wilkins?"

"It's Weaver," Billy said. "W-e-a-v-e-r."

"Oh, of course it is?" she cried, sitting down on the sofa. "How silly of me. I do apologize. In one ear and out the other, that's me, Mr Weaver."

"You know something?" Billy said. "Something that's really quite extraordinary about all this?"

"No, dear, I don't."

"Well, you see – both of these names, Mulholland and Temple, I not only seem to remember each one of them separately, so to speak, but somehow or other, in some peculiar way, they both appear to be sort of connected together as well. As though they were both famous for the same sort of thing, if you see what I mean – like ... well ... like Dempsey and Tunney, for example, or Churchill and Roosevelt."

"How amusing," she said. "But come over here now, dear, and sit down beside me on the sofa and I'll give you a nice cup of tea and a ginger biscuit before you go to bed."

"You really shouldn't bother," Billy said. "I didn't mean you to do anything like that." He stood by the piano, watching her as she fussed about with the cups and saucers. He noticed that she had small, white, quickly moving hands, and red finger-nails.

"I'm almost positive it was in the newspapers I saw them," Billy said. "I'll think of it in a second. I'm sure I will."

There is nothing more tantalizing than a thing like this which lingers just outside the borders of one's memory. He hated to give up.

"Now wait a minute," he said. "Wait just a minute. Mulholland ... Christopher Mulholland ... wasn't *that* the name of the Eton schoolboy who was on a walking-tour through the West Country, and then all of a sudden ..."

"Milk?" she said. "And sugar?"

"Yes, please. And then all of a sudden ..."

"Eton schoolboy?" she said, "Oh no, my dear, that can't possibly be right because *my* Mr Mulholland was certainly not an Eton schoolboy when he came to me. He was a Cambridge undergraduate. Come over here now and sit next to me and warm yourself in front of this lovely fire. Come on. Your tea's all ready for you." She patted the empty place beside her on the sofa, and she sat there smiling at Billy and waiting for him to come over.

He crossed the room slowly, and sat down on the edge of the sofa. She placed his teacup on the table in front of him.

"*There* we are," she said. "How nice and cosy this is, isn't it?"

Billy started sipping his tea. She did the same. For half a minute or so, neither of them spoke. But Billy knew that she was looking at him. Her body was half-turned towards him and he could feel her eyes resting on his face, watching him over the rim of her teacup. Now and again, he caught a whiff of a peculiar smell that seemed to emanate directly from her person. It was not in the least unpleasant, and it reminded him – well, he wasn't quite sure what it reminded him of. Pickled walnuts? New leather? Or was it the corridors of a hospital?

"Mr Mulholland was a great one for his tea," she said at length. "Never in my life have I seen anyone drink as much tea as dear, sweet Mr Mulholland."

"I suppose he left fairly recently," Billy said. He was still puzzling his head about the two names. He was positive now that he had seen them in the newspapers – in the headlines.

"Left?" she said, arching her brows. "But my dear boy, he never left. He's still here. Mr Temple is also here. They're on the third floor, both of them together."

Billy set down his cup slowly on the table, and stared at his landlady. She smiled back at him, and then she put out one of her white hands and patted him comfortingly on the knee. "How old are you, my dear?" she asked.

"Seventeen."

"Seventeen!" she cried. "Oh, it's the perfect age! Mr Mulholland was also seventeen. But I think he was a trifle shorter than you are, in fact I'm sure he was, and his teeth weren't *quite* so white. You have the most beautiful teeth, Mr Weaver, did you know that?"

"They're not as good as they look," Billy said. "They've got simply masses of fillings in them at the back."

"Mr Temple, of course, was a little older," she said, ignoring his remark. "He was actually twenty-eight. And yet I never would have guessed it if he hadn't told me, never in my whole life. There wasn't a *blemish* on his body."

"A what?" Billy said.

"His skin was *just* like a baby's."

There was a pause. Billy picked up his teacup and took another sip of his tea, then he set it down again gently in its saucer. He waited for her to say something else, but she seemed to have lapsed into another of her silences. He sat there staring ahead of him into the far corner of the room, biting his lower lip.

"That parrot," he said at last. "You know something? It had me completely fooled when I first saw it through the window from the street. I could have sworn it was alive."

"Alas, no longer."

"It's most terribly clever the way it's been done," he said. "It doesn't look in the least bit dead. Who did it?"

"I did."

"*You* did?"

"Of course," she said. "And have you met my little Basil as well?" She nodded towards the dachshund curled up so comfortably in front of the fire. Billy looked at it. And suddenly, he realized that this animal had all the time been just as silent and motionless as the parrot. He put out a hand and touched it gently on the top of its back. The back was hard and cold, and when he pushed the hair to one side with his fingers, he could see the skin underneath, greyish-black and dry and perfectly preserved.

"Good gracious me," he said, "How absolutely fascinating." He turned away from the dog and stared with deep admiration at the little woman beside him on the sofa. "It must be most awfully difficult to do a thing like that."

"Not in the least," she said. "I stuff *all* my little pets myself when they pass away. Will you have another cup of tea?"

"No, thank you," Billy said. The tea tasted faintly of bitter almonds, and he didn't much care for it.

"You did sign the book, didn't you?"

"Oh, yes."

"That's good. Because later on, if I happen to forget what you were called, then I can always come down here and look it up. I still do that almost every day with Mr Mulholland and Mr ... Mr ... "

"Temple," Billy said. "Gregory Temple. Excuse my asking, but haven't there been *any* other guests here except them in the last two or three years?"

Holding her teacup high in one hand, inclining her head slightly to the left, she looked up at him out of the corners of her eyes and gave him another gentle little smile.

"No, my dear," she said. "Only you."

● Role play: editing the story

A rather tiresome editor has worked on the story before publication and has suggested some changes. You are the sub-editor and have been allowed to comment on the effect these changes would have.

Set your work out like this:

Changes	Comments
1. **Omission:** Leave out the details of Billy's journey and begin with him ringing the bell of the house.	
2. **Reorganisation:** Let Billy discover that the parrot is stuffed as soon as he enters the room.	
3. **Alteration:** Make the landlady a landlord instead, and make Billy into a girl.	
4. **Clarification:** After saying that the tea tastes of bitter almonds, explain that arsenic has that taste.	

Next, working in small groups or pairs, take on the role of this insensitive editor, and prepare more changes to the story. Use the categories suggested above – omission, reorganisation, alteration and clarification. You also decide the ending is too vague and either change it altogether or make it clearer. Draft your suggestions as above.

Pass your suggestions to another group, asking them to write their reactions in the space provided. Meanwhile, write your comments on the suggestions passed to you by another group.

● Written assignments (literature): analysis of structure

1. A good storyteller knows how to select what is important and to leave out what is not, and when to disclose information to the reader. How does Roald Dahl meet these requirements in *The Landlady*?

2. 'The story *The Landlady* is like a jigsaw. Only when we reach the end do we see the full picture.' By close reference to the story, show how the pieces in the jigsaw gradually fit together.

● Close study of character: Billy Weaver

We are told about Billy in the first section of the story. Make a list of what we learn about his character and appearance in the section of the story up to the point where he rings the bell.

Now go through the rest of the story and see what else we learn about him. Does what we learn here merely confirm what we already know, or is there anything new?

● Close study of character: the landlady

Make a similar list for the landlady, but this time put the items in two columns, one headed *Pleasant*, the other *Suspicious*. How does the landlady's behaviour (a) conceal, and (b) reveal her true character?

● Appearance and reality in the story

In this story, many things are not what they seem to be. Look at the list below and, setting your work out like this, show how the appearance of each item is at odds with reality.

For example, offering somebody a cup of tea is usually seen as a hospitable gesture, not a threatening one.

	Appearance	Reality
The landlady		
The house		
The parrot		
The dachshund		
The cup of tea		
Anything else?		

- ## Parallels with fairy tales and nursery rhymes

Below are some characters and situations taken from various fairy tales and nursery rhymes. In your groups, try to identify the story they come from or guess what they might be about and then decide which you think bear some resemblance to elements in *The Landlady*.

1. A kind old woman invites two children into her cosy little cottage.

2. Two children are turned out by their parents and get lost.

3. A household is put to sleep for a hundred years.

4. A rather simple youth is taken in by an old woman. She wants him to kiss her.

5. Three brothers go off to seek their fortunes.

6. A poor, ragged girl becomes a princess.

7. An evil man murders his wives and keeps them locked away in a room which no-one is allowed to enter.

8. A man is lavishly entertained by a monster who turns out to be kind.

9. An ugly old woman is transformed into a beautiful princess by being kissed.

10. A girl is given a drink by an old woman, and it has an unexpected result.

- ## Written assignments (language): narrative

1. *Either* write a story in which appearances are deceptive. Try to keep the reader in suspense about the true nature of things for as long as possible. Choose your own title.

Or

2. Use one of the skeleton outlines above and write a fairy tale for modern times. Give it a realistic setting and convincing main characters, but try to keep some of the air of mystery which fairy tales have. Choose your own title.

- ## Group role play: adapting the story for television

You have been given the task of turning this story into a half-hour play for television. People are needed to do a variety of jobs:

Props/wardrobe manager, and assistant,

Design team,

Camera crew,

Scriptwriters,

Musical director,

Director.

You may think of others.

The props manager should compile a list of all props needed for the play – for instance, a stuffed parrot in a cage.

The design team should be responsible for providing drawings of the sets, both within and outside the house.

The camera crew should decide on the type of shots required for each scene – long or medium, what close-ups might be effective, the level of lighting, and so on.

The scriptwriters should write out the dialogue of the play, together with any stage directions evident from the story.

The musical director should time the scenes, select music and sound effects.

The director should act as coordinator, deciding on issues that arise as well as on how to convey anything that does not arise from the dialogue – such as Billy's thoughts as he tries to remember the significance of the names in the visitors' book.

● Written assignments (literature): narrative/ballad

1. Imagine you are the landlady's next intended victim. However, unlike the others you manage to escape. Write the story of your adventure, being sure to explain why you were in Bath, referring to the names in the visitors' book, and preserving the important framework of Roald Dahl's story.

2. Compose a ballad – a story in verse with simple rhyme scheme and four lines to each verse – entitled 'The Strange Tale of Billy Weaver'.

Here is a verse to start you off:

Billy Weaver was a lad
Who wanted to do well.
He went to Bath to please his boss,
And this is what befell ...

4

Reunion

This is intended to be a *controlled conditions assignment*, done without discussion.

Read the story and answer the following questions as fully and as carefully as possible. Remember the work you have done on other short stories.

Section A Answer all these questions.

1. Give a brief summary of the family circumstances of the narrator. Include the important facts as they emerge from the story.

2. In the first paragraph, the narrator says about his father 'as soon as I saw him I felt that he was my father, my flesh and blood, my future and my doom.' Explain as clearly as you can what you think the writer means by this statement.

3. Father and son enter a number of different kinds of restaurants. What impression do you get about each of the restaurants from the way the father addresses the waiters? Refer to the story to support what you have to say.

   (a) '"*Kellner!*" he shouted. "*Garçon! Cameriere! You!*"'

   (b) '"Master of the hounds! Tallyhoo and all that sort of thing. We'd like a little something in the way of a stirrup cup."'

   (c) '"You don't desire our patronage. Is that it? Well, the hell with you. *Vada all' inferno.*"'

4. Describe as fully as possible, in your own words, the character of the father. Do you think we are meant to like or dislike him?

5. What do you think are the boy's feelings about his father during the events of this story? How does he feel about him at the end?

Section B Your teacher will advise you which of these questions to answer.

6. What might the boy have wanted his father to tell him and ask him after the gap of three years? Write from the boy's point of view.

7. Re-tell any incident from the story from the point of view of two of the following people: (a) the father, (b) one of the waiters, (c) the newspaper seller.

8. When he gets to his grandmother's cottage the boy writes to his father. Write the letter he might have written.

9. When the boy eventually returns home, his mother asks him about the meeting with his father. Write an account of the conversation as you think it might develop.

10. Write a story of your own, entitled 'Reunion'.

Reunion

John Cheever

The last time I saw my father was in Grand Central Station. I was going from my grandmother's in the Adirondacks to a cottage on the Cape that my mother had rented, and I wrote my father that I would be in New York between trains for an hour and a half and asked if we could have lunch together. His secretary wrote to say that he would meet me at the information booth at noon, and at twelve o'clock sharp I saw him coming through the crowd. He was a stranger to me – my mother divorced him three years ago, and I hadn't been with him since – but as soon as I saw him I felt that he was my father, my flesh and blood, my future and my doom. I knew that when I was grown I would be something like him; I would have to plan my campaigns within his limitations. He was a big, good-looking man, and I was terribly happy to see him again. He struck me on the back and shook my hand. "Hi, Charlie," he said. "Hi, boy. I'd like to take you up to my club, but it's in the Sixties, and if you have to catch an early train I guess we'd better get something to eat around here." He put his arm around me, and I smelled my father the way my mother sniffs a rose. It was a rich compound of whiskey, after-shave lotion, shoe polish, woollens, and the rankness of a mature male. I hoped that someone would see us together. I wished that we could be photographed. I wanted some record of our having been together.

We went out of the station and up a side street to a restaurant. It was still early, and the place was empty. The bartender was quarrelling with a delivery boy, and there was one very old waiter in a red coat down by the kitchen door. We sat down, and my father hailed the waiter in a loud voice. "*Kellner!*" he shouted. "*Garçon! Cameriere! You!*" His boisterousness in the empty restaurant seemed out of place. "Could we have a little service here!" he shouted. "Chop-chop." Then he clapped his hands. This caught the waiter's attention, and he shuffled over to our table.

"Were you clapping your hands at me?" he asked.

"Calm down, calm down, *sommelier*," my father said. "If it isn't too much to ask of you – if it wouldn't be too much above and beyond the call of duty, we would like a couple of Beefeater Gibsons."

"I don't like to be clapped at," the waiter said.

"I should have brought my whistle," my father said. "I have a whistle that is audible only to the ears of old waiters. Now, take out your little pad and your little pencil and see if you can get this straight: two Beefeater Gibsons. Repeat after me: two Beefeater Gibsons."

"I think you'd better go somewhere else," the waiter said quietly.

"That," said my father, "is one of the most brilliant suggestions I have ever heard. Come on, Charlie, let's get the hell out of here."

I followed my father out of that restaurant into another. He was not so boisterous this time. Our drinks came, and he cross-questioned me about the baseball season. He then struck the edge of his empty glass with his knife and began shouting again. "*Garçon! Kellner! You!* Could we trouble you to bring us two more of the same."

"How old is the boy?" the waiter asked.

"That," my father said, "is none of your goddamned business."

"I'm sorry, sir," the waiter said, "but I won't serve the boy another drink."

"Well, I have some news for you," my father said. "I have some very interesting news for you. This doesn't happen to be the only restaurant in New York. They've opened another on the corner. Come on, Charlie."

He paid the bill, and I followed him out of that restaurant into another. Here the waiters wore pink jackets like hunting coats, and there was a lot of horse tack on the walls. We sat down, and my father began to shout again. "Master of the hounds! Tallyhoo and all that sort of thing. We'd like a little something in the way of a stirrup cup. Namely, two Bibson Geefeaters."

"Two Bibson Geefeaters?" the waiter asked, smiling.

"You know damned well what I want," my father said angrily. "I want two Beefeater Gibsons, and make it snappy. Things have changed in jolly old England. So my friend the duke tells me. Let's see what England can produce in the way of a cocktail."

"This isn't England," the waiter said.

"Don't argue with me," my father said. "Just do as you're told."

"I just thought you might like to know where you are," the waiter said.

"If there is one thing I cannot tolerate," my father said, "it is an impudent domestic. Come on, Charlie."

The fourth place we went to was Italian. "*Buon giorno*," my father said. "*Per favore, possiamo avere due cocktail americani, forti, forti. Molto gin, poco vermut.*"

"I don't understand Italian," the waiter said.

"Oh, come off it," my father said. "You understand Italian, and you know damned well you do. *Vogliamo due cocktail americani. Subito.*"

The waiter left us and spoke with the captain, who came over to our table and said, "I'm sorry, sir, but this table is reserved."

"All right," my father said. "Get us another table."

"All the tables are reserved," the captain said.

"I get it," my father said. "You don't desire our patronage. Is that it? Well, the hell with you. *Vada all' inferno.* Let's go, Charlie."

"I have to get my train," I said.

"I'm sorry, sonny," my father said. "I'm terribly sorry." He put his arm around me and pressed me against him. "I'll walk you back to the station. If there had only been time to go up to my club."

"That's all right, Daddy," I said.

"I'll get you a paper," he said. "I'll get you a paper to read on the train."

Then he went up to a newsstand and said, "Kind sir, will you be good enough to favor me with one of your goddamned, no-good, ten-cent afternoon papers?" The clerk turned away from him and stared at a magazine cover. "Is it asking too much, kind sir," my father said, "is it asking too much for you to sell me one of your disgusting specimens of yellow journalism?"

"I have to go, Daddy," I said. "It's late."

"Now, just wait a second, sonny," he said. "Just wait a second. I want to get a rise out of this chap."

"Goodbye, Daddy," I said, and I went down the stairs and got my train, and that was the last time I saw my father.

5

Great Uncle Crow

Taddy the Lamplighter

Here are two short stories with a number of superficial similarities but an
even greater number of features that make them quite different.
Both are about single old men, characters in their own right. Both stories are
told from the point of view of a much younger person. Both consider events
from the past, from an age that is gone.

We will leave you to explore the differences as you read and study
the stories.

Now read the first of the pair, *Great Uncle Crow*, paying particular attention to
the colours, sounds and smells of the scene.

Great Uncle Crow

H. E. Bates

Once in the summer time, when the water-lilies were in bloom and the wheat
was new in ear, his grandfather took him on a long walk up the river, to see his
Uncle Crow. He had heard so much of Uncle Crow, so much that was wonderful
and to be marvelled at, and for such a long time, that he knew him to be, even
before that, the most remarkable fisherman in the world.

"Masterpiece of a man, your Uncle Crow," his grandfather said. "He could
git a clothes-line any day and tie a brick on it and a mossel of cake and go out and
catch a pike as long as your arm."

When he asked what kind of cake his grandfather seemed irritated and said
it was just like a boy to ask questions of that sort.

"Any kind o' cake," he said. "Plum cake. Does it matter? Caraway cake.
Christmas cake if you like. Anything. I shouldn't wonder if he could catch a

pretty fair pike with a cold baked tater."

"Only a pike?"

"Times," his grandfather said, "I've seen him sittin' on the bank on a sweltering hot day like a furnace, when nobody was gittin' a bite not even off a bloodsucker. And there your Uncle Crow'd be a-pullin' 'em out by the dozen, like a man shellin' harvest beans."

"And how does he come to be my Uncle Crow," he said, "if my mother hasn't got a brother? Nor my father."

"Well," his grandfather said, "he's really your mother's own cousin, if everybody had their rights. But all on us call him Uncle Crow."

"And where does he live?"

"You'll see," his grandfather said. "All by hisself. In a little titty bit of a house, by the river."

The little titty bit of a house, when he first saw it, surprised him very much. It was not at all unlike a black tarred boat that had either slipped down a slope and stuck there on its way to launching or one that had been washed up and left there in a flood. The roof of brown tiles had a warp in it and the sides were mostly built, he thought, of tarred beer-barrels.

The two windows with their tiny panes were about as large as chessboards and Uncle Crow had nailed underneath each of them a sill of sheet tin that was still a brilliant blue, each with the words 'Bachache Pills' in white lettering on it, upside down.

On all sides of the house grew tall feathered reeds. They enveloped it like gigantic whispering corn. Some distance beyond the great reeds the river went past in a broad slow arc, on magnificent kingly currents, full of long white islands of water-lilies, as big as china breakfast cups, shining and yellow-hearted in the sun.

He thought, on the whole, that that place, the river with the water-lilies, the little titty bit of a house, and the great forest of reeds talking between soft brown beards, was the nicest place he had ever seen.

"Anybody about?" his grandfather called. "Crow! – anybody at home?"

The door of the house was partly open, but at first there was no answer. His grandfather pushed open the door still farther with his foot. The reeds whispered down by the river and were answered, in the house, by a sound like the creek of bed springs.

"Who is't?"

"It's me, Crow," his grandfather called. "Lukey. Brought the boy over to have a look at you."

A big gangling red-faced man with rusty hair came to the door. His trousers were black and very tight. His eyes were a smeary vivid blue, the same colour as the stripes of his shirt, and his trousers were kept up by a leather belt with brass escutcheons on it, like those on horses' harness.

"Thought very like you'd be out a-pikin'," his grandfather said.

"Too hot. How's Lukey boy? Ain't seed y' lately, Lukey boy."

His lips were thick and very pink and wet, like cow's lips. He made a wonderful erupting jolly sound somewhat between a belch and a laugh.

"Comin' in it a minute?"

In the one room of the house was an iron bed with an old red check horse-rug spread over it and a stone copper in one corner and a bare wooden table with dirty plates and cups and a tin kettle on it. Two osier baskets and a scythe stood in another corner.

Uncle Crow stretched himself full length on the bed as if he was very tired. He put his knees in the air. His belly was tight as a bladder of lard in his black trousers, which were mossy green on the knees and seat.

"How's the fishin'?" his grandfather said. "I bin tellin' the boy ..."

Uncle Crow belched deeply. From where the sun struck full on the tarred wall of the house there was a hot whiff of baking tar. But when Uncle Crow belched there was a smell like the smell of yeast in the air.

"It ain't bin all that much of a summer yit," Uncle Crow said. "Ain't had the rain."

"Not like that summer you catched the big 'un down at Archer's Mill. I recollect you a-tellin' on me ..."

"Too hot and dry by half," Uncle Crow said. "Gits in your gullet like chaff."

"You recollect that summer?" his grandfather said. "Nobody else a-fetching on 'em out only you ..."

"Have a drop o' neck-oil," Uncle Crow said.

The boy wondered what neck-oil was and presently, to his surprise, Uncle Crow and his grandfather were drinking it. It came out of a dark-green bottle and it was a clear bright amber, like cold tea, in the two glasses.

"The medder were yeller with 'em," Uncle Crow said. "Yeller as a guinea."

He smacked his lips with a marvellously juicy, fruity sound. The boy's grandfather gazed at the neck-oil and said he thought it would be a corker if it was kept a year or two, but Uncle Crow said, "Trouble is, Lukey boy, it's a terrible job to keep it. You start tastin' on it to see if it'll keep and then you taste on it again and you go on tastin' on it until they ain't a drop left as'll keep."

Uncle Crow laughed so much that the bed springs cackled underneath his bouncing trousers.

"Why is it called neck-oil?" the boy said.

"Boy," Uncle Crow said, "when you git older, when you git growed-up, you know what'll happen to your gullet?"

"No."

"It'll git sort o' rusted up inside. Like a old gutter pipe. So's you can't swaller very easy. Rusty as old Harry it'll git. You know that, boy?"

"No."

"Well, it will. I'm tellin', on y'. And you know what y' got to do then?"

"No."

"Every now and then you gotta git a drop o' neck-oil down it. So's to ease it. A drop o' neck-oil every once in a while – that's what you gotta do to keep the rust out."

The boy was still contemplating the curious prospect of his neck rusting up inside in later years when Uncle Crow said, "Boy, you go outside and jis' round the corner you'll see a bucket. You bring handful o' cresses out on it. I'll bet you're hungry, ain't you?"

"A little bit."

He found the watercresses in the bucket, cool in the shadow of the little house, and when he got back inside with them Uncle Crow said, "Now you put the cresses on that there plate there and then put your nose inside that there basin and see what's inside. What is't, eh?"

"Eggs."

"Ought to be fourteen on 'em. Four-apiece and two over. What sort are they, boy?"

"Moor-hens'."

"You got a knowin' boy here, Lukey," Uncle Crow said. He dropped the scaly red lid of one eye like an old cockerel going to sleep. He took another drop of neck-oil and gave another fruity, juicy laugh as he heaved his body from the bed. "A very knowin' boy."

Presently he was carving slices of thick brown bread with a great horn-handled shut-knife and pasting each slice with summery golden butter. Now and then he took another drink of neck-oil and once he said, "You get the salt pot, boy, and empty a bit out on that there saucer, so's we can all dip in."

Uncle Crow slapped the last slice of bread on to the buttered pile and then said, "Boy, you take that there jug there and go a step or two up the path and dip yourself a drop o' spring water. You'll see it. It comes out of a little bit of a wall, jist by a doddle-willer."

When the boy got back with the jug of spring water Uncle Crow was opening another bottle of neck-oil and his grandfather was saying, "God a-mussy man, goo steady. You'll have me agooin' one way and another ..."

"Man alive," Uncle Crow said, "and what's wrong with that?"

Then the watercress, the salt, the moor-hens' eggs, the spring water, and the neck-oil were all ready. The moor-hens' eggs were hard-boiled. Uncle Crow lay on the bed and cracked them with his teeth, just like big brown nuts, and said he thought the watercress was just about as nice and tender as a young lady.

"I'm sorry we ain't got the gold plate out though. I had it out a-Sunday." He closed his old cockerel-lidded eye again and licked his tongue backwards and forwards across his lips and dipped another peeled egg in salt. "You know what I had for my dinner a-Sunday, boy?"

"No."

"A pussy-cat on a gold plate. Roasted with broad-beans and new taters. Did you ever heerd talk of anybody eatin' a roasted pussy-cat, boy?"

"Yes."

"You did?"

"Yes," he said, "that's a hare."

"You got a very knowin' boy here, Lukey," Uncle Crow said. "A very knowin' boy."

Then he screwed up a big dark-green bouquet of watercress and dipped it in salt until it was entirely frosted and then crammed it in one neat wholesale bite into his soft pink mouth.

"But not on a gold plate?" he said.

He had to admit that.

"No, not on a gold plate," he said.

All that time he thought the fresh watercress, the moor-hens' eggs, the brown bread-and-butter, and the spring water were the most delicious, wonderful things he had ever eaten in the world. He felt that only one thing was missing.

It was that whenever his grandfather spoke of fishing Uncle Crow simply took another draught of neck-oil.

"When are you goin' to take us fishing?" he said.

"You et up that there egg," Uncle Crow said. "That's the last one. You et that there egg up and I'll tell you what."

"What about gooin' as far as that big deep hole where the chub lay?" grandfather said. "Up by the back-brook ..."

"I'll tell you what, boy," Uncle Crow said, "you git your grandfather to bring you over September time, of a morning, afore the steam's off the winders. Mushroomin' time. You come over and we'll have a bit o' bacon and mushroom for breakfast and then set into the pike. You see, boy, it ain't the pikin' season now. It's too hot. Too bright. It's too bright of afternoon, and they ain't a-bitin'."

He took a long rich swig of neck-oil.

"Ain't that it, Lukey? That's the time, ain't it, mushroom time?"

"Thass it," his grandfather said.

"Tot out," Uncle Crow said. "Drink up. My throat's jist easin' orf a bit."

He gave another wonderful belching laugh and told the boy to be sure to finish up the last of the watercress and the bread-and-butter. The little room was rich with the smell of neck-oil, and the tarry sun-baked odour of the beer-barrels that formed its walls. And through the door came, always, the sound of reeds talking in their beards, and the scent of summer meadows drifting in from beyond the great curl of the river with its kingly currents and its islands of full blown lilies, white and yellow in the sun.

"I see the wheat's in ear," his grandfather said. "Ain't that the time for tench, when the wheat's in ear?"

"Mushroom time," Uncle Crow said. "That's the time. You git mushroom time here, and I'll fetch you a tench out as big as a cricket bat."

He fixed the boy with an eye of wonderful watery, glassy blue and licked his lips with a lazy tongue, and said, "You know what colour a tench is, boy?"

"Yes," he said.

"What colour?"

"The colour of the neck-oil."

"Lukey," Uncle Crow said, "you got a very knowin' boy here. A very knowin' boy."

After that, when there were no more cresses or moor-hens' eggs or bread-and-butter to eat, and his grandfather said he'd get hung if he touched another drop of neck-oil, he and his grandfather walked home across the meadows.

"What work does Uncle Crow do?" he said.

"Uncle Crow? Work? ... well, he ain't ... Uncle Crow? Well, he works, but he ain't what you'd call a reg'lar worker ..."

All the way home he could hear the reeds talking in their beards. He could see the water-lilies that reminded him so much of the gold and white inside the moor-hens' eggs. He could hear the happy sound of Uncle Crow laughing and sucking at the neck-oil, and crunching the fresh salty cresses into his mouth in the tarry little room.

He felt happy, too, and the sun was a gold plate in the sky.

● Discussion: the creation of mood and atmosphere

Below are some extracts from the story. Discuss them and the notes that appear alongside. The aim of the work is to help you to identify some of the features of the story and to understand how Bates has created an atmosphere and a mood from the very beginning of his story. Use your discussion, and any notes you make, to help you with the work that follows.

fairy story?

'*Once in the summertime when the water-lilies were in bloom and the wheat was new in ear, his grandfather took him on a long walk up the river to see his Uncle Crow.* He had heard so much of Uncle Crow, so much that was *wonderful* and to

description

be *marvelled* at, and for such a long time, that he knew him to be, even before that, the most *remarkable* fisherman in the world.'

N.B.

exaggeration

'"*Masterpiece of a man,* your Uncle Crow," his grandfather said. "He could git a clothes-line any day and tie a brick

lots of similes

on it and a mossel of cake and go out and catch *a pike as long as your arm.*"'

figures of speech

sounds

'On all sides of the house grew tall *feathered reeds*. They enveloped it like *gigantic whispering corn*. Some distance beyond the great reeds the river went past in a broad slow arc, on magnificent *kingly currents* full of long white

why kingly?

similes	islands of water-lilies, *as big as china breakfast cups,* shining and *yellow-hearted* in the sun.'	colours
description	'A *big gangling red-faced man with rusty hair* came to the door. His trousers were black and very tight. *His eyes were*	
colours	*a smeary vivid blue,* the same colour as the stripes of his shirt, and his trousers were held up by a leather belt with *brass* escutcheons on it, *like those on horses' harness.'*	
language of conversation	'"Thought very like you'd be out a-pikin'," his grandfather said.	
	"Too hot. How's Lukey boy? Ain't seed y' lately, Lukey boy."	
animal comparisons	*His lips were thick and very pink and wet, like cow's lips. He made a wonderful erupting jolly sound somewhere between a belch and a laugh.'*	sounds
repetitions = patterns	'"*You got a knowin' boy here, Lukey,*" Uncle Crow said. *He dropped the scaly red lid of one eye like an old cockerel going to sleep. He took another drop of neck-oil and gave another fruity, juicy laugh as he heaved his body from the bed.*	
	A very knowin' boy.'''	
sounds	'All the way home he could hear *the reeds talking in their beards.* He could see *the water-lilies* that reminded him so	patterns repeated
colours	much of the *gold and white* inside the moorhens' eggs. He could hear *the happy sound* of Uncle Crow *laughing* and *sucking* at the neck-oil, and *crunching* the fresh salty	smell
sun on islands	cresses into his mouth in *the tarry little room.*	
breakfast cups – now plates	He felt happy, too, and *the sun was a gold plate in the sky.'*	colours

● Character portrayal through imagery

Imagery is a word frequently used in the discussion of literature. It has a number of meanings. *Chambers English Dictionary* gives the following:

imagery: the work of the imagination; mental pictures; figures of speech; images in general or collectively.

In *Great Uncle Crow* there is an abundance of imagery. Most of it is in the form of similes and metaphors.

What is Great Uncle Crow like? He appeals to our imagination, but more immediately to three of our senses.

(a) List words and phrases from the story that describe Uncle Crow. Put them under three headings: what we see, what we hear, what we smell.

(b) List the things Uncle Crow is compared to.

Put them under two headings: living things, non-living things.

When you have finished the two lists, write down the following question:

Why do we find Uncle Crow so attractive described as he is, and compared to the things we have listed?

Do not answer this question yet, but think about it as you continue with the following task. It is designed to help you arrive at a fuller answer than you would perhaps give now.

● Similes and metaphors

You have no doubt been told that a *simile* is a comparison between two things using words such as 'like' or 'as' when the two objects have something in common. A *metaphor* is a more definite comparison, in which we say that something 'is' something else. For example, in this story we read:

'"Times," his grandfather said, "I've seen him sittin' on the bank on *a sweltering hot day like a furnace*, when nobody was gettin' a bite not even off a bloodsucker. And there your Uncle Crow'd be apullin' 'em out by the dozen, *like a man shellin' harvest beans*."'

Also:

'"*Masterpiece of a man*, your Uncle Crow," his grandfather said.'

Look at these comparisons and explain why they are described as simile or metaphor. Write down all the ideas that occur to you because of this pictorial way of writing.

Similes are easier to spot than metaphors. This story contains far more similes than metaphors. Very little is described without the use of this figure of speech.

Make a list of similes from the story. Set them out as follows:

Simile	Objects compared
a pike as long as your arm	pike (fish) – human arm
it was not at all unlike a black tarred boat	shape of house – shape of boat
like a old gutter pipe	human throat – rusty pipe

When you have compiled this you should have a good list of the sounds, colours and smells of the story to add to the list you made when you examined the description of Uncle Crow himself. Read through the lists you have made, ticking those items you feel have something humorous about them.

Next, discuss briefly any changes you detect in the boy's feelings as the story progresses. Does the writer have a point of view different from that of the young boy?

● Written assignments (literature): descriptive writing

1. Describe Great Uncle Crow. Remember the question you wrote down earlier. *Why do we find Uncle Crow so attractive described as he is, and compared to the things we have listed?*
Your description should in some way answer this question and bring out the qualities that make Uncle Crow attractive.
Your title is: 'Great Uncle Crow'

2. We see everything in this story through the eyes of a young boy. Imagine you are that young boy ten or fifteen years later. Describe all you saw and learned on the day you visited Great Uncle Crow. Try to convey the way you felt when you were a young child and something of the glamour of his life as you saw it. What do you now feel about things you felt then? Your title is: 'Looking back at Great Uncle Crow'.

Taddy the Lamplighter
Bill Naughton

Through the dense narrow streets where I lived as a boy, there came every evening a man called Taddy the Lamplighter. A bunch of us lads would be huddled round the lamp-post at the corner of Alley Brew, shoving close up to each other for warmth, and telling 'Pat and Mick' tales in the darkness while waiting for him.

From a distance you could see the flicker of his light, held high in the air – fixed in a metal holder at the tip of his long pole – and we would all go silent as he drew near, and our eyes would watch upwards as he turned on the tap with a poke of his pole. The gas would hiss and he would thrust the torchlike tip through the glass door at the bottom of the lamp, and then, at the instant of the bright gaslight exploding over us, we would scatter with cries and cheers of "Hooray! Good old Taddy!"

Taddy always looked serious, but he seemed to enjoy our applause just the same. He would give a squint at the light, see if it was what it should be, whilst Ollie Baker, a serious-minded sort of lad, would always say something, "A champion light there tonight, Taddy!" To which Taddy would usually nod, "Aye, it is that an' all!" Or if the light were not so good Ollie would say, "Not up to the mark tonight, Taddy!" And Taddy would shake his head and sigh, "Them 'ometers must be low, me lad." Then on his way he would go, and Ollie, who was the leader, would decide what game we should play, perhaps 'Jumpy o'er back' or 'Ride or kench'.

One cold December evening there was a very light fall of snow – not enough for snow fights, but enough to make 'a slur'. This was a slide about two feet wide and twenty-five feet in length, starting at the lamp-post and running down the steep pavement of Alley Brew. In swift file we skated down, Ollie leading, and our clog-irons quickly brought up a slippery glass-like surface. And just as we were tiring a bit, Art Baines spotted Taddy's light.

"Quick!" he whispered, "let's lay a blind slur for Taddy!"

I could see Ollie wasn't for it, but all the others agreed that quick, that he didn't try to sway them. We dropped down on our knees, and with our caps we coaxed a thin coating of snow over our slur. And when it was hidden we got in

our usual position by the lamp, and we watched old Taddy as he came along.

His two flat feet slopped up the Brew in the snow, and by some lucky chance they kept just at the edge of the slur without stepping on to it. We had expected him to go arm over tip at every step, but he hadn't, and now we watched in silence as he lifted his pole to nudge the tap. Then, just as he was about to pop the torch up the lamp, he moved a foot — and that did for him. He let out a squeak, and in a flurried attempt to recover his balance as his foot slipped, he jerked his other foot on to the slur.

Poor old Taddy — his shout for help was drowned by our laughter and yells as we watched him slide backwards, his pole in the air, and faster he went until he fell flat on his face. And even then, stretched out, he went on sliding, while we ran off with yells and shrieks. But I think we all felt a bit ashamed.

After waiting by the chapel for twenty minutes, and there being no sign of Taddy coming to light his next lamp we got anxious.

"We'll hatta go back an' see," said Ollie.

There were about nine of us, and with Ollie in the lead we cautiously made our way back.

"Look!" I whispered, "the owd chap's lying where he fell!"

And sure enough he was, down on the snowy pavement, his pole swung some feet away. He wasn't unconscious, but he was groaning. We went to help him up, expecting him to curse us, but instead he began moaning about the lamps.

"Me lamps! ... all me lamps are out! ... an' I've busted me arm an' carn't light 'um." His right arm hung limp. "Tak' me watch outa m'pocket," he said. I put my hand in his waistcoat pocket and pulled out a big watch. "All but eight o'clock," I said.

"Oh, good grief," cried Taddy, "folk won't be able to see their way about without me lamps. I'll get sacked ... I will for a surety."

Ollie stood before the old man. "We was the instigators, Taddy," he said solemnly, "an' it's up to us to see that thy lamps are lit. But first we gotta take thee to Doctor Paddy Bryce to have thy arm fixed."

"Nay, nay," said Taddy, brightening up — "the lights come first! I can have my arm fettled afterwards."

We all marched round with Taddy and his pole, some supporting him, because he felt weak, and others competing for the job of lighting the lamps — which meant a few gas mantles were broken by our excited and inexpert hands.

Then we took him to Paddy Bryce's. We gathered outside the doctor's and discussed the situation while he was inside.

"It's not his lighting-up job as is the problem," said Ollie, "but his knocking-up job in the morning."

Taddy combined his job of lamplighter – which was very low paid – with that of knocker-up. Although a number of workers used the new-fangled alarum-clock, the majority relied on Taddy. Not only for the human touch but also because Taddy did not merely waken you, he took it as his responsibility to actually get you up. Many with clocks had been known to overlie, but that had never happened to one of Taddy's customers.

"Folk 'ull miss their work," said Art Baines.

To us, at that time, this seemed the worst thing that could possibly happen to anybody. We all went very quiet, and deadly serious. And when Taddy came out of the surgery, his arm bandaged beneath his topcoat, it was to confirm our fears. "I'm done," he said. "I carn't use my right hand, an' I'll not have strength enough in my left to whack with my knocking-up pole. There'll be eighty-three families miss their work tomorrow – unless a miracle happens."

"Give us the names an' lend us the pole," said Ollie, "an' we'll knock 'um up for thee."

"No use," said Taddy with a shake of his head, "I keep all the names an' times in me head. An' besides that, they every one expect their one special call. They won't get up without it. I've gotta bully some an' coax others, an' so on."

Ollie turned to me, "Let's volunteer to go with him in the morning, eh, Bill?"

"It's a late morning," put in Taddy eagerly. "My first customer isn't till haw past four. I could give you both a shout at twenty-past. You could whack an' I'd call."

Half-past four didn't seem so late to me, but with them all looking at me I had to say I would. But I was uneasy at what my mother would say about being wakened at that hour. To my surprise, however, she agreed with the idea, and since my father was on the night shift at pit I didn't have to worry over him.

The thought of so many families depending on me to get them up worried me out of my sleep, and when Taddy called I was already awake, and I ran downstairs in my bare feet. In two minutes I was dressed and out in the street with a butty in my hand.

"Ollie should be here in a minute," said Taddy, "so we'll give Harry Foster a call while we're waiting."

He handed me a long bamboo pole that had an end made of a fan of flexible wires, and when we got to Foster's I stood looking at the upstairs window, and waiting for Taddy to give me the signal.

"Right, me lad," he said, "let him have a tattoo of nice sharp raps, but not too heavy."

Feeling nervous, but willing, I tapped the wires against the window.

"Nay, nay, that'll never do!" snapped Taddy. "Sharp raps but not heavy ones."

The next time I did better, and when I had finished Taddy called up.

"'Arry! 'Arry! it wants a minute to haw-past."

I heard Harry let out a sigh, "What time did tha say it were?"

"Haw' past four. Nice morning, 'Arry, a topcoat warmer than it was yes'day. Snow's done it."

He waited, listening for Harry's footsteps on the bedroom floor. When he heard them clomp heavily he nodded, "I can trust Harry – he'll not go back to bed. But some of 'um jump straight in again once me back's turned."

The next customer was Steve Duckley, and Taddy had a change of tactics here. Ollie who had now arrived, was told, "Keep smattering till tha hears a voice."

Ollie almost rapped the window in, and both of us laughed because we could hear Steve's snoring above the sound of the wires.

"Steve!" growled Taddy, "Steve, you flamer – wilt' waken up!"

"Aw ... aw ..." grunted Steve.

"Come on," said Taddy, "we'll leave him for a few minutes an' go across to Miss Spood who works at the chemic' factory."

He warned me as I held the pole, "Very gently, me lad – like it were the breeze playing ont' glass." Then, after my very delicate tapping he called softly, "Are you awake, Florence? It's twenty minutes to five, my dear, an' it's a petticoat warmer till it was yes'day."

Florence replied, "Yerss!" And as we moved to the next house Taddy explained, "That girl needs coaxing. She's very sensitive – a sharp word would turn her back into bed for the day."

The next customer was a miner called Jack Beezer, and I was shocked at the language he used on Taddy. He cursed him for all he was worth, and refused to get up. We went to another customer and then returned to Jack, "Tha's missed the first winding," shouted Taddy, "an' tha's missed the second, an' I'll bet tha misses the third." Then he whispered to me, "Keep tapping an' don't stop till I tell thee." I kept at it, though when Jack jumped up with a roar I ran away.

"He's a good lad is Jack," said Taddy. "He allus pays me eightpence a week: fourpence for knocking him up an' fourpence for being cussed by him."

Twenty minutes later when we were passing Beezer's, Jack was waiting at the door with a pint pot of tea for Taddy. The busiest time was from five-thirty to six-thirty, and after that Taddy relaxed, bought a newspaper, and added an item of news to his greeting, "Twenty-to-seven, Sarah!" Pause. "I see they've nabbed that chap who chopped up his wife – he were in lodgings at Blackpoo'."

Taddy had very sharp eyes and he kept a constant watch for people going back to bed, and if there were no light downstairs he would go back and investigate. Nobody escaped.

At seven o'clock he let Ollie and myself go, saying that he could manage the remaining few without using his pole, and so, excited and slightly tired, we ran off home.

But as the days went on to weeks – and Taddy's arm seemed to get worse instead of better – the job, though interesting, lost most of its excitement. The other lads would go lighting the lamps, but none of them could be relied upon to get up at just after four in the morning, so that the job fell to Ollie and myself all the time.

Then when it seemed that we were destined to go round with Taddy for the rest of our days, it chanced that we bumped into Doctor Bryce one morning – when he was coming out of Ogden's, where the eldest daughter had been having a bad time over her first confinement. He was a very surly chap when sober and it seemed that he was about to pass us without speaking, were it not that he spotted Taddy's arm in the sling.

"What the devil's the matter with you?" he asked. "It's over a month since I told you to give that arm plenty of exercise." And being a blunt sort of a chap he grabbed Taddy's arm out of the sling and began to shake it violently up and down. "That's healed grand," he said, "so you keep it on the move – or I'll clout your lug if I catch you dodging."

Ollie and myself saw it all. The minute the doctor walked off Taddy put his hand out for the knocking-up pole.

"An' I should damn well think so!" snorted Ollie.

"Taddy,' I said, "you're a false 'un!"

"I were lonely," said Taddy sadly. "It's a lonely job. You lads were such company for me, I didn't like to be left on my own again. I hope you're not mad at me. Goodbye."

As we watched him trudge up the street Ollie said, "Poor chap, his working days are numbered."

"Why?" I asked.

"They've invented street lights that light themselves," said Ollie, "an' them cheap alarum-clocks will soon be all the vogue, so that nob'dy 'ull want a knocker-up."

I half-believed what he said about the lamps, but I could not believe what he said about the clocks. I thought about it walking home in the dark morning, and I could not imagine that any right-minded person would choose to be roused by the noisy racket of a cheap alarum-clock in preference to Taddy's sensitive window-tapping and his understanding of how folk feel when they're wakened up. By contrast the tin clock seemed a horrible way of being woke up, and I should have been right shaken had I known that it would triumph as swiftly as it did over old Taddy.

If you read this story after studying *Great Uncle Crow* the contrast in style should be obvious. But how has the writer created for us a memorable character with whom we sympathise? There are no lists of similes and other figures of speech to compile, no appeals to the senses of sight, smell and hearing to be appreciated.

● Character portrayal through dialogue and actions

The factual statements we can make about Taddy are few if we use only the direct evidence of the story. However, if we examine what he says and does very carefully, we can see true qualities of human warmth that do not depend upon poetic skills alone for appreciation.

Discuss the following extracts from the story. What do they reveal about Taddy? Make notes.

'... at the instant of the bright gaslight exploding over us, we would scatter with cries and cheers of "Hooray! Good old Taddy!"

Taddy always looked serious, but seemed to enjoy our applause just the same. He would give a squint at the light, see if it was what it should be ...'

'He wasn't unconscious, but he was groaning. We went to help him up, expecting him to curse us, but instead he began moaning about the lamps.'

'"Oh, good grief," cried Taddy, "folk won't be able to see their way about without me lamps. I'll get sacked ... I will for a surety."'

'Although a number of workers used the new-fangled alarum clock, the majority relied on Taddy. Not only for the human touch but also because Taddy did not merely waken you, he took it as his responsibility to actually get you up.'

'"There'll be eighty-three families miss their work tomorrow – unless a miracle happens."'

Compile a similar list of quotations. There is no need to write very long quotations. Make notes as before.

● **Written assignment (literature): appreciation**
Remember the way we got a picture of Great Uncle Crow. Describe Taddy the Lamplighter and show how his character is revealed.

● **Discussion and note-taking: comparison of the stories**
In pairs or groups, discuss and make notes on the following points, in preparation for a comparison between *Great Uncle Crow* and *Taddy the Lamplighter*.

(a) *The narrator*
Who is telling each story? What do we find out about him?

(b) *The setting*
Where is each story set? What period is each set in? What do we find out

about the lives of people like Taddy and those he served from the story?

(c) *The language*
What can be said about the language of each storyteller and his characters? Compare the different dialects used in each story. Make lists of dialect words or quaint phrases used e.g. 'fettled', 'for a surety' and 'clout your lug'. Distinguish between dialect and accent (the different ways words are pronounced). For example, 'haw-past' and ''Arry'.

(d) *The use of dialogue*
Dialogue is important in revealing character. Words that indicate how people speak can be compared. Bates uses 'said' most of the time but Naughton occasionally varies this, using words like 'snapped Taddy' and 'growled Taddy'. Make a list of other examples.

● Spoken assignment: talk

Prepare a talk, illustrated with quotations from both stories, to show the different methods and styles adopted by H. E. Bates and Bill Naughton in *Great Uncle Crow* and *Taddy the Lamplighter*.

The script of your talk may be submitted as a piece of written coursework.

● General assignments (language and literature)

Choose one of the following to write about. Which one you choose, and how you write, will determine whether the piece is seen as language or as literature coursework.

1. Which story do you prefer? Give reasons for your choice.

2. Retell each story from the point of view of the main character.
Either, or both, may be read onto tape in character and offered as spoken as well as written assignments.

3. 'Life in town or country can provide satisfaction and fulfilment.'
Write on this topic, using evidence from the two stories and any other evidence you wish to support your point of view.

4. If you could ask the two main characters about their lives, what questions would you ask them? What answers would you expect?
Write this up as magazine article or a TV chat show script.

5. Write another adventure or incident from the lives of these two characters. You must remain true to the two men as we know them from the stories we have studied. Taddy would not be lazy, for example, or Uncle Crow a workaholic! You can try to use a style that suits each character's view of the world.

6. To show you have appreciated the importance of dialogue in each story, write two conversations, in the styles of the two authors:

(a) between the Grandfather and the boy's mother when she reproaches him for taking the boy to see such an old reprobate,
(b) between Taddy and one of his clients, a mill girl, who doesn't like getting up early in the morning.

6

More Than Just the Disease

● Written activity: group identity

Every group has ways of signalling that its members belong together. The members of a group show their unity by the type of clothes they wear, their hairstyles, their taste in music, what they do with their leisure time, their ways of speaking, or what they choose to talk about.

If someone new came to join your English class, list five things that could make him or her an *outsider*.

What five things would make you feel someone was an *insider* or could belong to your circle of friends?

● Spoken assignment: anecdote

In front of the class, two minutes allowed, tell the class an anecdote. Tell of an occasion when you felt an outsider.

> What was the occasion?
>
> What made you feel an outsider?
>
> How did you feel during the incident?
>
> How did it end?
>
> Did you stay an outsider?

Often, a group does not mean to shut others out, but does – perhaps by something as simple as everyone else watching the same television programme; or because everybody has known each other so long that they can keep saying, 'Do you remember when ...?'; or because everybody wears a particular kind of training shoe, or goes to a particular club.

Everybody has experience of being an outsider in some group. Sometimes we don't care; sometimes we feel upset, but don't show it; sometimes we seem to dislike or dismiss the group; sometimes we worry about what is wrong with us; sometimes we become anxious to appear the same as others.

Now read the story, thinking about insiders and outsiders.

More Than Just the Disease
Bernard MacLaverty

As he unpacked his case Neil kept hearing his mother's voice. *Be tidy at all times, then no one can surprise you.* This was a strange house he'd come to, set in the middle of a steep terraced garden. Everything in it seemed of an unusual design; the wardrobe in which he hung his good jacket was of black lacquer with a yellow inlay of exotic birds. *A little too ornate for my taste – vulgar almost.* And pictures – there were pictures hanging everywhere, portraits, landscapes, sketches. *Dust gatherers.* The last things in his case were some comics and he laid them with his ironed and folded pyjamas on the pillow of the bottom bunk and went to join the others.

They were all sitting in the growing dark of the large front room, Michael drinking hot chocolate, Anne his sister with her legs flopped over the arm of the chair, Dr Middleton squeaking slowly back and forth in the rocking-chair while his wife moved around preparing to go out.

"Now, boys, you must be in bed by ten thirty at the latest. Anne can sit up until we come back if she wants. We'll not be far away and if anything does happen you can phone 'The Seaview'." She spent some time looking in an ornamental jug for a pen to write down the number. "I can find nothing in this house yet."

"We don't need Anne to babysit," said Michael. "We're perfectly capable of looking after ourselves. Isn't that right Neil?" Neil nodded. He didn't like Michael involving him in an argument with the rest of the family. He had to have the tact of a guest; sit on the fence yet remain Michael's friend.

"Can we not stay up as late as Anne?" asked Michael.

"Anne is fifteen years of age. Please, Michael, it's been a long day. Off to bed."

"But Mama, Neil and I ..."

"Michael." The voice came from the darkness of the rocking-chair and had enough threat in it to stop Michael. The two boys got up and went to their bedroom.

Neil lifted his pyjamas and went to the bathroom. He dressed for bed buttoning the jacket right up to his neck and went back with his clothes draped over his arm. Michael was half-dressed.

"That was quick," he said. He bent his thin arms, flexing his biceps. "I only wear pyjama bottoms. Steve McQueen, he-man," and he thumped his chest before climbing to the top bunk. They lay and talked and talked – about their first year at the school, how lucky they had been to have been put in the same form, who they hated most. The Crow with his black gown and beaky nose, the Moon with his pallid round face, wee Hamish with his almost mad preoccupation with ruling red lines. Once Neil had awkwardly ruled a line which showed the two bumps of his fingers protruding beyond the ruler and wee Hamish had pounced on it.

"What are these bumps? Is this a drawing of a camel, boy?" Everybody except Neil had laughed and if there was one thing he couldn't abide it was to be laughed at. A voice whispered that it was a drawing of his girlfriend's chest.

Neil talked about the Scholarship examination and the day he got his results. When he saw the fat envelope on the mat he knew his life would change – if you got the thin envelope you had failed, a fat one with coloured forms meant that you had passed. What Neil did not say was that his mother had cried, kneeling in the hallway hugging and kissing him. He had never seen anyone cry with happiness before and it worried him a bit. Nor did he repeat what she had said with her eyes shining. *Now you'll be at school with the sons of doctors and lawyers.*

Anne opened the door and hissed into the dark.

"You've got to stop talking right now. Get to sleep." She was in a cotton nightdress which became almost transparent with the light of the hallway behind her. Neil saw her curved shape outlined to its margins. He wanted her to stay there but she slammed the door.

After that they whispered and had a farting competition. They heard Michael's father and mother come in, make tea and go to bed. It was ages before either of them slept. All the time Neil was in agonies with his itch but he did not want to scratch in case Michael should feel the shaking communicated to the top bunk.

In the morning Neil was first awake and tiptoed to the bathroom with all his clothes to get dressed. He took off his pyjama jacket and looked at himself in the mirror. Every morning he hoped that it would have miraculously disappeared overnight but it was still there crawling all over his chest and shoulders: his psoriasis – a redness with an edge as irregular as a map and the skin flaking and scumming off the top. Its pattern changed from week to week but only once had it appeared above his collar line. That week his mother had kept him off school. He turned his back on the mirror and put on a shirt, buttoning it up to the neck. He wondered if he should wear a tie to breakfast but his mother's voice had nothing to say on the subject.

Breakfast wasn't a meal like in his own house when he and his mother sat down at table and had cereal and tea and toast with sometimes a boiled egg. Here people just arrived and poured themselves cornflakes and went off to various parts of the room, or even the house, to eat them. The only still figure was the doctor himself. He sat at the corner of the table reading the *Scotsman* and drinking coffee. He wore blue running shoes and no socks and had a T-shirt on. Except for his receding M-shaped hairline he did not look at all like a doctor. In Edinburgh anytime Neil had seen him he wore a dark suit and a spotted bow-tie.

Anne came in. "*Guten Morgen, mein Papa.* Hello Neil." She was bright and washed with her yellow hair in a knot on the top of her head. Neil thought she was the most beautiful girl he had ever seen up close. She wore a pair of denims cut down to shorts so that there were frayed fringes about her thighs. She also had what his mother called *a figure.* She ate her cornflakes noisily and the doctor did not even raise his eyes from the paper. *Close your mouth when you're eating, please. Others have to live with you.*

"Some performance last night, eh Neil?" she said.

"Pardon?"

"Daddy, they talked till all hours."

Her father turned a page of the paper and his hand groped out like a blind man's to find his coffee.

"Sorry," said Neil.

"I'm only joking," said Anne and smiled at him. He blushed because she looked directly into his eyes and smiled at him as if she liked him. He stumbled to his feet.

"Thank you for the breakfast," he said to the room in general and went outside to the garden where Michael was sitting on the steps.

"Where did you get to? You didn't even excuse yourself from the table," said Neil.

"I wasn't at the table, small Fry," said Michael. He was throwing pea-sized stones into an ornamental pond at a lower level.

"One minute you were there and the next you were gone."

"I thought it was going to get heavy."

"What?"

"I know the signs. The way the old man reads the paper. Coming in late last night."

"Oh."

Neil lifted a handful of multi-coloured gravel and fed the pieces singly into his other hand and lobbed them at the pool. They made a nice plip noise.

"Watch it," said Michael. He stilled Neil's throwing arm with his hand. "Here comes Mrs Wan."

"Who's she?"

An old woman in a bottle-green cardigan and baggy mouse-coloured trousers came stepping one step at a time down towards them. She wore a puce-coloured hat like a turban and, although it was high summer, a pair of men's leather gloves.

"Good morning, boys," she said. Her voice was the most superior thing Neil had ever heard, even more so than his elocution teacher's. "And how are you this year, Benjamin?"

"Fine. This is my friend Neil Fry." Neil stood up and nodded. She was holding secateurs and a flat wooden basket. He knew that she would find it awkward to shake hands so he did not offer his.

"How do you do? What do you think of my garden, young man?"

"It's very good. Tidy."

"Let's hope it remains that way throughout your stay," she said and continued her sideways stepping down until she reached the compost heap at the bottom beyond the ornamental pool.

"Who is she?" asked Neil.

"She owns the house. Lets it to us for the whole of the summer."

"But where does she live when you're here?"

"Up the back in a caravan. She's got ninety million cats." Mrs Wan's puce turban threaded in and out of the flowers as she weeded and pruned. It was a dull overcast day and the wind was moving the brightly-coloured rose blooms.

"Fancy a swim?" asked Michael.

"Too cold. Anyway I told you I can't swim."

"You don't have to swim. Just horse around. It's great."

"Naw."

Michael threw his whole handful of gravel chipping into the pond and went up the steps to the house.

That afternoon the shelf of cloud moved inland and the sky over the Atlantic became blue. The wind dropped and Dr Middleton observed that the mare's-tails were a good sign. The whole family went down the hundred yards to the beach, each one carrying something – a basket, a deckchair, a lilo.

"Where else in the world but Scotland would we have the beach to ourselves on a day like this?" said Mrs Middleton. The doctor agreed with a grunt. Michael got stripped to his swimming trunks and they taught Neil to play *boules* in the hard sand near the water. The balls were of bright grooved steel and he enjoyed trying to lob them different ways until he finally copied the doctor who showed him how to put back-spin on them. Anne wore a turquoise bikini and kept hooking her fingers beneath the elastic of her pants and snapping them out to cover more of her bottom. She did this every time she bent to pick up her boule and Neil came to watch for it. When they stopped playing Michael and his sister ran off to leap about in the breakers – large curling walls, glass-green, which nearly knocked them off their feet. From where he stood Neil could only hear their cries faintly. He went and sat down with the doctor and his wife.

"Do you not like the water?" she asked. She was lying on a sunbed, gleaming with suntan oil. She had her dress rucked up beyond her knees and her shoulder straps loosened.

"No. It's too cold."

"The only place *I'll* ever swim again is the Med," said the doctor.

"Sissy," said his wife, without opening her eyes. Neil lay down and tried to think of a better reason for not swimming. His mother had one friend who occasionally phoned for her to go to the Commonwealth Pool. When she really didn't feel like it there was only one excuse that seemed to work.

At tea Michael took a perverse pleasure out of telling him again and again how warm the water was and Anne innocently agreed with him.

The next day was scorching hot. Even at breakfast time they could see the heat corrugating the air above the slabbed part of the garden.

"You *must* come in for a swim today, Fry. I'm boiled already," said Michael.

"The forecast is twenty-one degrees," said the doctor from behind his paper. Anne whistled in appreciation.

Neil's thighs were sticking to the plastic of his chair. He said, "My mother forgot to pack my swimming trunks. I looked yesterday."

Mrs Middleton, in a flowing orange dressing-gown, spoke over her shoulder from the sink. "Borrow a pair of Michael's." Before he could stop her she had gone off with wet hands in search of extra swimming trunks.

"Couldn't be simpler," she said, setting a navy blue pair with white side panels on the table in front of Neil.

"I'll get mine," said Michael and dashed to his room. Anne sat opposite Neil on the Formica kitchen bench-top swinging her legs. She coaxed him to come swimming, again looking into his eyes. He looked down and away from them.

"Come on, Neil. Michael's not much fun in the water."

"The fact is," said Neil, "I've got my period."

There was a long silence and a slight rustle of the *Scotsman* as Dr Middleton looked over the top of it. Then Anne half-slid, half-vaulted off the bench and ran out. Neil heard her make funny snorts in her nose.

"That's too bad," said the doctor and got up and went out of the room shutting the door behind him. Neil heard Anne's voice and her father's, then he heard the bedroom door shut. He folded his swimming trunks and set them on the sideboard. Mrs Middleton gave a series of little coughs and smiled at him.

"Can I help you with the dishes?" he asked. There was something not right.

"Are you sure you're well enough?" she said smiling. Neil nodded and began to lift the cups from various places in the room. She washed and he dried with a slow thoroughness.

"Neil, nobody is going to force you to swim. So you can feel quite safe."

Michael came in with his swimming gear in a roll under his arm.

"Ready, small Fry?"

"Michael, could I have a word? Neil, could you leave those bathing trunks back in Michael's wardrobe?"

On the beach the boys lay down on the sand. Michael hadn't spoken since they left the house. He walked in front, he picked the spot, he lay down and Neil followed him. The sun was hot and again they had the beach to themselves. Neil picked up a handful of sand and examined it as he spilled it out slowly.

"I bet you there's at least one speck of gold on this beach," he said.

"That's a bloody stupid thing to say."

"I'll bet you there is."

Michael rolled over turning his back. "I can pick them."

"What?"

"I can really pick them."

"What do you mean?"

"I might as well have asked a girl to come away on holiday."

Neil's fist bunched in the sand.

"What's the use of somebody who won't go in for a dip?"

"I can't, that's all."

"My Mum says you must have a very special reason. What is it, Fry?"

Neil opened his hand and some of the damp, deeper sand remained in little segments where he had clenched it. He was almost sure Anne had laughed.

"I'm not telling you."

"Useless bloody Mama's boy," said Michael. He got up flinging a handful of sand at Neil and ran down to the water. Some of the sand went into Neil's eyes, making him cry. He knuckled them clear and blinked, watching Michael jump, his elbows up, as each glass wave rolled at him belly-high.

Neil shouted hopelessly towards the sea. "That's the last time I'm getting you into the pictures."

He walked back towards the house. He had been here a night, a day and a morning. It would be a whole week before he could get home. Right now he felt he *was* a Mama's boy. He just wanted to climb the stair and be with her behind the closed door of their house. This had been the first time in his life he had been away from her and, although he had been reluctant because of this very thing, she had insisted that he could not turn down an invitation from the doctor's family. *It will teach you how to conduct yourself in good society.*

At lunch time Michael did not speak to him but made up salad rolls and took them on to the patio. Anne and her father had gone into the village on bicycles. Neil sat at the table chewing his roll with difficulty and staring in front of him. *If there is one thing I cannot abide it's a milk bottle on the table.* Mrs Middleton was the only one left for him to talk to.

"We met Mrs Wan this morning," he said.

"Oh did you? She's a rum bird – feeding all those cats."

"How many has she?"

"I don't know. They're never all together at the same time. She's a Duchess, you know?"

"A real one?"

"Yes. I can't remember her title – from somewhere in England. She married some Oriental and lived in the Far East. Africa too for a time. When he died she came home. Look." She waved her hand at all the bric-à-brac. "Look at this."

She went to a glass-fronted cabinet and took out what looked like a lace ball. It was made of ivory and inside was another ball with just as intricately carved mandarins and elephants and palm leaves, with another one inside that again.

"The question is how did they carve the one inside. It's all one piece."

Neil turned it over in his hands marvelling at the mystery. He handed it carefully back.

"You wouldn't want to play boules with that," he said.

"Isn't it exquisitely delicate?"

He nodded and said, "Thank you for the lunch. It was very nourishing."

He wandered outside in the garden and sat for a while by the pool. It was hot and the air was full of the noise of insects and bees moving in and out the flowers. He went down to the beach and saw that his friend Michael had joined up with some other boys to play cricket. He sat down out of sight of them at the side of a sand-dune. He lay back and closed his eyes. They had laughed at him in school when he said he didn't know what l.b.w. meant. He had been given a free cricket bat but there was hardly a mark on it because he couldn't seem to hit the ball. It was so hard and came at him so fast that he was more interested in getting out of its way than playing any fancy strokes. Scholarship boys were officially known as foundationers but the boys called them 'fundies' or 'fundaments'. When he asked what it meant somebody told him to look it up in a dictionary. 'Part of body on which one sits; buttocks; anus.'

He lifted his head and listened. At first he thought it was the noise of a distant seagull but it came again and he knew it wasn't. He looked up to the top of the sand-dune and saw a kitten, its tiny black tail upright and quivering.

"Pshhh-wshhh."

He climbed the sand and lifted it. It miaowed thinly. He stroked its head and back and felt the frail fish bones of its ribs. It purred and he carried it back to the house. He climbed the steps behind the kitchen and saw a caravan screened by a thick hedge. The door was open and he had to hold it steady with his knee before he could knock on it.

"Come in," Mrs Wan's voice called. Neil stepped up into the van. After the bright sunlight it was gloomy inside. It smelt of old and cat. He saw Mrs Wan sitting along one wall with her feet up.

"I found this and thought maybe it was yours," said Neil handing the cat over to her. She scolded it.

"You little monkey," she said and smiled at Neil. "This cat is a black sheep.

He's always wandering off. Thank you, young man. It was very kind of you to take the trouble to return him."

"It was no trouble."

She was dressed as she had been the day before except for the gloves. Her hands were old and her fingers bristled with rings. She waved at him as he turned to go.

"Just a minute. Would you like something to drink – as a reward?" She stood up and rattled in a cupboard above the sink.

"I think some tonic water is all I can offer you. Will that do?" She didn't give him a clean glass but just rinsed one for a moment under the thin trickle from the swan-neck tap at the tiny sink. She chased three cats away from the covered bench seat and waved him to sit down. Because the glass was not very clean the bubbles adhered to its sides. He saw that nothing was clean as he looked about the place. There were several tins of Kit-e-Kat opened on the draining-board and a silver fork encrusted with the stuff lay beside them. There were saucers all over the floor with milk which had evaporated in the heat leaving yellow rings. Everything was untidy. He set his glass between a pile of magazines and a marmalade pot on the table. She asked him his name and about his school and where he lived and about his father. Neil knew that his mother would call her nosey but he thought that she seemed interested in all his answers. She listened intently, blinking and staring at him with her face slightly turned as if she had a deaf ear.

"My father died a long time ago," he said.

"And your mother?"

"She's alive."

"And what does she do for a living?"

"She works in the cinema."

"Oh how interesting. Is she an actress?"

"No. She just works there. With a torch. She gets me in free – for films that are suitable for me. Sometimes I take my friend Michael with me."

"Is that the boy below?"

"Yes."

"I thought his name was Benjamin. But how marvellous that you can see all these films free." She clapped her ringed hands together and seemed genuinely excited. "I used to love the cinema. The cartoons were my favourite. And the newsreels. I'll bet you're very popular when a good picture comes to town."

"Yes I am," said Neil and smiled and sipped his tonic.

"Let's go outside and talk. It's a shame to waste such a day in here." Neil offered his arm as she lowered herself from the step to the ground.

"What a polite young man."

"That's my mother's fault."

They sat on the deckchairs facing the sun and she lit a cigarette, holding it between her jewelled fingers. Her face was brown and criss-crossed with wrinkles.

"Why aren't you in swimming on such a day?" she asked.

Neil hesitated, then heard himself say, "I can't. I've got a disease."

"What is it?"

Again he paused but this old woman seemed to demand the truth.

"A thing – on my chest."

"Let me see?" she said and leaned forward. He was amazed to find himself unbuttoning his shirt and showing her his mark. In the sunlight it didn't look so red. She scrutinized it and hummed, pursing her mouth and biting her lower lip.

"Why does it stop you bathing?"

Neil shrugged and began to button up when she stopped him.

"Let the sun at it. I'm sure it can do no harm." He left his shirt lying open. "When I was in Africa I worked with lepers."

"Lepers?"

"Yes. So the sight of you doesn't worry me," she said. "Watch that you don't suffer from more than just the disease."

"I don't understand."

"It's bad enough having it without being shy about it as well."

"Have you got leprosy now?"

"No. It's not as contagious as everybody says."

Neil finished his tonic and lay back in the chair. The sun was bright and hot on his chest. He listened to Mrs Wan talking about leprosy, of how the lepers lost their fingers and toes, not because of the disease but because they had lost all feeling in them and they broke and damaged them without knowing. Eventually they got gangrene. Almost all the horrible things of leprosy, she said, were secondary. Suddenly he heard Michael's voice.

"Mrs Wan, Mum says could you tell her where ..." his voice tailed off seeing Neil's chest, "... the cheese grater is?"

"Do you know, I think I brought it up here." She got up and stepped slowly into the caravan. Neil closed over his shirt and began to button it. Neither boy said a word.

At tea Michael spoke to him as if they were friends again and in bed that night it was Neil's suggestion that they go for a swim.

"Now? Are you mad?"

"They say it's warmer at night."

"Yeah and we could make dummies in the beds like Clint Eastwood."

"They don't *have* to look like Clint Eastwood." They both laughed quiet sneezing laughs.

After one o'clock they dropped out of the window and ran to the beach. For almost half an hour in the pale darkness Neil thrashed and shivered. Eventually he sat down to wait in the warmer shallows, feeling the withdrawing sea hollow the sand around him. Further out, Michael whooped and rode the breakers like a shadow against their whiteness.

● Close study of character: Neil

Characters have an inner and an outer life. In this story the only inner life that is communicated to us is Neil's. His inner thoughts are the only ones we are told about.

He wants others to understand him. No opportunity is given to him to communicate clearly, so he ends up expressing his inner self in actions that can be misunderstood. For example, Neil refuses to swim because he is embarrassed about the disfigurement on his chest. Michael thinks the refusal is because he is too feeble to join in any fun.

Neil suffers from psoriasis and he is a scholarship boy.
Psoriasis is defined in *Chambers English Dictionary* as: 'a skin disease in which red scaly papules and patches appear.' It can be made worse by heat and stress. Neil might say, 'I suffer from psoriasis.' Others might say, 'He's got spots.'
A *scholarship boy* is one who has passed an examination at the age of eleven to attend a school which charges fees. The scholarship boy has obtained such high marks in the examination that the school is willing to accept him without fees.
Neil might say, 'I am a scholarship boy. I got very high marks in the entrance

exam.' Others might say, 'He shouldn't be at this school. His mother can't afford the fees.'

● **Neil's emotions**

We share Neil's emotions for much of the story. Here is a list of emotions or feelings. Copy the list out and note next to each emotion an occasion in the story when Neil feels that emotion. For example, he would certainly have felt pleasure when he received the result of his examination.

Emotion:		*Occasion:*
	anxiety	
	happiness	
	inadequacy	
	jealousy	
	misery	
	relief	

Discuss and add to this list four other emotions and occasions for which you feel there is evidence in the story.

Your completed list now has ten entries.

Discuss each entry and decide for each one whether it is *positive* or *negative* i.e. does it make Neil feel *good* or *bad* about himself?

Next, ask yourself whether these emotions depend on the presence or actions of another character. If you find that several emotions are linked to the same character, discuss what you think are the reasons.

● **Written assignment (literature): description of character**

Neil is a misunderstood character. Describe him and explain some of the problems that face him.

Your title is: 'A Study of Neil Fry – Part One'.

● **Other characters and Neil**

Although we don't see into their inner thoughts and feelings, we can tell something about the feelings of other characters from their actions.

In your groups, make one statement about what these people think of Neil at any point in the story: Michael, Dr Middleton, Mrs Middleton, Anne.

As before, give your evidence by referring to a specific occasion.

You may find this selection of incidents useful:

1. Just after Neil has said that he won't go to play in the sea for the first time:

   'Michael threw his whole handful of gravel chipping into the pond and went up the steps to the house.'

2. After Neil has used the excuse his mother uses when she does not want to go swimming:

   '"The fact is," said Neil, "I've got my period."

   There was a long silence and a slight rustle of the *Scotsman* as Dr Middleton looked over the top of it. Then Anne half-slid, half-vaulted off the bench and ran out. Neil heard her make funny snorts in her nose.

   "That's too bad," said the doctor and got up and went out of the room shutting the door behind him. Neil heard Anne's voice and her father's, then he heard the bedroom door shut. He folded his swimming trunks and set them on the sideboard. Mrs Middleton gave a series of little coughs and smiled at him.'

   'At lunch time Michael did not speak to him but made up salad rolls and took them on to the patio.'

4. '"Mrs Wan, Mum says could you tell her where ..." his voice tailed off seeing Neil's chest, "... the cheese grater is?"'

● Neil's mother

Although Neil's mother does not appear, we learn about her through Neil's thoughts. He uses her words to guide himself through the new experience of life with the Middleton family.

Below are some of her sayings. Using these as evidence, construct as full and accurate a picture as you can of the person behind the sayings.

'Be tidy at all times, then no one can surprise you.'

'A little too ornate for my taste – vulgar almost.'

'Dust gatherers.'

'Now you'll be at school with the sons of doctors and lawyers.'

'Close your mouth when you're eating, please. Others have to live with you.'

'It will teach you how to conduct yourself in good society.'

'If there is one thing I cannot abide it's a milk bottle on the table.'

• Mrs Wan

When Neil visits Mrs Wan, he does not hear his mother's voice. Why do you think this is so?

As the director of a film of this short story you are to give instructions to the actress playing Mrs Wan. What directions would you give about

(a) voice,

(b) way of sitting,

(c) way of walking,

(d) way of looking?

What directions would you give concerning the part of Mrs Wan to:

(a) the make-up artist,

(b) the props collector,

(c) the costume maker?

Remember the Middletons are renting Mrs Wan's house for the summer, so the contents of the house, the furnishings and the garden all reflect her taste.

Make up three things that Neil's mother might say if she met Mrs Wan or visited her house.

• Written assignment (literature): description of events and actions

Describe the experience Neil has when he goes to stay with the Middletons and how he tries to cope with things.

Your title is: 'A Study of Neil Fry – Part Two'.

• Spoken assignment: discussion

Mrs Wan says to Neil, 'Watch that you don't suffer from more than just the disease.'

Discuss what she means by this. Would this piece of advice be useful in other circumstances?

• Written assignment (literature): appreciation

Does the story have a happy ending for Neil? If you think it does, explain why and how this has happened.

Your title is: 'A Study of Neil Fry – Part Three'.

● Close study of text: the author's style

Some parts of the writing of this story seem to work at more than one level. Although what is being described is part of the story's action, we find the description helps us to understand the experience.

Example 1

'She went to a glass-fronted cabinet and took out what looked like a lace ball. It was made of ivory and inside was another ball with just as intricately carved mandarins and elephants and palm leaves, with another one inside that again.

"The question is how did they carve the one inside. It's all one piece."

Neil turned it over in his hands marvelling at the mystery. He handed it carefully back.

"You wouldn't want to play boules with that," he said.

"Isn't it exquisitely delicate?"

He nodded and said, "Thank you for the lunch. It was very nourishing."'

What ideas do you get which can apply to the whole story from this description of the 'lace ball'?

You might feel that the intricacy, the mystery, the differences, and yet the strange unity of the 'lace ball' are meant to make us aware of these aspects of life – as shown in the story where the very different lives of Neil, the Middletons and Mrs Wan nevertheless have a strange sense of relationship one to another.

Can you find ideas from the following pieces of description? What is MacLaverty trying to make us aware of, other than the simple action?

Example 2

'He looked up to the top of the sand-dune and saw a kitten, its tiny black tail upright and quivering.

"Pshhh-wshhh."

He climbed the sand and lifted it. It miaowed thinly. He stroked its head and back and felt the frail fish bones of its ribs. It purred and he carried it back to the house.'

Example 3

'For almost half an hour in the pale darkness Neil thrashed and shivered. Eventually he sat down to wait in the warmer shallows, feeling the withdrawing sea hollow the sand around him. Further out, Michael whooped and rode the breakers like a shadow against their whiteness.'

● Written assignment (literature): appreciation

What aspects of MacLaverty's style interest you in *More Than Just the Disease*? You must refer closely to the text to back up your ideas. You may want to deal with such points as:

    use of setting,
    use of significant detail to convey character,
    communication of viewpoint,
    use of contrast,
    use of descriptive writing,
    the importance of the title.

Your title is: 'MacLaverty's Style'.

● General assignments

1. A writer can use many different ways to help us see the characters of a story. Show how some of the characters in this story – Neil, the Middletons, Mrs Wan and Neil's mother – are created for us.

2. Describe two characters from the story and explain how we come to know and understand them.

3. When Neil returns home he finds his mother's instructions much more irksome than before. He tries to tell her about his experiences at the Middletons, above all trying to communicate his feelings about himself, the Middletons and Mrs Wan.

   Write the conversation they have as a play, putting in any stage directions and scene setting you think appropriate. Bring out the characters as you think of them, both in what is said and how it is said.

4. Neil and Michael return to school with a deeper understanding of each other. Write a sequel to the story in which they discuss the events of the holiday.

5. Neil's mother – Mrs Fry – writes to Dr and Mrs Middleton thanking them for giving Neil a holiday where he enjoyed himself and learned much about himself. Write the letter.

7

War of the Worlds

● **Author's introduction to *War of the Worlds***

Most of my work is unplanned. I start with a sentence; this sentence becomes the foundation on which to build the rest of the story. War of the Worlds started with the mother reminiscing about her eccentric grandmother, who had an obsession with growing prizewinning mangoes. (Remember the mangoes at the end of the story!)

However the real work of writing only starts once the first draft is finished. This is brutally trimmed, so that the main story and its ideas come over clear and unencumbered by excess baggage. What remains is then endlessly reworked, with a continual search for the right phrase, the right word, the right image to ensure that the story will come vibrantly alive in the mind of the reader.

I believe that all writers are products of their society and environment, therefore writing is not something divorced from real life but arises directly from the people, ideas and events around us.

I wanted to show life through British Asian eyes, because we're always being asked to see life through British/English eyes, and to demonstrate that British Asians also have opinions and views on the 'sacred cows' of English culture such as romantic love, 'freedom', etc. I also wanted to show that views can be the same even if people come from different backgrounds. For example, the scene in the Gurudwara could just as well have been set in a church. There is hypocrisy in every religion.

And lastly – maybe because I'm a woman? – I know that women are vastly more intelligent and capable than men will ever admit, or allow them to be. You may not see the chains but most women walk around in shackles. (Why do you think they're always suffering from backache, bellyache, headache and heartache?) Therefore my main characters are always (Asian) women who are intelligent, articulate: engaging in acts of adventure, rebellion, derring-do, and who sometimes manage to have a bit of fun along the way.

Ravinder Randhawa

War of the Worlds
Ravinder Randhawa

"You two want to do what you want? Behave as you please?" Mum's voice hard and strained, refusing to shed the tears flooding her eyes. "If you don't like living here, you can leave. Both of you." It was like being given ECT. Little shockwaves burned through us. I could see Suki's eyes growing larger and larger, expanding exponentially. Mum had never said anything like this to us before.

She'd never blamed us before, she'd blamed the nurse in the hospital when we were born. "Twin daughters," she'd told Mum, bearing one on each arm. "Aren't they sweet? Sweet on the outside, acid on the inside," she'd said sing-song. "Oh, they're going to be terrible. The Terrible Twins!" chuckling away.

"Because your father isn't around any more ..." Mum still couldn't bring herself to use words like dead ... "you think you no longer need to watch your tongue, or have respect for other people. And you never have to come back. Have your freedom." Scooping up the baby, marching off upstairs.

It wasn't that we'd changed, things had. We'd been wilder than wild even when Dad was alive: running round town like we were urban guerrillas of the Asian kind. No part of town we didn't know, no person we didn't suss out, no action we didn't know about. The town was our battleground. Our Frontline. Dad would rave and rant at us, tell us we were shameless, not fit to live in civilised society and did we know what happened to women like us? Dad wanted us to be accommodating, to fit in, to live like decent people. We know what 'decent' people get up to when they think no one's looking, we argued back, like there seems to be one set of rules people use if they think they're going to be found out and another set if they think they can do whatever they want in safe secrecy. And it's not as if everyone doesn't know what's going on. They're all happy to shut their eyes to it 'cos they don't want to rock the boat and they don't want to grass on anyone else in case they get grassed on themselves.

Mum and Dad copped it from us every time. We were part of them and they were part of us and that's why we could never be soft with them. If we got them to agree with us, just once, it was like the gates were opened for us to take on the whole world.

And now Mum was saying we could leave. Go. Do what we want. Walk out the front door. We both swivelled our heads to look towards it, though of course we couldn't see it from where we were sitting. Suki and I didn't look at each other; we didn't have to. Mum's ultimatum was ticking like a time-bomb in our brains.

Freedom!

We both stood up, went towards the front door and opened it. It was a beautiful summer evening: balmy, cool, fragrant. Real tourist brochure stuff. We stepped out, over the threshold.

"Charlie's having her party tonight," said Suki.

"Probably be the same old crowd."

"We should go to London. Thousands of new people there."

"Millions. And new things to do."

"Living on our own."

"Making it in the Metropolis."

A car drove by and the bloke in it waved to us. We both waved back, our arms like enthusiastic windscreen wipers. We could hear him reversing his car further up the road, the gravel crunching under his tyres. The blokes loved doing that. Made them feel like Action Man come alive. His engine noise zoomed towards us and then stopped as the car came to a body-shaking, gravel-crunching stop outside our gate.

"You gonna go?" asked Suki.

"I did him last time. He won't know the difference."

She sauntered off towards him and I sat peeling grass blades, till a pile of curled green strips lay at my feet.

Their voices rose and fell, scraps of sentences floated back to me followed by occasional riffs of laughter; Suki was leading him on, making him think he had a chance. He didn't of course. He was too ordinary. His flash car and trendy clothes couldn't make up for the mediocre stuff in his brain. I was surprised he hadn't heard of us, hadn't been warned off going near the terrible twins. We had a whole pack of enemies in town, not least among them, the blokes who'd sworn they loved us madly and couldn't live without us. Until we put our reject stamp on them.

Suki and I always compared notes and it was always the same old story: unimaginative, unintelligent. Men who thought they were God's special gift to Asian women. The white blokes wanted to liberate us from our 'primitive' traditions and customs; the Asian blokes thought weren't we lucky to be loved by them in spite of our dubious reputations and bad style of life. Nothing guaranteed

to make us run faster and further than blokes imagining themselves to be 'In Love' with us. We'd seen enough of the after-effects of 'In Love' to make us avoid it like the proverbial plague.

First there was Janet, whose bloke had been 'In Love' with her, had chased her for months till she'd finally come round, as they say; come to her senses, he'd said. And Paul had been ever so romantic, insisting on a church wedding, white dress, whisking her off to a grand honeymoon. Janet don't talk about Love no more though – bit difficult when half your teeth been knocked out, and all the other bits of your body knocked in.

Then there was our cousin, Jeeta. Got to be fair, he hadn't said he loved Kulwinder. Just that he forgot to tell her that he'd promised his love to the *gori* next door; just that he didn't have the guts to tell his mother, either, as she busily went about arranging his marriage to Kulwinder. Kulwinder who was sweet, obedient and modest, the perfect Indian girl, the perfect Indian bride.

"Being perfect didn't stop her getting messed up, did it?" said Suki in one of her sarky moods.

Kulwinder did her best. We know she tried hard, but she was too innocent, too simple for his tactics, and he knew she didn't know how to fight back. He wanted to drive her away by driving her to a nervous breakdown; that much she sussed out and flew the nest before the rot could set in.

Suki and I couldn't believe it. The whole family, even our Mum and Dad, sided with him: they said she should have tried harder, been more patient, understanding. Marriage wasn't the easy option the West made it out to be. It had to be worked at, sacrifices and compromises made. "Sita-Savitri doesn't live here any more, don't you know?" I said. Wasted my inter-cultural mythical allusions, didn't I, 'cos they all turned round and looked as blank as blank at me.

Suki and I wanted to make Halal meat out of Jeeta and serve him up to Kulwinder on a platter, but she wouldn't have none of it. She was too good an Indian girl to get mixed up in revenge and justice, and anyway her father had to think of her future. He'd have to start looking for another marriage for her. She mustn't jeopardise her chances.

Then there was the time we brought Shanti and her baby home.

"They've been thrown out of their home, Mum, and an English woman was trying to help her, but you know how none of these *goras* can speak Punjabi ..."

"Illiterate lot," added Suki, interrupting my grand speech. Mum took her in and Mum and Mum's friends all gathered round to help. They brought clothes for

Shanti and the baby, they cooked food for them, they condoled, they consoled, they commiserated and then stood back as Shanti and baby went back to her horrible husband. We couldn't understand it and attacked Mum for driving her back.

"Shanti thought it over and made her own choice," said Mum.

"Some choice," muttered Suki.

"That's all some women get."

"It's wrong."

"Yes," replied Mum, seeming to agree with us for once, "but it won't be for long, will it? You two are going to change the world, aren't you?" She could be dead sarcastic, our mum.

We couldn't let it go, could we? We decided on direct action: decided to get them at the Gurudwara. Anyone could get up and speak. The men did it all the time, giving long lectures on righteous living and long-winded explanations of God's thoughts and intentions; they all talked like they had a hot line to the heavens.

We'd made sure we were dressed proper and started off by reading a verse from Suki's *Gotka* (no, she hadn't got religion, just thought it was 'bootiful' poetic stuff. Mum and Dad would get ever so pleased when they saw her reading it – thinking that the light of goodness had finally touched their wayward daughter). I've done a lot of things in my (short) life, but getting up there in front of all them Sunday-come-to-worship-people was the toughest. It started off all sweet and nice, the mothers and grandmothers smiling at us, whispering among themselves about how nice it was to see us young women taking part. I sneaked a glance at Dad. Shouldn't have. His eyes were sending out laser beams of anger. He knew we were up to something.

Finishing the verse, we started in on our talk, speaking our best Punjabi and careful not to let our dupattas slip off our heads. We began by saying that there was much suffering in our community and that we, as the Gurudwara, should organise to do something about it. For instance there should be a fund for women who have to leave home because they are being beaten or ill-treated; the Gurudwara should arrange accommodation as well as helping them with education and training and make sure they weren't outcast by the rest of the community. Rather the Gurudwara should praise them for having the courage to liberate themselves from cruelty, just as India had liberated herself from the cruelty of the Raj (rather a neat touch, I thought: the linking of the personal to the political, the micro to

the macro). It was as if the windows had banged open and let in a hot strong
wind; a susurration of whispers eddied to and fro.

They didn't know we'd only given them the hors d'oeuvre. We then suggested that the problem should be tackled at the root: men were not going to
have respect for women unless they had respect for women's work; therefore the
boys should be taught cooking, cleaning, babycare, etc. The men sniggered, some
laughed out loud.

"Men who beat or mistreat their wives should be heavily fined by the
Gurudwara, and if they persist should be cast out from our society. And if they've
taken a dowry they should be made to return it, in double. Blokes who make girls
pregnant and then leave them in the lurch should never be allowed to have an
arranged marriage . . ." We had to stop 'cos Pati's dad, Harcharan Singh, stood up
and launched into an attack on us. We were really disgusted! That man spent
more money on his drinking and smoking than he did on his family, and still
wanted them to be grateful for whatever scraps he threw their way. This man was
now standing up and accusing us of being corrupt and dangerous; others were
nodding their heads in agreement.

"Are you saying these things don't happen?" we asked, all innocent-like.

I don't think he even heard, just carried on with his diatribe against 'children who don't know their place and women who have no respect for tradition
and custom.' Others couldn't wait and interrupted until there were several voices
all speaking at once. One voice strained above the others and accused us of
bringing dirt and filth into the house of God and getting a bit carried away he let
slip a couple of nasty words. Mistake, because Mrs Gill, who was a Moral
Majority in her own right, got up immediately and rounded on him like a 40-ton
truck. Adjusting her dupatta like a gunslinger adjusting his holster, she told him
it was his rotten tongue defiling the house of God and why couldn't the men sit
quiet and let the girls finish what they were saying.

"We should listen to our young sometimes," she said. "We may learn
something." She gave us the all-clear nod and sat back down among the women.

This was the crunch, the lunge for the jugular vein, and as I formed the
words and reached for the microphone I found my voice, Suki's voice, reaching
out, spreading across the hall: "It's no good coming to the Gurudwara once a
week to show how clean and pure you are, it doesn't hide all the sordid, under-
hand things that have been happening all week. The Gurudwara isn't the disinfec-
tant that kills 99 per cent of all germs. It should be treated with more respect. In

turn we who are the Gurudwara should get tough on those men who harass us women, whistle at us, touch us up, attempt to force us into their cars ... Some of them are sitting right here and they know who they are." Like a storm among the trees angry, aggrieved whispers were rustling around the men ... "What about the man who's started a prostitution racket? He's here. And those who can't tell the difference between their daughters and their wives ..." The place exploded, most rising to their feet, some raising their fists to us, others moving forward, pushing through towards us.

Dad had saved us. Defused the danger. The crowd had parted to let him through.

"I suppose we'll have to call him Moses after this," whispered Suki. He stopped by us and turned round to face the others.

"It's late. I'm going to take my daughters home. But we can't go without having Prasad." Picking up the covered bowl of warm Prasad Dad served us each with a round ball of the gorgeous delicious sweet, whispering to us to meet him by the car. He turned round and started serving those nearest to us. Prasad is God's food and you're not supposed to refuse it. You should be glad it's offered to you.

"D-a-d is O-u-r C-h-a-m-p-i-o-n." All the way home we wanted to chant "D-a-d is O-u-r C-h-a-m-p-i-o-n," like the football fans do, but he was in a foul mood so we shut up and kept quiet.

"We think what you did was really brave," said Preeti during the dinner break at school.

"Yeah. Those things really needed to be said," added Bhupinder, her short pigtails swishing round her face; she never had been able to grow her hair below shoulder length, despite all the creams and lotions she poured on to it.

"So why didn't you say anything?" asked Suki. "We could have used some help."

"You kidding? Mum would have come down on me like Two Tons of Bricks."

"Gutless goons always want other people to do their fighting for them," I said, hoping it sounded as sarky as I felt.

"No-one asked you to do it," put in Preeti, coming to her best friend's aid. "Anyway you two fancy yourselves as Revolutionaries."

"Freedom Fighters," added stupid Bhupinder with a stupid giggle. "We wouldn't want to take your glory from you."

"And not everyone's got liberal parents like yours." Poison Preeti again.

Liberal parents! That sure was history, what with Mum as good as throwing us out of the house! Suki was trying to say goodbye to the thing at the gate, his arms stretching out to hold her back, impress her with his burning passion. She moved back towards him once, twice, and I thought, this is silly, why's she wasting her time on him when we've got to talk and make decisions?

"You were right. He's a dead loss." Her skirt swished by me as she sat down.

"There must be some who aren't."

"We'll have to go looking for them, won't we?"

"Mum doesn't want us here if we don't change."

"You want to leave?" Suki turned round to look at me, face on, full frontal.

"I'm not scared of leaving."

"Not the point."

"There's always white people and white society ...?" My voice sounded as if posing a maths problem.

"They'll want us to change to their ways ..." Suki came back as sharp as a knife.

Silence between the two of us. For a change! I picked up the shredded bits of grass and shifted them through my fingers. "Not much choice, is there? I guess it's a case of Here to Stay–Here to Fight."

Suki giggled. "Old slogans never die, eh?"

I had an idea. I thought it was brilliant. "Let's go to Patel's." Suki caught on as I knew she would. "And see if he's got any mangoes for Mum? Right."

We closed the gate very carefully behind us, in case Mum heard and wondered.

● Note-taking and discussion: the title and language of the story

The narrator of this story is obviously very angry. This anger is seen first of all in the title and then in some of the language and imagery used.

The title of this story is similar to the title of a famous novel by H. G. Wells. In that novel, *The War of the Worlds*, the earth is invaded by hostile forces from outer space, chaos ensues and there is a continuing battle for control of the planet.

If this title is to be appropriate for this story, then we must be clear as to what worlds are at war. Make notes under the following headings and discuss your ideas with your partner or group:

    (a)   the world of young people,

    (b)   the adult world,

    (c)   man's world,

    (d)   woman's world,

    (e)   the white world,

    (f)   A British/Asian's world.

Discussion: 'Which worlds are at war in this story?'

When you feel you have arrived at an understanding of the worlds involved in this story, write another heading: 'the language of war'. Skim the story noting down where the author uses the imagery and vocabulary of war. Some examples are given to start you off:

    shockwaves,

    we were urban guerrillas,

    the town was our battleground,

    our frontline.

You should end up with quite a long list of individual words or short phrases.

Using the items on your list, discuss the following questions and make brief answers in note form:

    (a)   How was the town a battleground?

    (b)   Why was mother's ultimatum like a time-bomb?

    (c)   Which seems to you to be more important: the fact that the twins are girls; the fact that they are teenagers; the fact that they are Asian?

    (d)   Were the girls at war with themselves?

- **Written assignment (literature): essay**

Using the notes you have made, the ideas discussed and the brief answers written, write an essay.

Your title is: 'War of the Worlds'.

● Discussion and close study of the text: the different worlds people live in

A very bleak picture of the lives some people have to lead emerges from this story. For example, Shanti and her baby are thrown out of their home by a horrible husband.

Here are some extracts from the story that hint at a problem or do not fully explain why there is a problem. Discuss each one and decide: (a) what the problem is, (b) whether there is an easy solution, (c) whether people are likely to want the solution you come up with.

1. 'We know what "decent" people get up to when they think no one's looking, we argued back, like there seems to be one set of rules people use if they think they're going to be found out and another set if they think they can do whatever they want in safe secrecy.'

2. 'We could hear him reversing his car further up the road, the gravel crunching under his tyres. The blokes loved doing that. Made them feel like Action Man come alive.'

3. 'His flash car and trendy clothes couldn't make up for the mediocre stuff in his brain.'

4. 'Men who thought they were God's special gift to Asian women. The white blokes wanted to liberate us from our "primitive" traditions and customs; the Asian blokes thought weren't we lucky to be loved by them in spite of our dubious reputations and bad style of life.'

5. 'Janet don't talk about Love no more though – bit difficult when half your teeth been knocked out, and all the other bits of your body knocked in.'

6. 'He wanted to drive her away by driving her to a nervous breakdown; that much she sussed out and flew the nest before the rot could set in.'

7. 'Marriage wasn't the easy option the West made it out to be. It had to be worked at, sacrifices and compromises made.'

8. '... they commiserated and then stood back as Shanti went back to her horrible husband. We couldn't understand it and attacked Mum for driving her back.

"Shanti thought it over and made her own choice," said Mum.

"Some choice," muttered Suki.

"That's all some women get."' "

When you have discussed these passages and arrived at some definition of the problem, you should be ready to undertake a similar exercise in reverse. Make a list of other problems you feel exist, and select short extracts from the story to support your point of view.

Here are some ideas of other problems:

(a) cruelty to women,

(b) different education for boys and girls,

(c) women bearing sole responsibility for pregnancy outside marriage,

(d) too much money being spent on drink and other pleasures,

(e) little respect for religion,

(f) prostitution

As before, decide what the problem is, whether there is an easy solution, and whether people want that solution.

● Spoken assignment (language): talk

Using the ideas and information accumulated, prepare the script for a short talk: 'Modern problems and some possible solutions'.

Decide before you start what your target audience is, as this will affect what you write. For example, you could talk to a group of younger pupils, your own class, a meeting of the local Spare Rib group, a mixed gathering of people from the neighbourhood or a political party.

State your target audience below the title of your script title.

● Discussion and close study of the text: the sequence of events

The events in a story do not always happen in the order in which the writer tells them. Sometimes there are flashbacks or other movements back and forth in time.

What is the order of events in this story? Is there a 'normal' beginning, middle and end?

How can the father of the twins be both dead and alive in the story?

Here are some major events from the story. Try to put them:

(1) in the order that they happened,

(2) in the order they occur in the story.

Do this, if possible, without looking back at the story.

(a) the mother's ultimatum: 'You can leave.',

(b) Janet getting married and beaten by her husband,

(c) the father saving the girls 'like Moses' at the Gurudwara,

(d) Shanti taking refuge with her baby then going back to her husband,

(e) Suki talking to the man in the car,

(f) the narrator sitting peeling grass blades, thinking.

How easy is the task of putting these events in order? If it is difficult you may look back at the story. This will help you with (2) but not with (1). Why is this? Perhaps because it is very difficult to put into order our thoughts and feelings, our reasons and justifications for what we say and do.

What you may need to do to help you with (1) is to construct a list under different headings:

Events that happened before the story begins and that we are not told about

e.g. the death of the twins' father

Events that the narrator remembers and tells us about

e.g. what took place at the Gurudwara

Events that are taking place while the narrator tells us her thoughts

e.g. Suki talking to the man in the car

The problem arises because all these events and details exist in the mind of the narrator and help to make her what she is.

● **Written assignment (literature): diary entries**

Imagine that the narrator of this story keeps a diary. What kind of entries would there be?

Because she has such strong feelings about what happens to her and what she sees happening to people around her, it is probable that her diary entries would be concerned with these feelings.

Write the diary entries for *five* days in the life of the narrator. Here are some suggestions, but they are not necessarily in the order in which things happened:

> the day the twins spoke at the Gurudwara,
>
> the day the mother gave the ultimatum,
>
> the day the father died,
>
> the day cousin Jeeta married Kulwinder,
>
> the day Shanti and her baby went back to the horrible husband.

You may choose other days. Think carefully about the order in which you write your entries because your thoughts will reflect what has happened to you in your life.

Much of your factual information will come from the story. Where you have to invent things, do so in a way that is true to the story. Much other information about the way you as narrator feel is also to be found in the story, but in a less clear form than factual details. What you feel on the day your father dies, how he dies and the way you react to the event, you will have to imagine. In this entry show the quality of your identification with the narrator, your understanding and appreciation of the story

8

The Destructors

Graham Greene

I

It was on the eve of August Bank Holiday that the latest recruit became the leader of the Wormsley Common Gang. No one was surprised except Mike, but Mike at the age of nine was surprised by everything. "If you don't shut your mouth," somebody once said to him, "you'll get a frog down it." After that Mike had kept his teeth tightly clamped except when the surprise was too great.

The new recruit had been with the gang since the beginning of the summer holidays, and there were possibilities about his brooding silence that all recognized. He never wasted a word even to tell his name until that was required of him by the rules. When he said "Trevor" it was a statement of fact, not as it would have been with the others a statement of shame or defiance. Nor did anyone laugh except Mike, who, finding himself without support and meeting the dark gaze of the newcomer, opened his mouth and was quiet again. There was every reason why T., as he was afterwards referred to, should have been an object of mockery – there was his name (and they substituted the initial because otherwise they had no excuse not to laugh at it), the fact that his father, a former architect and present clerk, had 'come down in the world' and that his mother considered herself better than the neighbours. What but an odd quality of danger, of the unpredictable, established him in the gang without any ignoble ceremony of initiation?

The gang met every morning in an impromptu car-park, the site of the last bomb of the first blitz. The leader, who was known as Blackie, claimed to have heard it fall, and no one was precise enough in his dates to point out that he would have been one year old and fast asleep on the down platform of Wormsley Common Underground Station. On one side of the car-park leant the first occupied house, No. 3, of the shattered Northwood Terrace – literally leant, for it had suffered from the blast of the bomb and the side walls were supported on wooden struts. A smaller bomb and some incendiaries had fallen beyond, so that the house stuck up like a jagged tooth and carried on the further wall relics of its neighbour, a dado, the remains of a fireplace. T., whose words were almost confined to voting "Yes" or "No" to the plan of operations proposed each day by Blackie, once startled the whole gang by saying broodingly, "Wren built that house, father says."

"Who's Wren?"

"The man who built St Paul's."

"Who cares?" Blackie said. "It's only old Misery's."

Old Misery – whose real name was Thomas – had once been a builder and decorator. He lived alone in the crippled house, doing for himself; once a week you could see him coming back across the common with bread and vegetables, and once as the boys played in the car-park he put his head over the smashed wall of his garden and looked at them.

"Been to the loo," one of the boys said, for it was common knowledge that since the bombs fell something had gone wrong with the pipes of the house and Old Misery was too mean to spend money on the property. He could do the redecorating himself at cost price, but he had never learnt plumbing. The loo was a wooden shed at the bottom of the garden with a star-shaped hole in the door: it had escaped the blast which had smashed the house next door and sucked out the window-frames of No. 3.

The next time the gang became aware of Mr Thomas was more surprising. Blackie, Mike, and a thin yellow boy, who for some reason was called by his surname Summers, met him on the common coming back from the market. Mr Thomas stopped them. He said glumly, "You belong to the lot that play in the car-park?"

Mike was about to answer when Blackie stopped him. As the leader he had responsibilities. "Suppose we are?" he said ambiguously.

"I got some chocolates," Mr Thomas said. "Don't like 'em myself. Here you are. Not enough to go round, I don't suppose. There never is," he added with sombre conviction. He handed over three packets of Smarties.

The gang were puzzled and perturbed by this action and tried to explain it away. "Bet someone dropped them and he picked 'em up," somebody suggested.

"Pinched 'em and then got in a bleeding funk," another thought aloud.

"It's a bribe," Summers said. "He wants us to stop bouncing balls on his wall."

"We'll show him we don't take bribes," Blackie said, and they sacrificed the whole morning to the game of bouncing that only Mike was young enough to enjoy. There was no sign from Mr Thomas.

Next day T. astonished them all. He was late at the rendezvous, and the voting for that day's exploit took place without him. At Blackie's suggestion the gang was to disperse in pairs, take buses at random and see how many free rides could be snatched from unwary conductors (the operation was to be carried out in pairs to avoid cheating). They were drawing lots for their companions when T. arrived.

"Where you been, T.?" Blackie asked. "You can't vote now. You know the rules."

"I've been *there*," T. said. He looked at the ground, as though he had thoughts to hide.

"Where?"

"At Old Misery's." Mike's mouth opened and then hurriedly closed again with a click. He had remembered the frog.

"At Old Misery's?" Blackie said. Ther was nothing in the rules against it, but he had a sensation that T. was treading on dangerous ground. He asked hopefully, "Did you break in?"

"No. I rang the bell."

"And what did you say?"

"I said I wanted to see his house."

"What did he do?"

"He showed it me."

"Pinch anything?"

"No."

"What did you do it for then?"

The gang had gathered round: it was as though an impromptu court were about to form and to try some case of deviation. T. said, "It's a beautiful house," and still watching the ground, meeting no one's eyes, he licked his lips first one way, then the other.

"What do you mean, a beautiful house?" Blackie asked with scorn.

"It's got a staircase two hundred years old like a corkscrew. Nothing holds it up."

"What do you mean, nothing holds it up. Does it float?"

"It's to do with opposite forces, Old Misery said."

"What else?"

"There's panelling."

"Like in the Blue Boar?"

"Two hundred years old."

"Is Old Misery two hundred years old?"

Mike laughed suddenly and then was quiet again. The meeting was in a serious mood. For the first time since T. had strolled into the car-park on the first day of the holidays his position was in danger. It only needed a single use of his real name and the gang would be at his heels.

"What did you do it for?" Blackie asked. He was just, he had no jealousy, he was anxious to retain T. in the gang if he could. It was the word 'beautiful' that worried him – that belonged to a class world that you could still see parodied at the Wormsley Common Empire by a man wearing a top hat and a monocle, with a haw-haw accent. He was tempted to say, "My dear Trevor, old chap," and unleash his hell hounds. "If you'd broken in," he said sadly – that indeed would have been an exploit worthy of the gang.

"This was better," T. said. "I found out things." He continued to stare at his feet, not meeting anybody's eye, as though he were absorbed in some dream he was unwilling – or ashamed – to share.

"What things?"

"Old Misery's going to be away all tomorrow and Bank Holiday."

Blackie said with relief, "You mean we could break in?"

"And pinch things?" somebody asked.

Blackie said, "Nobody's going to pinch things. Breaking in – that's good enough, isn't it? We don't want any court stuff."

"I don't want to pinch anything," T. said. "I've got a better idea."

"What is it?"

T. raised eyes as grey and disturbed as the drab August day. "We'll pull it down," T. said. "We'll destroy it."

Blackie gave a single hoot of laughter and then, like Mike, fell quiet, daunted by the serious implacable gaze. "What'd the police be doing all the time?" he said.

"They'd never know. We'd do it from inside. I've found a way in." He said with a sort of intensity, "We'd be like worms, don't you see, in an apple. When we came out again there'd be nothing there, no staircase, no panels, nothing but just walls, and then we'd make the walls fall down – somehow."

"We'd go to jug," Blackie said.

"Who's to prove? And anyway we wouldn't have pinched anything." He added, without the smallest flicker of glee, "There wouldn't be anything to pinch after we'd finished."

"I've never heard of going to prison for breaking things," Summers said.

"There wouldn't be time," Blackie said. "I've seen housebreakers at work."

"There are twelve of us," T. said. "We'd organize."

"None of us know how..."

"I know," T. said. He looked across at Blackie, "Have you got a better plan?"

"Today," Mike said tactlessly, "we're pinching free rides ..."

"Free rides," T. said. "You can stand down, Blackie, if you'd rather ..."

"The gang's got to vote."

"Put it up then."

Blackie said uneasily, "It's proposed that tomorrow and Monday we destroy Old Misery's house."

"Hear! Hear!" said a fat boy called Joe.

"Who's in favour?"

T. said, "It's carried."

"How do we start?" Summers asked.

"He'll tell you," Blackie said. It was the end of his leadership. He went away to the back of the car-park and began to kick a stone, dribbling it this way and that. There was only one old Morris in the park, for few cars were left there except lorries: without an attendant there was no safety. He took a flying kick at the car and scraped a little paint off the rear mudguard. Beyond, paying no more attention to him than to a stranger, the gang had gathered round T.; Blackie was dimly aware of the fickleness of favour. He thought of going home, of never returning, of letting them all discover the hollowness of T.'s leadership, but suppose after all what T. proposed was possible – nothing like it had ever been done before. The fame of the Wormsley Common car-park gang would surely reach around London. There would be headlines in the papers. Even the grown-up gangs who ran the betting at the all-in wrestling and the barrow-boys would hear with respect of how Old Misery's house had been destroyed. Driven by the pure, simple, and altruistic ambition of fame for the gang, Blackie came back to where T. stood in the shadow of Misery's wall.

T. was giving his orders with decision: it was as though this plan had been with him all his life, pondered through the seasons, now in his fifteenth year crystallized with the pain of puberty. "You," he said to Mike, "bring some big

nails, the biggest you can find, and a hammer. Anyone else who can better bring a hammer and a screwdriver. We'll need plenty of them. Chisels too. We can't have too many chisels. Can anybody bring a saw?"

"I can," Mike said.

"Not a child's saw," T. said. "A real saw."

Blackie realized he had raised his hand like any ordinary member of the gang.

"Right, you bring one, Blackie. But now there's a difficulty. We want a hacksaw."

"What's a hacksaw?" someone asked.

"You can get 'em at Woolworth's," Summers said.

The fat boy called Joe said gloomily, "I knew it would end in a collection."

"I'll get one myself," T. said. "I don't want your money. But I can't buy a sledge-hammer."

Blackie said, "They are working on No. 15. I know where they'll leave their stuff for Bank Holiday."

"Then that's all," T. said. "We meet here at nine sharp."

"I've got to go to church," Mike said.

"Come over the wall and whistle. We'll let you in."

II

On Sunday morning all were punctual except Blackie, even Mike. Mike had had a stroke of luck. His mother felt ill, his father was tired after Saturday night, and he was told to go to church alone with many warnings of what would happen if he strayed. Blackie had had difficulty in smuggling out the saw, and then in finding the sledge-hammer at the back of No. 15. He approached the house from a lane at the rear of the garden, for fear of the policeman's beat along the main road. The tired evergreens kept off a stormy sun; another wet Bank Holiday was being prepared over the Atlantic, beginning in swirls of dust under the trees. Blackie climbed the wall into Misery's garden.

There was no sign of anybody anywhere. The loo stood like a tomb in a neglected graveyard. The curtains were drawn. The house slept. Blackie lumbered nearer with the saw and the sledge-hammer. Perhaps after all nobody had turned up: the plan had been a wild invention: they had woken wiser. But when he came close to the back door he could hear a confusion of sound, hardly louder than a hive in swarm: a clickety-clack, a bang bang bang, a scraping, a creaking, a sudden painful crack. He thought: it's true, and whistled.

They opened the back door to him and he came in. He had at once the impression of organization, very different from the old happy-go-lucky ways under his leadership. For a while he wandered up and down stairs looking for T. Nobody addressed him: he had a sense of great urgency, and already he could begin to see the plan. The interior of the house was being carefully demolished without touching the outer walls. Summers with hammer and chisel was ripping out the skirting-boards in the ground floor dining-room: he had already smashed the panels of the door. In the same room Joe was heaving up the parquet blocks, exposing the soft wood floorboards over the cellar. Coils of wire came out of the damaged skirting and Mike sat happily on the floor, clipping the wires.

On the curved stairs two of the gang were working hard with an inadequate child's saw on the banisters – when they saw Blackie's big saw they signalled for it wordlessly. When he next saw them a quarter of the banisters had been dropped into the hall. He found T. at last in the bathroom – he sat moodily in the least cared-for room in the house, listening to the sounds coming up from below.

"You've really done it," Blackie said with awe. "What's going to happen?"

"We've only just begun," T. said. He looked at the sledge-hammer and gave his instructions. "You stay here and break the bath and the wash-basin. Don't bother about the pipes. They come later."

Mike appeared at the door. "I've finished the wire, T.," he said.

"Good. You've just got to go wandering round now. The kitchen's in the basement. Smash all the china and glass and bottles you can lay hold of. Don't turn on the taps – we don't want a flood – yet. Then go into all the rooms and turn out drawers. If they are locked get one of the others to break them open. Tear up any papers you find and smash all the ornaments. Better take a carving-knife with you from the kitchen. The bedroom's opposite here. Open the pillows and tear up the sheets. That's enough for the moment. And you, Blackie, when you've finished in here crack the plaster in the passage up with your sledge-hammer."

"What are you going to do?" Blackie asked.

"I'm looking for something special," T. said.

It was nearly lunch-time before Blackie had finished and went in search of T. Chaos had advanced. The kitchen was a shambles of broken glass and china. The dining-room was stripped of parquet, the skirting was up, the door had been taken off its hinges, and the destroyers had moved up a floor. Streaks of light came in through the closed shutters where they worked with the seriousness of creators – and destruction is after all a form of creation. A kind of imagination had seen this house as it had now become.

Mike said, "I've got to go home for dinner."

"Who else?" T. asked, but all the others on one excuse or another had brought provisions with them.

They squatted in the ruins of the room and swapped unwanted sandwiches. Half an hour for lunch and they were at work again. By the time Mike returned, they were on the top floor, and by six the superficial damage was completed. The doors were all off, all the skirtings raised, the furniture pillaged and ripped and smashed – no one could have slept in the house except on a bed of broken plaster. T. gave his orders – eight o'clock next morning, and to escape notice they climbed singly over the garden wall, into the car-park. Only Blackie and T. were left: the light had nearly gone, and when they touched a switch, nothing worked – Mike had done his job thoroughly.

"Did you find anything special?" Blackie asked.

T. nodded. "Come over here," he said, "and look." Out of both pockets he drew bundles of pound notes. "Old Misery's savings," he said. "Mike ripped out the mattress, but he missed them."

"What are you going to do? Share them?"

"We aren't thieves," T. said. "Nobody's going to steal anything from this house. I kept these for you and me – a celebration." He knelt down on the floor and counted them out – there were seventy in all. "We'll burn them," he said, "one by one," and taking it in turns they held a note upwards and lit the top corner, so that the flame burnt slowly towards their fingers. The grey ash floated above them and fell on their heads like age. "I'd like to see Old Misery's face when we are through," T. said.

"You hate him a lot?" Blackie asked.

"Of course I don't hate him," T. said. "There'd be no fun if I hated him." The last burning note illuminated his brooding face. "All this hate and love," he said, "it's soft, it's hooey. There's only things, Blackie," and he looked round the room crowded with the unfamiliar shadows of half things, broken things, former things. "I'll race you home, Blackie," he said.

III

Next morning the serious destruction started. Two were missing – Mike and another boy whose parents were off to Southend and Brighton in spite of the slow warm drops that had begun to fall and the rumble of thunder in the estuary like the first guns of the old blitz. "We've got to hurry," T. said.

Summers was restive. "Haven't we done enough?" he said. "I've been given a bob for slot machines. This is like work."

"We've hardly started," T. said. "Why there's all the floors left, and the stairs. We haven't taken out a single window. You voted like the others. We are going to *destroy* this house. There won't be anything left when we've finished."

They began again on the first floor picking up the top floorboards next to the outer wall, leaving the joists exposed. Then they sawed through the joists and retreated into the hall, as what was left of the floor heeled and sank. They had learnt with practice, and the second floor collapsed more easily. By the evening an odd exhilaration seized them as they looked down the great hollow of the house. They ran risks and made mistakes: when they thought of the windows it was too late to reach them. "Cor," Joe said, and dropped a penny down into the dry rubble-filled well. It cracked and span among the broken glass.

"Why did we start this?" Summers asked with astonishment; T. was already on the ground, digging at the rubble, clearing a space along the outer wall. "Turn on the taps," he said. "It's too dark for anyone to see now, and in the morning it won't matter." The water overtook them on the stairs and fell through the floorless rooms.

It was then they heard Mike's whistle at the back. "Something's wrong," Blackie said. They could hear his urgent breathing as they unlocked the door.

"The bogies?" Summers asked.

"Old Misery," Mike said. "He's on his way." He put his head between his knees and retched. "Ran all the way," he said with pride.

"But why?" T. said. "He told me..." He protested with the fury of the child he had never been, "It isn't fair."

"He was down at Southend," Mike said, "and he was on the train coming back. Said it was too cold and wet." He paused and gazed at the water. "My, you've had a storm here. Is the roof leaking?"

"How long will he be?"

"Five minutes. I gave Ma the slip and ran."

"We better clear," Summers said. "We've done enough, anyway."

"Oh no, we haven't. Anybody could do this" – 'this' was the shattered hollowed house with nothing left but the walls. Yet walls could be preserved. Façades were valuable. They could build inside again more beautifully than before. This could again be a home. He said angrily, "We've got to finish. Don't move. Let me think."

"There's no time," a boy said.

"There's got to be a way," T. said. "We couldn't have got thus far ..."

"We've done a lot," Blackie said.

"No. No, we haven't. Somebody watch the front."

"We can't do any more."

"He may come in at the back."

"Watch the back too." T. began to plead. "Just give me a minute and I'll fix it. I swear I'll fix it." But his authority had gone with his ambiguity. He was only one of the gang. "Please," he said.

"Please," Summers mimicked him, and then suddenly struck home with the fatal name. "Run along home, Trevor."

T. stood with his back to the rubble like a boxer knocked groggy against the ropes. He had no words as his dreams shook and slid. Then Blackie acted before the gang had time to laugh, pushing Summers backward.

"I'll watch the front, T.," he said, and cautiously he opened the shutters of the hall. The grey wet common stretched ahead, and the lamps gleamed in the puddles. "Someone's coming, T. No, it's not him. What's your plan, T.?"

"Tell Mike to go out to the loo and hide close beside it. When he hears me he's got to count ten and start to shout."

"Shout what?"

"Oh, 'Help,' anything."

"You hear, Mike," Blackie said. He was the leader again. He took a quick look between the shutters. "He's coming, T."

"Quick, Mike. The loo. Stay here, Blackie, all of you till I yell."

"Where are you going, T.?"

"Don't worry. I'll see to this. I said I would, didn't I?"

Old Misery came limping off the common. He had mud on his shoes and he stopped to scrape them on the pavement's edge. He didn't want to soil his house, which stood jagged and dark between the bomb-sites, saved so narrowly, as he believed, from destruction. Even the fanlight had been left unbroken by the bomb's blast. Somewhere somebody whistled. Old Misery looked sharply round. He didn't trust whistles. A child was shouting: it seemed to come from his own garden. Then a boy ran into the road from the car-park. "Mr Thomas," he called, "Mr Thomas."

"What is it?"

"I'm terribly sorry, Mr Thomas. One of us got taken short, and we thought you wouldn't mind, and now he can't get out."

"What do you mean, boy?"

"He's got stuck in your loo."

"He'd no business... Haven't I seen you before?"

"You showed me your house."

"So I did. So I did. That doesn't give you the right to ..."

"Do hurry, Mr Thomas. He'll suffocate."

"Nonsense. He can't suffocate. Wait till I put my bag in."

"I'll carry your bag."

"Oh, no you don't. I carry my own."

"This way, Mr Thomas."

"I can't get in the garden that way. I've got to go through the house."

"But you can get in the garden this way, Mr Thomas. We often do "

"You often do?" He followed the boy with a scandalized fascination. "When? What right ...?"

"Do you see ...? The wall's low."

"I'm not going to climb walls into my own garden. It's absurd."

"This is how we do it. One foot here, one foot there, and over." The boy's face peered down, an arm shot out, and Mr Thomas found his bag taken and deposited on the other side of the wall.

"Give me back my bag," Mr Thomas said. From the loo a boy yelled and yelled. "I'll call the police."

"Your bag's all right, Mr Thomas. Look. One foot there. On your right. Now just above. To your left." Mr Thomas climbed over his own garden wall. "Here's your bag, Mr Thomas."

"I'll have the wall built up," Mr Thomas said. "I'll not have you boys coming over here, using my loo." He stumbled on the path, but the boy caught his elbow and supported him. "Thank you, thank you, my boy," he murmured automatically. Somebody shouted again through the dark. "I'm coming, I'm coming," Mr Thomas called. He said to the boy beside him, "I'm not unreasonable.

Been a boy myself. As long as things are done regular. I don't mind you playing round the place Saturday mornings. Sometimes I like company. Only it's got to be regular. One of you asks leave and I say Yes. Sometimes I'll say No. Won't feel like it. And you come in at the front door and out at the back. No garden walls."

"Do get him out, Mr Thomas."

"He won't come to any harm in my loo," Mr Thomas said, stumbling slowly down the garden. "Oh, my rheumatics," he said. "Always get 'em on Bank Holiday. I've got to go careful. There's loose stones here. Give me your hand. Do you know what my horoscope said yesterday? 'Abstain from any dealings in first half of week. Danger of serious crash.' That might be on this path," Mr Thomas said. "They speak in parables and double meanings." He paused at the door of the loo. "What's the matter in there?" he called. There was no reply.

"Perhaps he's fainted," the boy said.

"Not in my loo. Here, you, come out," Mr Thomas said, and giving a great jerk at the door he nearly fell on his back when it swung easily open. A hand first supported him and then pushed him hard. His head hit the opposite wall and he sat heavily down. His bag hit his feet. A hand whipped the key out of the lock and the door slammed. "Let me out," he called, and heard the key turn in the lock. "A serious crash," he thought, and felt dithery and confused and old.

A voice spoke to him softly through the star-shaped hole in the door. "Don't worry, Mr Thomas," it said, "we won't hurt you, not if you stay quiet."

Mr Thomas put his head between his hands and pondered. He had noticed that there was only one lorry in the car-park, and he felt certain that the driver would not come for it before the morning. Nobody could hear him from the road in front, and the lane at the back was seldom used. Anyone who passed there would be hurryng home and would not pause for what they would certainly take to be drunken cries. And if he did call "Help," who, on a lonely Bank Holiday evening, would have the courage to investigate? Mr Thomas sat on the loo and pondered with the wisdom of age.

After a while it seemed to him that there were sounds in the silence – they were faint and came from the direction of his house. He stood up and peered through the ventilation-hole – between the cracks in one of the shutters he saw a light, not the light of a lamp, but the wavering light that a candle might give. Then he thought he heard the sound of hammering and scraping and chipping. He thought of burglars – perhaps they employed the boy as a scout, but why should burglars engage in what sounded more and more like a stealthy form of carpentry? Mr Thomas let out an experimental yell, but nobody answered. The noise could not even have reached his enemies.

IV

Mike had gone home to bed, but the rest stayed. The question of leadership no longer concerned the gang. With nails, chisels, screwdrivers, anything that was sharp and penetrating they moved around the inner walls worrying at the mortar between the bricks. They started too high, and it was Blackie who hit on the damp course and realized the work could be halved if they weakened the joints immediately above. It was a long, tiring, unamusing job, but at last it was finished. The gutted house stood there balanced on a few inches of mortar between the damp course and the bricks.

There remained the most dangerous task of all, out in the open at the edge of the bomb-site. Summers was sent to watch the road for passers-by, and Mr Thomas, sitting on the loo, heard clearly now the sound of sawing. It no longer came from his house, and that a little reassured him. He felt less concerned. Perhaps the other noises too had no significance.

A voice spoke to him through the hole. "Mr Thomas."

"Let me out," Mr Thomas said sternly.

"Here's a blanket," the voice said, and a long grey sausage was worked through the hole and fell in swathes over Mr Thomas's head.

"There's nothing personal," the voice said. "We want you to be comfortable tonight."

"Tonight," Mr Thomas repeated incredulously.

"Catch," the voice said. "Penny buns – we've buttered them, and sausage-rolls. We don't want you to starve, Mr Thomas."

Mr Thomas pleaded desperately. "A joke's a joke, boy. Let me out and I won't say a thing. I've got rheumatics. I got to sleep comfortable."

"You wouldn't be comfortable, not in your house, you wouldn't. Not now."

"What do you mean, boy?" but the footsteps receded. There was only the silence of night: no sound of sawing. Mr Thomas tried one more yell, but he was daunted and rebuked by the silence – a long way off an owl hooted and made away again on its muffled flight through the soundless world.

At seven next morning the driver came to fetch his lorry. He climbed into the seat and tried to start the engine. He was vaguely aware of a voice shouting, but it didn't concern him. At last the engine responded and he backed the lorry until it touched the great wooden shore that supported Mr Thomas's house. That way he could drive right out and down the street without reversing. The lorry moved forward, was momentarily checked as though something were pulling it from behind, and then went on to the sound of a long rumbling crash. The driver was astonished to see bricks bouncing ahead of him, while stones hit the roof of his cab. He put on his brakes. When he climbed out the whole landscape had suddenly altered. There was no house beside the car-park, only a hill of rubble. He went round and examined the back of his car for damage, and found a rope tied there that was still twisted at the other end round part of a wooden strut.

The driver again became aware of somebody shouting. It came from the wooden erection which was the nearest thing to a house in that desolation of broken brick. The driver climbed the smashed wall and unlocked the door. Mr Thomas came out of the loo. He was wearing a grey blanket to which flakes of pastry adhered. He gave a sobbing cry. "My house," he said. "Where's my house?"

"Search me," the driver said. His eye lit on the remains of a bath and what had once been a dresser and he began to laugh. There wasn't anything left anywhere.

"How dare you laugh," Mr Thomas said. "It was my house. My house."

"I'm sorry," the driver said, making heroic efforts, but when he remembered the sudden check to his lorry, the crash of bricks falling, he became convulsed again. One moment the house had stood there with such dignity between the bomb-sites like a man in a top hat, and then, bang, crash, there wasn't anything left – not anything. He said, "I'm sorry. I can't help it, Mr Thomas. There's nothing personal, but you got to admit it's funny."

● Group discussion and decision-making: the title of the story

Below are five words and five definitions all adapted from *Chambers English Dictionary*.

In groups, decide which definition goes with which word. Discuss the words until you all agree that you have matched them up correctly.

Words:

Construct

Create

Destroy

Destruction

Destructor

Definitions: A destroyer; a furnace for burning up refuse

To bring into being or form out of nothing; to bring into

being by force of imagination; to make, produce or form;

to design

To unbuild or pull down; to overturn; to ruin; to put an end to

To build up; to put together the parts of; to compose

Act or process of destroying; overthrow; physical or moral ruin

When you have finished your discussion, answer these two questions as a
group. Remember that the opinion of each member of the group is important
and your answers should reflect that.

1. Why do you think the story is called *The Destructors* rather than *The
Destroyers*?

2. What do you think the author means when he says 'destruction is a
kind of creation'? Do you agree?

Report your group's answers back to the whole class.

● Discussion and written activity: newspaper headlines

Before carrying out this assignment, discuss the following headlines. Then,
write headlines of your own, appropriate to different kinds of newspapers.
(If you are not sure of the different styles newspapers have, examine copies of
tabloid and broadsheet newspapers. Compare, for example, *The Sun* and *The
Star* with *The Guardian* and *The Daily Telegraph*.)

● Written assignment (language): newspaper reports

Discuss, draft and prepare two front pages that report the destruction of the
house. One front page will be in the style of a 'tabloid', one in the style of a
'quality' newspaper.

Ensure that there is a contrast, easily appreciated by the reader, between
headlines, styles of reporting and layout. Leave space for pictures.

Articles should include interviews with and/or quotations from Mr Thomas,
the lorry driver and others as appropriate.

The headlines

NOTHING PERSONAL, MATE!

You've gorra laugh!

Boys Destroy House

'It was my house', says aged victim

OLD MAN HOMELESS AFTER POINTLESS DESTRUCTION

Council to Re-House
Homeless Victim

T. Takes after Architect Dad

LOO VIGIL ORDEAL

Kid Gang Hits
Old Misery's Pad

HOUSE DONE TO A T!

● **Group discussion: the plot**

In a short story, a writer only mentions things which are necessary to the story in some way – perhaps for the plot, perhaps for atmosphere, perhaps to help a reader understand a character.

In groups of five, discuss the importance of the following facts and put them in order of importance to the plot. Make notes on the points made by the group. All must agree with the group's final order.

The facts:

1. The existence of an outside toilet.
2. The fact that Mr Thomas lived alone.
3. The isolation of the house.
4. Trevor's father's profession.
5. The Bank Holiday week-end.
6. The lorry in the car park.

When you have done this, elect one member of the group to be a spokesperson. This person moves to the next group in the room, telling that group the reasons for your choice and listening to the group's reasons for their choice.

Your delegate returns with new points of view.

While this has been going on, you have received another spokesperson from another group.

When you have re-grouped, discuss any changes you want to make to your order. Report back to the whole class.

Remember, there are no right or wrong answers. There are opinions supported by reference to the story.

● Written assignments (literature): appreciation

After this activity you should be in a position to use your notes and the opinions you heard expressed to help you complete a piece of written work.

Either

1. 'Good short stories are so well constructed that every detail is important to the final effect.' By giving examples, show that this statement is true of *The Destructors*. Use examples of your own as well as those discussed here.

Or

2. A teacher has asked you for a written assessment of *The Destructors* in order to assist with the planning of next year's work. In your assessment deal with aspects of the story you find interesting.

● Close study of character: Trevor

We gradually build up a picture of a character from what he or she says, does and thinks; from what others say and think about him or her; from the way others react; and, of course, from the way he or she is described by the author.

Read and discuss each of these extracts from the story carefully and write down what we learn about Trevor from them.

1. 'The new recruit had been with the gang since the beginning of the summer holidays, and there were possibilities about his brooding silence that all recognized. He never wasted a word even to tell his name until that was required of him by the rules.'

2. 'T., whose words were almost confined to voting "Yes" or "No" to the plan of operations proposed each day by Blackie, once startled the whole gang by saying broodingly, "Wren built that house, father says."

   "Who's Wren?"

   "The man who built St Paul's."'

3. '"I don't want to pinch anything," T. said. "I've got a better idea."

   "What is it?"

   T. raised eyes, as grey and disturbed as the drab August day. "We'll pull it down," he said. "We'll destroy it."'

4. 'T. was giving his orders with decision: it was as though this plan had been with him all his life, pondered through the seasons.'

5. '"We aren't thieves," T. said. "Nobody's going to steal anything from this house. I kept these for you and me – a celebration." He knelt down on the floor and counted them out – there were seventy in all. "We'll burn them," he said, "one by one," and taking it in turns they held a note upwards and lit the top corner, so that the flame burnt slowly towards their fingers. The grey ash floated above them and fell on their heads like age. "I'd like to see Old Misery's face when we are through," T. said.

   "You hate him a lot?" Blackie asked.

   "Of course I don't hate him," T. said. "There'd be no fun if I hated him." The last burning note illuminated his brooding face. "All this hate and love," he said, "it's soft, it's hooey. There's only things, Blackie," and he looked round the room crowded with the unfamiliar shadows of half things, broken things, former things. "I'll race you home, Blackie," he said.'

6. '"We better clear," Summers said. "We've done enough, anyway."

   "Oh no, we haven't. Anybody could do this" – 'this' was the

shattered hollowed house with nothing left but the walls. Yet walls could be preserved. Façades were valuable. They could be built inside again more beautifully than before. This could again be a home. He said angrily, "We've got to finish. Don't move. Let me think."''

Choose more extracts you consider to be important to the revelation of Trevor's character. Write down what we learn from your extracts.

● **Class role play: what motivates Trevor**

Choose someone to be T. Question T. about his motivation. Speculate on his relationship with his father. Try to find out exactly why he did what he did.

● **Written assignment (literature): character study**

When you have done this, use what you have found out to write a character study of Trevor.

● **Role play: the police investigation**

Following the destruction of 3, Northwood Terrace on Monday 3rd August 1954, a police investigation is mounted. Its aim is to discover:

    (a)   the perpetrators of the crime,

    (b)   what motivated it,

    (c)   exactly how it was carried out.

You are the detective assigned to the case. You and your colleagues are to prepare a dossier of evidence for presentation at Wormsley Common Magistrates' Court.

Your first lead is that a boy called Blackie is bragging about the Wormsley Common Car Park Gang.

The owner of the house, Mr Thomas, is at present suffering from shock and rheumatism in Wormsley Infirmary, but will be available for interview soon. Meanwhile, you are to sift through the debris looking for clues. You are also following up a report of a missing sledge hammer at number 15, and you wish to interview the driver of the lorry. Later you may wish to call on the help of a psychiatrist.

● **Written assignment (language): report writing**

Compile your dossier.

Your title is: 'Report of Investigation'.

- ## Role play: the court hearing

Using all the evidence gathered while doing the previous assignments, organise the court hearing that takes place following the police investigation.

Characters

Mr Thomas

Lorry driver

Gang members: Blackie, Summers, Mike, and others unnamed

Trevor

Trevor's father

Expert witness – a psychiatrist

Magistrate

Clerk of the Court

Police witnesses

Press – representatives from at least two contrasting newspapers

You will need to decide the charges and who is to be charged. Prepare for your role by making notes to help you in court.

- ## Written assignment (language): newspaper reports

Discuss, draft and prepare two front pages that report the court hearing. One front page will be in the style of a 'tabloid', one in the style of a 'quality' newspaper.

Ensure that there is a contrast, easily appreciated by the reader, between headlines, styles of reporting and layout. Leave space for pictures. Articles may include interviews and quotations from the characters concerned. Remember, you are not reporting the events of the story alone, but also the events of your creation of a trial.

9

The Personal Touch

This is intended to be a *controlled conditions assignment*, done without discussion. Read the story and answer the following questions as fully and as carefully as possible. Remember the work you have done on other short stories.

1. This is a very short story, and the writer has included only the most important details. Explain why he considered the following things to be significant:

    (a)   that Joe Priddy and his brother-in-law have watched the Quincy girl undress, with the aid of binoculars,

    (b)   that Hank gave Joe the subscription to *Snoop* as a birthday present,

    (c)   that Joe was sitting by his wife when he opened the second letter from *Snoop*,

    (d)   that Joe has $428.05 hidden in a box under the bed,

    (e)   that the return envelope in the second letter is not pre-paid.

2. It is clear that someone from the *Snoop* office was detailed to spy on Joe Priddy. Compose the memo this person might have sent to David Michaelson, the subscription director, containing the results of the surveillance of Priddy.

    Include information from the story only – do not invent anything. Remember, a memo is written in note form.

3. In his letter to *Snoop*, Priddy objects to 'computer-typed messages that try to appear personal'. What features of the *Snoop* letters qualify them for this criticism, and for his comment that they are 'phony garbage'?

    Write a letter in the same style on one of the following subjects:
(a) mail order sports clothes, (b) burglar alarms which bark like a dog.

4. The second letter from *Snoop* is a sophisticated blackmail concealing its true meaning. Write a different version of the letter, making the meaning perfectly clear.

5. The next time Joe sees his brother-in-law, he tells him about the problems he has had with *Snoop*. Write the conversation they might have had.

6. Below are two statements about junk mail. Which is closest to your own opinion? Write a short list of points which might serve as the basis of a talk on the subject. Give your talk a title, according to the point of view you would take.

> – It's a free society; if people don't like junk mail they can always throw it in the bin.
>
> – junk mail is an intrusion into people's privacy, and can be used for undesirable purposes.

The Personal Touch
Chet Williamson

Seed catalog – toss; Acme flier – keep for Mary; *Sports Illustrated* – keep; phone bill, electric bill, gas bill – keep, keep, keep. Damn it. Subscription-renewal notice to *Snoop* – toss...

Joe Priddy tossed, but the envelope landed face up, balanced on the edge of the wastebasket. He was about to tip it in when he noticed the words PERSONAL MESSAGE INSIDE on the lower-left front.

Personal, my ass, he thought, but he picked it up and read it.

Dear Mr Pridy,

We have not yet received your subscription renewal to SNOOP, the Magazine of Electronic and Personal Surveillance. We trust that, after having been a loyal subscriber for 9 months, you will renew your subscription so that we may continue to send SNOOP to you at 19 Merrydale Drive.

We do not have to remind you, Mr Pridy, of the constant changes in surveillance technology and techniques. We are sure that in your own town of Sidewheel, NY, you have seen the consequences for yourself. So keep up to date on the latest in surveillance, Mr Pridy, by sending $11.95 in the enclosed pre-paid envelope today. As one involved and/or interested in the field of law enforcement, you cannot afford to be without SNOOP, Mr Pridy.

Best regards,

David Michaelson
Subscription Director

P.S.: If you choose not to resubscribe, Mr Pridy, would you please take a moment and tell us why, using the enclosed post-paid envelope? Thank you, Mr Pridy.

Joe shook his head. Who did they think they were fooling? 'Pridy,' said Joe to himself. 'Jesus.'

Mary's brother Hank had given Joe the subscription to *Snoop* for his birthday. 'As a joke,' he'd said, winking at Joe lasciviously, a reference to the evening he and Hank had watched the Quincy girl undress in the apartment across the courtyard with the aid of Joe's binoculars. It had taken some imagination to satisfy Mary's curiosity about Hank's joke, and Joe still felt uncomfortable each time *Snoop* hit his mailbox. And now they wanted him to resubscribe?

He was about to toss the letter again when he thought about the P.S. 'Tell us why.' Maybe he'd do just that. It would get all his feelings about *Snoop* out of his system to let them know just how he felt about their 'personal message.'

Dear MR. MICHELSON,

I have chosen not to resubscribe to SNOOP after having received it for 9 MONTHS because I am sick and tired of computer-typed messages that

try to appear personal. I would much rather
receive an honest request to 'Dear Subscriber'
than the phony garbage that keeps turning up in
my mailbox. So do us both a favor and don't send any
more subscription-renewal notices to me at 19
MERRYDALE DRIVE in my lovely town of
SIDEWHEEL, NY. OK?

Worst regards,

Joseph H. Priddy

P.S.: And it's Priddy, not Pridy. Teach your
word processor to spell.

Joe pulled the page out of the typewriter and stuffed it into the post-paid
envelope.

Two weeks later, he received another subscription-renewal notice. As
before, PERSONAL MESSAGE INSIDE was printed on the envelope. He was about to
throw it away without opening it when he noticed his name was spelled correctly. "Small favors," he muttered, sitting on the couch with Mary and tearing
the envelope open. Could they, he wondered, be responding to his letter?

Dear Mr Priddy,

Christ, another word-processor job... At least they got the name right...

We received your recent letter and are sorry
that you have chosen not to resubscribe to
SNOOP, the Magazine of Electronic and Personal
Surveillance. We hope, however, that you will
reconsider, for if you resubscribe now at the
low price of $427.85 for the next nine issues

$427.85? What the hell? What happened to $11.95?

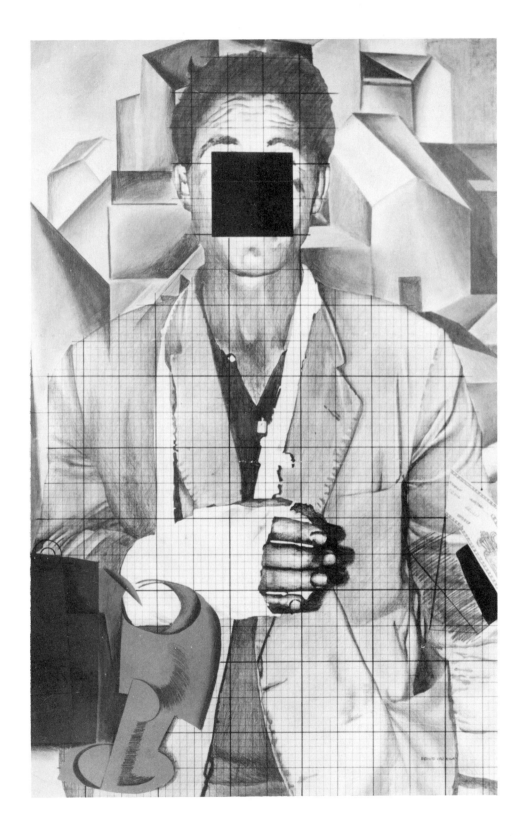

we will be able to continue your subscription
uninterrupted, bringing you all the latest
news and updates on surveillance technology
and techniques. And in today's world, Mr
Priddy, such knowledge should not be taken
lightly. You'll learn techniques similar to
those that led New York City law-enforcement
officials to the biggest heroin bust in
history, that told members of the FBI of a plan
to overthrow the state government of Montana
by force, that alerted us to your own four-
month affair with Rayette Squires.

Wha – Joe could feel the blood leave his face.

Youll get tips on photographic surveillance,
as well, and learn techniques that will let
your own efforts equal that of the enclosed 2 by
2 showing you and Miss Squires at The Sidewheel
Motel in the lovely town of Sidewheel, NY.

Joe dove for the envelope, which was lying dangerously close to Mary's
McCall's. He peeked as surreptitiously as possible into the envelope and found,
between the slick paper flier and the return envelope, a well-lit color photo of
him and Rayette in a compromising and fatiguing position. His wife looked up in
response to his high-pitched whine, and he smacked the envelope shut, giggled
weakly, and finished the letter.

We sincerely hope, Mr Priddy, that you'll
rejoin our family of informed subscribers by
mailing your check for $427.85 very soon.
Shall we say within 10 days?

Regards,

David Michaelson
Subscription Director

Joe got up, envelope and letter in hand, and went to the bedroom to get out the shoe box he'd hidden – the one with the money he'd been squirreling away for an outboard motor, the money even Mary didn't know about.

When he counted it, it totaled $428.05. Which made sense. This time, the return envelope wasn't pre-paid.

I O

Uncle Ernest

● **Written activity and discussion: stereotypes**

A. This is the first sentence of the story. Read it carefully several times:

'A middle-aged man wearing a dirty raincoat, who badly needed a shave and looked as though he hadn't washed for a month, came out of a public lavatory with a cloth bag of tools folded beneath his arm.'

Write down your first impression of the type of man this is.
Discuss your written impressions with the group and the expectations you have of this man's behaviour.

Next, write down your impressions and expectations of the following people:

1. Old man with untidy, straggling moustache, wearing jersey with holes,
2. Smartly dressed woman with leather briefcase and filofax,
3. Fat woman, with spectacles, in home-made jersey and skirt,
4. Teenage boys with close-cropped hair, wearing football hats and scarves,
5. Middle-aged man with short hair cut, in pin-stripe suit,
6. Teenage girl with punk hairstyle.

Discuss your comments with the group.

What has been discussed will probably come under the definition of the word 'stereotype'. The word originally meant a solid metallic plate for printing, cast from a mould of type. In other words, the product was always predictable. The cast was only made when the typesetter or printer was sure that what would be printed was what was intended or expected.

What is a 'stereotype' when we apply the word to people?

Now, if you feel you understand the idea of a stereotype, read the story. If you do not feel quite at ease with the idea use the work in Section B to help you further.

B. A lot of television depends on stereotypes.

Name television characters who fit these stereotypes:

  (a) barmaid with heart of gold,

  (b) strong silent type, very masculine,

  (c) rich, spoilt, beautiful, dangerous person,

  (d) unpleasant, moody person,

  (e) woman, very successful, who never forgets human emotions we all share.

You may not have an answer for all these.

Write more brief stereotyped descriptions. Pass them on to the next group, asking them to guess names. You guess names of characters to fit the descriptions passed to you.

Now work individually. Make a chart that looks like the one below. Write down any stereotypes *you* might be thought to fit into. Write down how you would be expected to behave according to stereotype, and what you feel about being labelled in this way.

Stereotype	How I'm expected to behave	What I feel about this
e.g. Liverpudlian	To be witty, lively, always funny, never down-hearted.	I'm not like a simple-minded character out of *Bread* or *Brookside*.
Class joker		
Loving grandson		
Heavy Metal fan		

Now read the story.

Uncle Ernest

Alan Sillitoe

A middle-aged man wearing a dirty raincoat, who badly needed a shave and looked as though he hadn't washed for a month, came out of a public lavatory with a cloth bag of tools folded beneath his arm. Standing for a moment on the edge of the pavement to adjust his cap – the cleanest thing about him – he looked casually to left and right and, when the flow of traffic had eased off, crossed the road. His name and trade were always spoken in one breath, even when the nature of his trade was not in question: Ernest Brown the upholsterer. Every night before returning to his lodgings he left the bag of tools for safety with a man who looked after the public lavatory near the town centre, for he felt there was a risk of them being lost or stolen should he take them back to his room, and if such a thing were to happen his living would be gone.

Chimes to the value of half past ten boomed from the Council-house clock. Over the theatre patches of blue sky held hard-won positions against autumnal clouds, and a treacherous wind lashed out its gusts, sending paper and cigarette packets cartwheeling along unswept gutters. Empty-bellied Ernest was ready for his breakfast, so walked through a café doorway, instinctively lowering his head as he did so, though the beams were a foot above his height.

The long spacious eating-place was almost full. Ernest usually arrived for his breakfast at nine o'clock, but having been paid ten pounds for re-covering a three-piece in a public house the day before, he had stationed himself in the Saloon Bar for the rest of the evening to drink jar after jar of beer, in a slow, prolonged and concentrated way that lonely men have. As a result it had been difficult to drag himself from drugged and blissful sleep this morning. His face was pale and his eyes an unhealthy yellow: when he spoke only a few solitary teeth showed behind his lips.

Having passed through the half-dozen noisy people standing about he found himself at the counter, a scarred and chipped haven for hands, like a littered invasion beach extending between two headlands of tea urns. The big fleshy brunette was busy, so he hastily scanned the list written out in large white letters on the wall behind. He made a timid gesture with his hand. "A cup of tea, please."

The brunette turned on him. Tea swilled from a huge brown spout – into a cup that had a crack emerging like a hair above the layer of milk – and a spoon clinked after it into the stream. "Anything else?"

He spoke up hesitantly. "Tomatoes on toast as well." Picking up the plate pushed over to him he moved slowly backwards out of the crowd, then turned and walked towards a vacant corner table.

A steamy appetizing smell rose from the plate: he took up the knife and fork and, with the sharp clean action of a craftsman, cut off a corner of the toast and tomato and raised it slowly to his mouth, eating with relish and hardly noticing people sitting roundabout. Each wielding of his knife and fork, each geometrical cut of the slice of toast, each curve and twist of his lips joined in a complex and regular motion that gave him great satisfaction. He ate slowly, quietly and contentedly, aware only of himself and his body being warmed and made tolerable once more by food. The leisurely movement of spoon and cup and saucer made up the familiar noise of late breakfast in a crowded café, sounded like music flowing here and there in variations of rhythm.

For years he had eaten alone, but was not yet accustomed to loneliness. He could not get used to it, had only adapted himself to it temporarily in the hope that one day its spell would break. Ernest remembered little of his past, and life moved under him so that he hardly noticed its progress. There was no strong memory to entice him to what had gone by, except that of dead and dying men straggling barbed wire between the trenches in the first world war. Two sentences had dominated his lips during the years that followed: "I should not be here in England. I should be dead with the rest of them in France." Time bereft him of these sentences, till only a dull wordless image remained.

People, he found, treated him as if he were a ghost, as if he were not made of flesh and blood – or so it seemed – and from then on he had lived alone. His wife left him – due to his too vile temper, it was said – and his brothers went to other towns. Later he had thought to look them up, but decided against it: for even in this isolation only the will to go forward and accept more of it seemed worthwhile. He felt in a dim indefinite way that to go back and search out the slums and landmarks of his youth, old friends, the smells and sounds that beckoned him tangibly from better days, was a sort of death. He argued that it was best to leave them alone, because it seemed somehow probable that after death – whenever it came – he would meet all these things once again.

No pink scar marked his flesh from shellshock and a jolted brain, and so what had happened in the war warranted no pension book, and even to him the word 'injury' never came into his mind. It was just that he did not care any more: the wheel of the years had broken him, and so had made life tolerable. When the next war came his back was not burdened at first, and even the fines and days in prison that he was made to pay for being without Identity Card or Ration Book – or for giving them away with a glad heart to deserters – did not lift him from his tolerable brokenness. The nightmare hours of gunfire and exploding bombs revived a dull image long suppressed as he stared blankly at the cellar wall of his boarding house, and even threw into his mind the scattered words of two insane sentences. But, considering the time-scale his life was lived on, the war ended quickly, and again nothing mattered. He lived from hand to mouth, working cleverly at settees and sofas and chairs, caring about no one. When work was difficult to find and life was hard, he did not notice it very much, and now that he was prosperous and had enough money, he also detected little difference, spending what he earned on beer, and never once thinking that he needed a new coat or a solid pair of boots.

He lifted the last piece of toast and tomato from his plate, then felt dregs of tea moving against his teeth. When he had finished chewing he lit a cigarette and was once more aware of people sitting around him. It was eleven o'clock and the low-roofed café was slowly emptying, leaving only a dozen people inside. He knew that at one table they were talking about horse-racing and at another about war, but words only flowed into his ears and entered his mind at a low pitch of comprehension, leaving it calm and content as he vaguely contemplated the positions and patterns of tables about the room. There would be no work until two o'clock, so he intended sitting where he was until then. Yet a sudden embarrassment at having no food on the table to justify a prolonged occupation of it sent him to the counter for tea and cakes.

As he was being served two small girls came in. One sat at a table but the second and elder stood at the counter. When he returned to his place he found the younger girl sitting there. He was confused and shy, but nevertheless sat down to drink tea and cut a cake into four pieces. The girl looked at him and continued to do so until the elder one came from the counter carrying two cups of steaming tea.

They sat talking and drinking, utterly oblivious of Ernest, who slowly felt their secretive, childish animation enter into himself. He glanced at them from time to time, feeling as if he should not be there, though when he looked at them he did so in a gentle way, with kind, full-smiling eyes. The elder girl, about twelve years old, was dressed in a brown coat that was too big for her, and though she was talking and laughing most of the time he noticed the paleness of her face and her large round eyes that he would have thought beautiful had he not detected the familiar type of vivacity that expressed neglect and want.

The smaller girl was less lively and merely smiled as she answered her sister with brief curt words. She drank her tea and warmed her hands at the same time without putting the cup down once until she had emptied it. Her thin red fingers curled round the cup as she stared into the leaves, and gradually the talk between them died down and they were silent, leaving the field free for traffic that could be heard moving along the street outside, and for inside noises made by the brunette who washed cups and dishes ready for the rush that was expected at mid-day dinner-time.

Ernest was calculating how many yards of rexine would be needed to cover the job he was to do that afternoon, but when the younger girl began speaking he listened to her, hardly aware that he was doing so.

"If you've got any money I'd like a cake, our Alma."

"I haven't got any more money," the elder one replied impatiently.

"Yes you have, and I'd like a cake."

She was adamant, almost aggressive. "Then you'll have to want on, because I've only got tuppence."

"You can buy a cake with that," the young girl persisted, twining her fingers round the empty cup. "We don't need bus fares home because it ain't far to walk."

"We can't walk home: it might rain."

"No it won't."

"Well *I* want a cake as well, but I'm not walking all that way," the elder girl said conclusively, blocking any last gap that might remain in her defences. The younger girl gave up and said nothing, looked emptily in front of her.

Ernest had finished eating and took out a cigarette, struck a match across the iron fastening of a table leg and, having inhaled deeply, allowed smoke to wander from his mouth. Like a gentle tide washing in under the moon, a line of water flowing inwards and covering the sand, a feeling of acute loneliness took hold of him, an agony that would not let him weep. The two girls sat before him wholly engrossed in themselves, still debating whether they should buy a cake or whether they should ride home on a bus.

"But it'll be cold," reasoned the elder, "walking home."

"No it won't," the other said, but with no conviction in her words. The sound of their voices told him how lonely he was, each word feeding him with so much more loneliness that he felt utterly unhappy and empty.

Time went slowly: the minute-hand of the clock seemed as if it were nailed immovably at one angle. The two girls looked at each other and did not notice him: he withdrew into himself and felt the emptiness of the world and wondered how he would spend all the days that seemed to stretch vacantly, like goods on a broken-down conveyor belt, before him. He tried to remember things that had happened and felt panic when he discovered a thirty-year vacuum. All he could see behind was a grey mist and all he could see before him was the same unpredictable fog that would hide nothing. He wanted to walk out of the café and find some activity so that he would henceforth be able to mark off the passage of his empty days, but he had no will to move. He heard someone crying so shook himself free of such thoughts and saw the younger girl with hands to her eyes, weeping. "What's the matter?" he asked tenderly, leaning across the table.

The elder girl replied for her, saying sternly, "Nothing. She's acting daft."

"But she must be crying for some reason. What is it?" Ernest persisted, quietly and soothingly, bending closer still towards her. "Tell me what's wrong." Then he remembered something. He drew it like a live thread from a mixture of reality and dream, hanging on to vague words that floated back into his mind. The girl's conversation came to him through an intricate process of recollection. "I'll get you something to eat," he ventured. "Can I?"

She unscrewed clenched fingers from her eyes and looked up, while the elder girl glared at him resentfully and said, "We don't want anything. We're going now."

"No, don't go," he cried. "You just sit down and see what I'm going to get for you." He stood up and walked to the counter, leaving them whispering to each other.

He came back with a plate of pastries and two cups of tea, which he set before the girls, who looked on in silence. The younger was smiling now. Her round eager eyes were fascinated, yet followed each movement of his hands with some apprehension. Though still hostile the elder girl was gradually subdued by the confidently working actions of his hands, by caressing words and the kindness that showed in his face. He was wholly absorbed in doing good and, at the same time, fighting the feeling of loneliness that he still remembered, but only as a nightmare is remembered.

The two children fell under his spell, began to eat cakes and sip the tea. They glanced at each other, and then at Ernest as he sat before them smoking a cigarette. The café was still almost empty, and the few people eating were so absorbed in themselves, or were in so much of a hurry to eat their food and get out that they took little notice of the small company in the corner. Now that the atmosphere between himself and the two girls had grown more friendly Ernest began to talk to them. "Do you go to school?" he asked.

The elder girl automatically assumed control and answered his questions. "Yes, but today we had to come down town on an errand for our mam."

"Does your mother go out to work, then?"

"Yes," she informed him. "All day."

Ernest was encouraged. "And does she cook your dinners?"

She obliged him with another answer. "Not until night."

"What about your father?" he went on.

"He's dead," said the smaller girl, her mouth filled with food, daring to speak outright for the first time. Her sister looked at her with disapproval, making it plain that she had said the wrong thing and that she should only speak under guidance.

"Are you going to school then this afternoon?" Ernest resumed.

"Yes," the spokesman said.

He smiled at her continued hard control. "And what's your name then?"

"Alma," she told him, "and hers is Joan." She indicated the smaller girl with a slight nod of the head.

"Are you often hungry?"

She stopped eating and glanced at him, uncertain how to answer. "No, not much," she told him non-committally, busily eating a second pastry.

"But you were today?"

"Yes," she said, casting away diplomacy like the crumpled cake paper she let fall to the floor.

He said nothing for a few moments, sitting with knuckles pressed to his lips. "Well, look" – he began suddenly talking again – "I come in here every day for my dinner, just about half past twelve, and if ever you're feeling hungry, come down and see me."

They agreed to this, accepted sixpence for their bus fares home, thanked him very much, and said goodbye.

During the following weeks they came to see him almost every day. Sometimes, when he had little money, he filled his empty stomach with a cup of tea while Alma and Joan satisfied themselves on five shillings'-worth of more solid food. But he was happy and gained immense satisfaction from seeing them bending hungrily over eggs, bacon, and pastries, and he was so smoothed at last into a fine feeling of having something to live for that he hardly remembered the lonely days when his only hope of being able to talk to someone was by going into a public house to get drunk. He was happy now because he had his 'little girls' to look after, as he came to call them.

He began spending all his money to buy them presents, so that he was often in debt at his lodgings. He still did not buy any clothes, for whereas in the past his money had been swilled away on beer, now it was spent on presents and food for the girls, and he went on wearing the same old dirty mackintosh and was still without a collar to his shirt; even his cap was no longer clean.

Every day, straight out of school, Alma and Joan ran to catch a bus for the town centre and, a few minutes later, smiling and out of breath, walked into the café where Ernest was waiting. As days and weeks passed, and as Alma noticed how much Ernest depended on them for company, how happy he was to see them, and how obviously miserable when they did not come for a day – which was rare now – she began to demand more and more presents, more food, more money, but only in a particularly naïve and childish way, so that Ernest, in his oblivious contentment, did not notice it.

But certain customers of the café who came in every day could not help but see how the girls asked him to buy them this and that, and how he always gave in with a nature too good to be decently true, and without the least sign of realizing what was really happening. He would never dream to question their demands, for to him these two girls whom he looked upon almost as his own daughters were the only people he had to love.

Ernest, about to begin eating, noticed two smartly-dressed men sitting at a table a few yards away. They had sat in the same place the previous day, and also the day before that, but he thought no more about it because Joan and Alma came in and walked quickly across to his table.

"Hello, Uncle Ernest!" they said brightly. "What can we have for dinner?" Alma looked across at the chalk-written list on the wall to read what dishes were available.

His face changed from the blank preoccupation of eating, and a smile of happiness infused his cheeks, eyes, and the curve of his lips. "Whatever you like," he answered.

"But what have they got?" Alma demanded crossly. "I can't read their scrawl."

"Go up to the counter and ask for a dinner," he advised with a laugh.

"Will you give me some money then?" she asked, her hand out. Joan stood by without speaking, lacking Alma's confidence, her face timid, and nervous because she did not yet understand this regular transaction of money between Ernest and themselves, being afraid that one day they would stand there waiting for money and Ernest would quite naturally look surprised and say there was nothing for them.

He had just finished repairing an antique three-piece and had been paid that morning, so Alma took five shillings and they went to the counter for a meal. While they were waiting to be served the two well-dressed men who had been watching Ernest for the last few days stood up and walked over to him.

Only one of them spoke; the other held his silence and looked on. "Are those two girls your daughters, or any relation to you?" the first asked, nodding towards the counter.

Ernest looked up and smiled. "No," he explained in a mild voice, "they're just friends of mine, why?"

The man's eyes were hard, and he spoke clearly. "What kind of friends?"

"Just friends. Why? Who are you?" he shuddered, feeling a kind of half guilt growing inside him for a half-imagined reason that he hoped wasn't true.

"Never mind who we are. I just want you to answer my question."

Ernest raised his voice slightly, yet did not dare to look into the man's arrogant eyes. "Why?" he cried. "What's it got to do with you? Why are you asking questions like this?"

"We're from the police station," the man remarked dryly, "and we've had complaints that you're giving these little girls money and leading them the wrong way!"

Ernest wanted to laugh, but only from misery. Yet he did not want to laugh in case he should annoy the two detectives. He started to talk, "But ... but ..." – then found himself unable to go on. There was much that he wanted to say, yet he could enunciate nothing, and a bewildered animal stare moved slowly into his eyes.

"Look," the man said emphatically, "we don't want any of your 'buts'. We know all about you. We know who you are. We've known you for years in fact, and we're asking you to leave those girls alone and have nothing more to do with them. Men like you shouldn't be giving money to little girls. You should know what you're doing, and have more sense."

Ernest protested loudly at last. "I tell you they're friends of mine. I mean no harm. I look after them and give them presents just as I would daughters of my own. They're the only company I've got. In any case why shouldn't I look after them? Why should you take them away from me? Who do you think you are? Leave me alone ... leave me alone." His voice had risen to a weak scream of defiance, and the other people in the crowded café were looking around and staring at him wondering what was the cause of the disturbance.

The two detectives acted quickly and competently, yet without apparent haste. One stood on each side of him, lifted him up, and walked him by the counter, out on to the street, squeezing his wrists tightly as they did so. As Ernest passed the counter he saw the girls holding their plates, looking in fear and wonder at him being walked out.

They took him to the end of the street, and stood there for a few seconds talking to him, still keeping hold of his wrists and pressing their fingers hard into them.

"Now look here, we don't want any more trouble from *you*, but if ever we see you near those girls again you'll find yourself up before a magistrate." The tone of finality in his voice possessed a physical force that pushed Ernest to the brink of sanity.

He stood speechless. He wanted to say so many things, but the words would not come to his lips. They quivered helplessly with shame and hatred, and so were incapable of making words. "We're asking you in a peaceful manner," the detective went on, "to leave them alone. Understand?"

"Yes," Ernest was forced to answer.

"Right. Go on then. And we don't want to see you with those girls again."

He was only aware of the earth sliding away from under his feet, and a wave of panic crashing into his mind, and he felt the unbearable and familiar emptiness that flowed outwards from a tiny and unknowable point inside him. Then he was filled with hatred for everything, then intense pity for all the movement that was going on around him, and finally even more intense pity for himself. He wanted to cry but could not: he could only walk away from his shame.

Then he began to shed agony at each step. His bitterness eddied away and a feeling the depth of which he had never known before took its place. There was now more purpose in the motion of his footsteps as he went along the pavement through mid-day crowds. And it seemed to him that he did not care about anything any more as he pushed through the swing doors and walked into the crowded and noisy bar of a public house, his stare fixed by a beautiful heavily baited trap of beer pots that would take him into the one and only best kind of oblivion.

● Close study of the text: the author's narrative technique

In what stereotyped way do the police see Uncle Ernest? We do not see him as they do because of the knowledge and understanding given to us by the author.

How does an author like Alan Sillitoe help us to understand in such a brief space a character as complicated as Uncle Ernest? We probably thought we knew what he would be like when we read the first sentence of the story, so the author has had the even more difficult task of removing a stereotype from our minds.

Here are some of the means the writer uses:

(a)   observation,

(b)   explanation of an action,

(c)   creation of Ernest's inner life, including his memories,

(d)   use of conversation to show character and relationships.

Here are some quotations from the story, examples of these things in action. Discuss them and identify what the writer is doing in each case:

1. 'His face was pale and his eyes an unhealthy yellow: when he spoke only a few solitary teeth showed behind his lips.'
2. 'Ernest remembered little of his past, and life moved under him so that he hardly noticed its progress. There was no strong memory to entice him to what had gone by, except that of dead and dying men straggling barbed wire between the trenches in the first world war. Two sentences had dominated the years that followed: "I should not

be here in England. I should be dead with the rest of them in France." Time bereft him of these sentences, till only a dull wordless image remained.'

3. 'No pink scar marked his flesh from shell-shock and a jolted brain, and so what had happened in the war warranted no pension book, and even to him the word 'injury' never came into his mind. It was just that he did not care any more: the wheel of the years had broken him, and so had made life tolerable.'

4. 'There would be no work until two o'clock, so he intended sitting where he was until then. Yet a sudden embarrassment at having no food on the table to justify a prolonged occupation of it sent him to the counter for tea and cakes.'

5. 'The two girls looked at each other and did not notice him: he withdrew into himself and felt the emptiness of the world and wondered how he would spend all the days that seemed to stretch vacantly, like goods on a broken-down conveyor belt, before him.'

6. '"I'll get you something to eat," he ventured. "Can I?"

She unscrewed clenched fingers from her eyes and looked up, while the elder girl glared at him resentfully and said, "We don't want anything. We're going now."

"No, don't go," he cried. "You just sit down and see what I'm going to get for you."'

7. '"Right. Go on then. And we don't want to see you with those girls again."

He was only aware of the earth sliding away from under his feet, and a wave of panic crashing into his mind, and he felt the unbearable and familiar emptiness that flowed outwards from a tiny and unknowable point inside him. Then he was filled with hatred for everything, then intense pity for all the movement that was going on around him, and finally even more intense pity for himself. He wanted to cry but could not: he could only walk away from his shame.'

● Written assignment (language or literature): character description

To follow up the last piece of work in which you identified some of the ways in which Alan Sillitoe creates a character, choose one of the following assignments and decide on your own title.

1. Give a full description of a character who could have featured in this story, and try to arouse in the reader a feeling of sympathy and understanding for this character.

Use some of the techniques you have studied: observation, explanation of an action, creating a character's inner life and memories, use of conversation to show character and relationships.

You might want to write about any of the following: the mother, the café owner, a neighbour.

2. Give a full description of a character who is usually dismissed as a stereotype. For example, write about a rebellious teenager, a bored housewife, a pompous official.

You must try to create in the reader an understanding of a character we usually do not think deeply about.

In either case, use the techniques you have studied in Alan Sillitoe's writing. The following activity will help you plan how to use these techniques. You should do it first as a preparation for your written assignment.

● Planning a character description

Draw up a table like the one below to help you plan how to use some of the techniques:

Name of character	
Technique	What I wish to convey using this technique
Observation	
Explanation	
Inner thoughts	
Use of	
dialogue	
Reaction to	
events	
Action	

Here are two examples to think about and discuss:

1. Your character might be a teenager at a disco.

Observation	Clad in the bright stripes of the latest fashion, with dyed hair over swinging ear-rings, the girl looked over the floor filled with swarming shadows.
Explanation	She had arrived with her friends but somehow had got separated from them.
Inner thoughts	She wondered if their desertion had been deliberate, but tried to dismiss the thought. She felt almost frozen with shyness; she could not think of the right thing to do, and tried to shrink back against the wall.
Use of dialogue	Suddenly, out of the gloom to her right, a voice forced itself through her almost trance-like retreat. "Hey, Janet, isn't it? Wouldn't have expected to see you here!" She gazed painfully round, amazed at their being any personality left in her to be recognised. "Hmm, I've never been here before."
Reaction to events	The very act of speaking, however automatically, made her feel more secure, more in touch.
Action	She smiled with a real warmth towards the wizened face of the boy from down the road.

2. Your character might be this poor mother.

Observation	The buttons on the old corduroy coat worn by the woman who stood waiting to cross the road were missing, and the belt that held it closed was from a gent's black raincoat. The colours and materials clashed.
Explanation	Homelessness had been thrust upon this poor woman and her child by an inflexible and unforgiving father.
Inner thoughts	A warming meal for the child was at the centre of the poor woman's mind. "If only I can get to the hostel I have heard about before seven o'clock," she thought, "then at least there will be soup."
Use of dialogue	"Don't cry, darling," she said. "Mummy will see you don't go hungry for a second night."

"I'm tired, Mummy," the child said. "Tired."

"I know, my love, but just be patient."

Reaction to events	The wait at the lights was uncomfortable as the bright shop window opposite was being dressed for Christmas by two smart young men who stared out at passers-by. As their gaze fell on her, the young woman looked down and saw, as if with their eyes, the poorly cared-for child that clung to her for warmth. Anger flared and died. The two young men were not to blame for the child's poverty and need.
Action	Pulling the child closer to her she moved across the road as the lights changed.

● Written assignment (language or literature): letter writing

Many magazines invite readers to write in seeking advice on their problems. Problems are printed with a reply. The person replying is often called an agony aunt.

Either

1. A customer has watched Uncle Ernest and the girls and is not sure what to do. Write his/her letter outlining the problem, and a reply giving possible courses of action that he/she might take.

Or

2. Joan later becomes upset about the incident and writes to a problem page of a magazine or newspaper asking for advice. Compose her letter and the reply.

● Spoken assignment: role play in pairs

Either

1. Take the parts of Police Interviewer and Customer, working through the problem posed by the situation.

Or

2. Take the parts of Police Interviewer or Social Worker and Alma, working through the problem, discussing the issues posed by the situation.

Or

3. Take the part of the detective reporting the events of the case to his superior officer, answering any questions posed on his report.

I I

The Fly

Little fly,
Thy summer's play
My thoughtless hand
Has brushed away ...

Read the story.

The Fly

Katherine Mansfield

"Y'are very snug in here," piped old Mr Woodifield, and he peered out of the great, green-leather armchair by his friend the boss's desk as a baby peers out of its pram. His talk was over; it was time for him to be off. But he did not want to go. Since he had retired, since his ... stroke, the wife and the girls kept him boxed up in the house every day of the week except Tuesday. On Tuesday he was dressed and brushed and allowed to cut back to the City for the day. Though what he did there the wife and girls couldn't imagine. Made a nuisance of himself to his friends, they supposed... Well, perhaps so. All the same, we cling to our last pleasures as the tree clings to its last leaves. So there sat old Woodifield, smoking a cigar and staring almost greedily at the boss, who rolled in his office chair, stout, rosy, five years older than he, and still going strong, still at the helm. It did one good to see him.

Wistfully, admiringly, the old voice added, "It's snug in here, upon my word!"

"Yes, it's comfortable enough," agreed the boss, and he flipped the *Financial Times* with a paper-knife. As a matter of fact he was proud of his room; he liked to have it admired, especially by old Woodifield. It gave him a feeling of deep, solid satisfaction to be planted there in the midst of it in full view of that frail old figure in the muffler.

"I've had it done up lately," he explained, as he had explained for the past – how many? – weeks. "New carpet," and he pointed to the bright red carpet with a pattern of large white rings. "New furniture," and he nodded towards the massive bookcase and the table with legs like twisted treacle. "Electric heating!" He waved almost exultantly towards the five transparent, pearly sausages glowing so softly in the tilted copper pan.

But he did not draw old Woodifield's attention to the photograph over the table of a grave-looking boy in uniform standing in one of those spectral photographers' parks with photographers' storm-clouds behind him. It was not new. It had been there for over six years.

"There was something I wanted to tell you," said old Woodifield, and his eyes grew dim remembering. "Now what was it? I had it in my mind when I started out this morning." His hands began to tremble, and patches of red showed above his beard.

Poor old chap, he's on his last pins, thought the boss. And, feeling kindly, he winked at the old man, and said jokingly, "I tell you what. I've got a little drop of something here that'll do you good before you go out into the cold again. It's beautiful stuff. It wouldn't hurt a child." He took a key off his watch-chain, unlocked a cupboard below his desk, and drew forth a dark, squat bottle. "That's the medicine," said he. "And the man from whom I got it told me on the strict Q.T. it came from the cellars at Windsor Castle."

Old Woodifield's mouth fell open at the sight. He couldn't have looked more surprised if the boss had produced a rabbit.

"It's whisky, ain't it?" he piped feebly.

The boss turned the bottle and lovingly showed him the label. Whisky it was.

"D'you know," said he, peering up at the boss wonderingly, "they won't let me touch it at home." And he looked as though he was going to cry.

"Ah, that's where we know a bit more than the ladies," cried the boss, swooping across for two tumblers that stood on the table with the water-bottle, and pouring a generous finger into each. "Drink it down. It'll do you good. And don't put any water with it. It's sacrilege to tamper with stuff like this. Ah!" He tossed off his, pulled out his handkerchief, hastily wiped his moustaches, and cocked an eye at old Woodifield, who was rolling his in his chaps.

The old man swallowed, was silent a moment, and then said faintly, "It's nutty!"

But it warmed him; it crept into his chill old brain – he remembered.

"That was it," he said, heaving himself out of his chair. "I thought you'd like to know. The girls were in Belgium last week having a look at poor Reggie's grave, and they happened to come across your boy's. They're quite near each other, it seems."

Old Woodifield paused, but the boss made no reply. Only a quiver in his eyelids showed that he heard.

"The girls were delighted with the way the place is kept," piped the old voice. "Beautifully looked after. Couldn't be better if they were at home. You've not been across, have yer?"

"No, no!" For various reasons the boss had not been across.

"There's miles of it,' quavered old Woodifield, "and it's all as neat as a garden. Flowers growing on all the graves. Nice broad paths." It was plain from his voice how much he liked a nice broad path.

The pause came again. Then the old man brightened wonderfully.

"D'you know what the hotel made the girls pay for a pot of jam?" he piped. "Ten francs! Robbery, I call it. It was a little pot, so Gertrude says, no bigger than a half-crown. And she hadn't taken more than a spoonful when they charged her ten francs. Gertrude brought the pot away with her to teach 'em a lesson. Quite right, too; it's trading on our feelings. They think because we're over there having a look round we're ready to pay anything. That's what it is." And he turned towards the door.

"Quite right, quite right!" cried the boss, though what was quite right he hadn't the least idea. He came round by his desk, followed the shuffling footsteps to the door, and saw the old fellow out. Woodifield was gone.

For a long moment the boss stayed, staring at nothing, while the grey-haired office messenger, watching him, dodged in and out of his cubby-hole like a dog that expects to be taken for a run. Then, "I'll see nobody for half an hour, Macey," said the boss. "Understand? Nobody at all."

"Very good, sir."

The door shut, the firm heavy steps recrossed the bright carpet, the fat body plumped down in the spring chair, and leaning forward, the boss covered his face with his hands. He wanted, he intended, he had arranged to weep...

It had been a terrible shock to him when old Woodifield sprang that remark upon him about the boy's grave. It was exactly as though the earth had opened and he had seen the boy lying there with Woodifield's girls staring down at him. For it was strange. Although over six years had passed away, the boss never thought of the boy except as lying unchanged, unblemished in his uniform, asleep for ever. "My son!" groaned the boss. But no tears came yet. In the past, in the first months and even years after the boy's death, he had only to say those words to be overcome by such grief that nothing short of a violent fit of weeping could relieve him. Time, he had declared then, he had told everybody, could make no difference. Other men perhaps might recover, might live their loss down, but not he. How was it possible? His boy was an only son. Ever since his birth the boss had worked at building up this business for him; it had no other meaning if it was not for the boy. Life itself had come to have no other meaning. How on earth could he have slaved, denied himself, kept going all those years without the promise for ever before him of the boy's stepping into his shoes and carrying on where he left off?

And that promise had been so near being fulfilled. The boy had been in the office learning the ropes for a year before the war. Every morning they had started off together; they had come back by the same train. And what congratulations he had received as the boy's father! No wonder; he had taken to it marvellously. As to his popularity with the staff, every man jack of them down to old Macey couldn't make enough of the boy. And he wasn't in the least spoilt. No, he was just his bright natural self, with the right word for everybody, with that boyish look and his habit of saying, 'Simply splendid!'

But all that was over and done with as though it never had been. The day had come when Macey had handed him the telegram that brought the whole place crashing about his head. 'Deeply regret to inform you ...' And he had left the office a broken man, with his life in ruins.

Six years ago, six years ... How quickly time passed! It might have happened yesterday. The boss took his hands from his face; he was puzzled. Something seemed to be wrong with him. He wasn't feeling as he wanted to feel. He decided to get up and have a look at the boy's photograph. But it wasn't a favourite photograph of his; the expression was unnatural. It was cold, even stern-looking. The boy had never looked like that.

At that moment the boss noticed that a fly had fallen into his broad inkpot, and was trying feebly but desperately to clamber out again. Help! help! said those struggling legs. But the sides of the inkpot were wet and slippery; it fell back

again and began to swim. The boss took up a pen, picked the fly out of the ink, and shook it on to a piece of blotting-paper. For a fraction of a second it lay still on the dark patch that oozed round it. Then the front legs waved, took hold, and, pulling its small, sodden body up, it began the immense task of cleaning the ink from its wings. Over and under, over and under, went a leg along a wing as the stone goes over and under the scythe. Then there was a pause, while the fly, seeming to stand on the tips of its toes, tried to expand first one wing and then the other. It succeeded at last, and, sitting down, it began, like a minute cat, to clean its face. Now one could imagine that the little front legs rubbed against each other lightly, joyfully. The horrible danger was over; it had escaped; it was ready for life again.

But just then the boss had an idea. He plunged his pen back into the ink, leaned his thick wrist on the blotting-paper, and as they fly tried its wings down came a great heavy blot. What would it make of that? What indeed! The little beggar seemed absolutely cowed, stunned, and afraid to move because of what would happen next. But then, as if painfully, it dragged itself forward. The front legs waved, caught hold, and, more slowly this time, the task began from the beginning.

He's a plucky little devil, thought the boss, and he felt a real admiration for the fly's courage. That was the way to tackle things; that was the right spirit. Never say die; it was only a question of ... But the fly had again finished its laborious task, and the boss had just time to refill his pen, to shake fair and square on the new-cleaned body yet another dark drop. What about it this time? A painful moment of suspense followed. But behold, the front legs were again waving; the boss felt a rush of relief. He leaned over the fly and said to it tenderly, "You artful little b ..." And he actually had the brilliant notion of breathing on it to help the drying process. All the same, there was something timid and weak about its efforts now, and the boss decided that this time should be the last, as he dipped the pen deep into the inkpot.

It was. The last blot fell on the soaked blotting-paper, and the draggled fly lay in it and did not stir. The back legs were stuck to the body; the front legs were not to be seen.

"Come on," said the boss. "Look sharp!" And he stirred it with his pen – in vain. Nothing happened or was likely to happen. The fly was dead.

The boss lifted the corpse on the end of the paper-knife and flung it into the waste-paper basket. But such a grinding feeling of wretchedness seized him that he felt positively frightened. He started forward and pressed the bell for Macey.

"Bring me some fresh blotting-paper," he said sternly, "and look sharp about it." And while the old dog padded away he fell to wondering what it was he had been thinking about before. What was it? It was ... He took out his handkerchief and passed it inside his collar. For the life of him he could not remember.

● Written activities: first impressions of the story

1. After reading the story, write down what you think it is about in no more than twenty words. Compare your statement with your neighbour's.

2. Now write down a quick response to the following question: Why is this story entitled *The Fly*?

3. Suggest an alternative title. Be prepared to justify your suggestion to the class.

● Close study of the text: the author's 'voices'

Katherine Mansfield is such an accomplished writer of short stories that it is sometimes difficult to appreciate how much skill there is in her writing. She makes it look easy. Read and discuss the first four paragraphs to see what she has achieved. The aim of this task is to help you identify and understand the different 'voices' a writer can use.

Woodifield, wife and girls all 'speak' here	*"'Y'are very snug in here*," piped old Mr Woodifield, and he peered out of the great, green-leather armchair by his friend the boss's desk as a baby peers out of its pram. His talk was over; it was time for him to be off. But he did not want to go. Since he had retired, since his ...
Who says what?	stroke, *the wife and girls kept him boxed up* in the house every day of the week except Tuesday. On Tuesday *he was dressed and brushed and allowed to cut back to the City for the day. Though what he did there the wife and girls couldn't imagine. Made a nuisance of himself to his friends, they*
Is this the author or someone else?	supposed... Well, perhaps so. *All the same, we cling to our last pleasures as the tree clings to its last leaves.* So there sat old Woodifield, smoking a cigar and staring almost greedily at

Who says this?

The boss and the author: who says what?

The boss speaks

Is this the boss?

the boss, who rolled in his office chair, stout, rosy, five years older than he, and still going strong, still at the helm. *It did one good to see him.*'

'Wistfully, admiringly, the old voice added, *"It's snug in here, upon my word!"*'

"Yes, it's comfortable enough," agreed the boss, and he flipped the *Financial Times* with a paper-knife. *As a matter of fact he was proud of his room; he liked to have it admired, especially by old Woodifield. It gave him a feeling of deep, solid satisfaction to be planted there in the midst of it in full view of that frail old figure in the muffler.*'

'"*I've had it done up lately,*" he explained, as he had explained for the past – how many? – weeks. "*New carpet,*" and he pointed to the bright red carpet with a pattern of large white rings. "*New furniture,*" and he nodded towards the massive bookcase and the table with legs like twisted treacle. "*Electric heating!*" *He waved almost exultantly towards the five transparent, pearly sausages glowing so softly in the tilted copper pan.*'

Woodifield, the wife and daughters, and the author all speak in the first two paragraphs. Identify something each says. (The italics and the questions in the margin are intended to help you.)

In the next two paragraphs the boss speaks. What he says is easy to identify because of the direct speech. The author speaks too, recounting thoughts and words in such a way as to imply criticism. Make notes on how you think this is done.

● **The boss's office**

We learn in the fourth paragraph that the boss is very proud of his office. Copy the following list out and write down any additional information we are given about each item. For example, next to 'bookcase' you should write 'massive'.

> armchair
>
> office chair

carpet

bookcase

desk

fire

table

Is there anything in the story to suggest that we are not expected to share the boss's high opinion of his office?

● Woodifield and his relationship with the boss

Here is the first sentence of the story:

'"Y'are very *snug* in here," *piped old Mr Woodifield*, and he *peered* out of the *great, green-leather* armchair by his *friend* the boss's desk *as a baby peers out of its pram*.'

Certain words and phrases have been put in italics. Rewrite the sentence, substituting different words and phrases for those in italics. Your aim is to create, in an opening sentence, a different but consistent character and setting. For example, you might want to substitute 'colleague' for 'friend'. If you did this, how would this change the relationship between the two men?

Asking yourself a few questions about the two men may help you in this task. Similes and metaphors are rather like riddles. You could ask yourself: 'Why is old Woodifield like a baby in a pram?'

Your answer might be long and complicated:

because he is small and baby-faced,

because the chair he is in is very large, so he can only just see out,

like a baby in a big pram sitting up and peering round the hood,

because he has the same innocent curiosity that a baby has.

Whatever your answer, the original comparison has provided you with material to help you understand the character and his relationship with the boss.

Discuss with your partner or your group the relationship between these two men as you understand it so far.

● The boss: symbols of power and control

Re-read any notes you made before reading the story. Discuss the following points which are designed to clarify further the reasons for believing from the start that the relationship between these two men is strange.

The boss is a strange figure – you have made notes about his office and furniture.

He has no name. What is strange about this fact?

His office is the centre of his world. Discuss the furniture. Does this tell us anything about the boss?

In front of him, dwarfed by the armchair, is Mr Woodifield, who peers out 'as a baby peers out of its pram,' staring, 'almost greedily at the boss, who rolled in his office chair, stout, rosy, five years older than he, and still going strong, still at the helm'.

How does this description enforce your impression of the relationship between the two men?

As he reads the *Financial Times*, the boss flips over the pages with a paper-knife. Any menace here?

He is proud of the room, and 'liked to have it admired'. Why?

'It gave him a feeling of deep, solid satisfaction to be planted there in the midst of it in full view of that frail old figure in the muffler.'

How does he then treat Woodifield?

Unlocking a cupboard, he offers him whisky, which he is not allowed to have at home, and says, '... we know a bit more than the ladies,' and '... don't put any water with it. It's sacrilege to tamper with stuff like this'.

Conversation follows, before the boss sees Woodifield out. Enter the grey-haired office messenger who dodges in and out of his cubby-hole 'like a dog that expects to be taken for a run'.

Are we then surprised at the treatment of the fly?

● Narrative technique: a summary

In the opening four paragraphs, Katherine Mansfield conjures up two characters, and places them in a setting which is easy to visualise and which reinforces aspects of the boss's character. We get a good idea of the opinion each character has of the other, and realise the author's view of them is not the same as their own. She uses four different voices to tell the story – her own, old Woodifield's, that of wife and daughters, and the boss's – but moves so smoothly from one to the other that we are hardly aware of the change. In the course of the story she continues to choose words carefully to suit her purpose and varies the viewpoint while retaining the controlling voice herself.

- ## Written assignment (literature): appreciation

Show how Katherine Mansfield, from the very beginning of the story, prepares us for what follows old Mr Woodifield's departure.

- ## Discussion and note-making: comparison of the two characters

Discuss and make notes on the contrasting characters of the two men, under the headings suggested here. Some notes are given to help you.

	The boss	Woodifield
How he speaks:		
How he moves:		'shuffling footsteps'
How he drinks:		
How he looks at things:		
Attitude to women:	' "… we know a bit more than the ladies!" '	
Outlook on life:		

- ## Spoken assignment: discussion

Discuss the different characters of the two men. How has each reacted to the death of a son in the First World War?

- ## Further study of the author's 'voices'

In an earlier task you identified four different voices in the opening paragraphs. Look now at the following quotations, and, working with a partner or in a group, decide whose voice we are hearing in each case.

(a) 'He nodded towards the massive bookcase and the table with legs like twisted treacle.'

(b) 'He couldn't have looked more surprised if the boss had produced a rabbit.'

(c) 'Life itself had come to have no other meaning. How on earth could he have slaved, denied himself, kept going all those years …'

(d) 'The horrible danger was over; it had escaped; it was ready for life again.'

(e) 'The little beggar seemed absolutely cowed, stunned, and afraid to move because of what would happen next.'

● Character revealed through attitudes and behaviour

Central to this story is the character of the boss. We have already seen aspects of it revealed through the way he speaks and moves, the way he differs from old Woodifield and the way the office betrays something about his taste. We have not yet looked at what his attitudes and behaviour tell us.

Below is a brief summary of how the boss behaves during the story. Write a sentence or two about what is revealed about him in each case.

(a) He 'rolled in his office chair ...'

(b) He 'flipped the *Financial Times* with a paper-knife.'

(c) He 'did not draw old Woodifield's attention to the photograph over the table ...'

(d) He poured a generous finger of whisky for them both, ignoring the fact that old Woodifield was not allowed to drink at home.

(e) He loses concentration when he is told about his son's grave, but he betrays nothing.

(f) He tries to weep, but fails, even after gazing at the photograph of his son.

(g) He rescues the fly from the ink, only to drop blots on it until it dies of exhaustion.

Consider also the statement: '... he had left the office a broken man, with his life in ruins.' Does this statement fit the picture we get of him at the start of the story?

Now try to decide what his attitude is to:

(a) himself,

(b) his son,

(c) old Woodifield,

(d) the fly.

● **Written assignment (literature): character study**

Describe the character of the boss, attempting to explain why he behaves as he does. What are your own feelings about him?

● **Group discussion: the significance of the title**

The episode with the fly is apparently unconnected to the rest of the story, and yet Katherine Mansfield thought it important enough to feature as the title, so it must provide a key to what the story is about. Earlier on you made suggestions about an alternative title. Look again at that suggestion and see whether you can add any others.

Now see what connection you can make between the fly episode and the fact that the boss is unable to weep for his son any more. Here are some clues:

(a) The fly wallows in the ink. What other sort of wallowing is there in the story?

(b) The boss has a thick wrist as he drops ink on the fly. Is he heavy-handed about anything else?

(c) The fly, after laboriously cleaning itself, is ready for life again. The boss's life is supposed to be in ruins, yet he has just redecorated and refurnished his office...

(d) The boss prolongs the fly's misery until he totally exhausts it. What else could this apply to?

Discuss your ideas in groups, then present your conclusions to the class.

● **Class role play: adapting the story for television**

The Head of BBC Drama is thinking of making this story into a short play for television. You have been asked to make a feasibility study. Working in groups you are to complete the following tasks:

(a) Give a brief description of the appearance of the two characters for casting purposes,

(b) Suggest a design for the set,

(c) Draw up a list of props needed.

Next, you are to divide the story into four sections, as follows:

(a) Opening sentence up to 'It had been there for over six years.'

(b) '"There was something I wanted to tell you,"' up to 'Woodifield was gone.'

(c) 'For a long moment the boss stayed, ...' up to 'The boy had never looked like that.'

(d) 'At that moment the boss noticed ...,' up to the end of the story.

Someone from the group should work on each section to produce a storyboard (such as the one below) giving details of camera shots, and sound where appropriate. When the group comes together, discuss whether it has in fact been possible to convey the story faithfully, or whether because some things have been very difficult to convey, you need to resort to having a narrator.

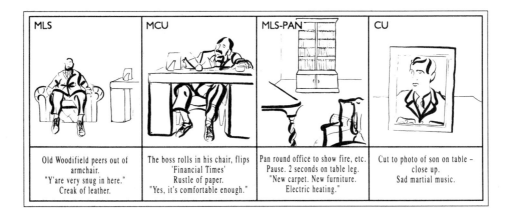

MLS	MCU	MLS-PAN	CU
Old Woodifield peers out of armchair. "Y'are very snug in here." Creak of leather.	The boss rolls in his chair, flips 'Financial Times' Rustle of paper. "Yes, it's comfortable enough."	Pan round office to show fire, etc. Pause. 2 seconds on table leg. "New carpet. New furniture. Electric heating."	Cut to photo of son on table – close up. Sad martial music.

You might wish to submit your notes and your contribution to the storyboard exercise as part of the following written assignment.

● Written assignment (language): report writing

Write a report on the findings of the feasibility study.

● General assignments (language and literature)

You should have enough ideas and information about the story to enable you to tackle any of these assignments. Which one you choose, and how you write, will determine whether the piece is seen as language or as literature coursework.

1. After the unsettling experience with the fly, the boss consults a

psychiatrist. Under hypnosis he reveals what took place on the Tuesday of old Woodifield's visit, and also some other things. Write up a full report, interpreting what happened so as to throw light on the boss's state of mind. Offer some professional advice as well.

2. Write an essay on what you have learned from this story about Katherine Mansfield's skill as a writer of short stories. Mention such things as her ability to create character economically, her use of language and imagery to establish the tone of the story, and the way she varies the narrative point of view by using different voices.

3. You may have read some of the poetry of the First World War or studied the events in a History course. Use your knowledge to write a letter from the boss's son to his family, describing conditions at the Front and stating his feelings about the war.

4. Use the structure of this story to write a short story of your own. Limit yourself to two main characters and one setting which you describe at the beginning. The story should develop from some good or bad tidings brought by one of the characters to the other.

5. Explain your first reactions to this story and how your first impressions have been altered, modified or reinforced by the further work you have done on it. Refer closely to the story, and in conclusion say what you think is the significance of the title.

12

Weekend

The work which follows aims to help you to think about the concerns of the story before you begin to read.

● Written activity: male and female roles

Below is a list of tasks. In a household where both partners work, which would you expect to be done by the man, and which by the woman?
Divide your page into three columns, heading one M, another F and the third one Notes.

Decide the frequency with which you think each task might be performed: put 3 for very frequent; 2 for regular but less frequent; 1 for occasional. Use the final column to note down any qualifications you would want to make.

Driving long distances F 1

Making breakfast M 2

Taking children to doctor's M 2

Shopping for children's clothes M 3

Lighting fires F 2

Cutting grass F 3

Laying concrete for paths, etc. F 3

Getting coal in F 3

Ironing clothes M 2

Washing dishes M 2

Cleaning blocked drains F 3

Pruning roses M 1

Decorating house F/M 1

Making curtains M 3

Taking dog for a walk F 1

Changing lightbulbs F 2

Washing car F 2 3

Feeding animals F 2

Deciding on holiday F 2

Buying birthday presents M 2

Bleeding radiators F

Shopping for food M

Mending roof F

Putting plugs on F

Putting clothes away M

Hoovering M

Mopping floors M

Cleaning bathroom M

Speaking to teachers F

What conclusions can you draw? Discuss them.

● Written activity: 'holding your tongue'

Often people find themselves in situations where they cannot say what they think. They have to 'hold their tongue', as we say.

In pairs, write down examples of such situations, and beside each write a reason for the person not being able to explain his or her point of view.
For example
Situation: pupil given a detention for being late for school.
Reason: teacher on late duty gets cross at long-winded explanations.
Or
Situation: nurse with complaining patient.
Reason: his/her job is to help patient not to show personal feelings.
Or
Situation: teenager in family argument over coming home late.
Reason: if he/she argues, parents will become upset and forbid any outings for a month.

● Written assignment (language): imagined thoughts

Choose one situation from your list and write down the person's thoughts when silence has to be maintained, or when true thoughts remain unspoken.

● Spoken activity: reading the story

A reader is selected to be narrator. Others are selected to read the parts of the characters where they use direct speech. The narrator reads the 'said Martha' or 'Katie confided' parts of the text.

The following readers will be required: narrator, Martha, Martin, Colin, Katie, Beryl.
Read the first three paragraphs. Pause and, by yourself, note down your first impressions of the people concerned – Martha, Martin, the children – and their life style.

What kind of story do you think this is going to be? What will the writer be interested in as she develops the story?

Now read the whole story.

Weekend

Fay Weldon

By seven-thirty they were ready to go. Martha had everything packed into the car and the three children appropriately dressed and in the back seat, complete with educational games and wholewheat biscuits. When everything was ready in the car Martin would switch off the television, come downstairs, lock up the house, front and back, and take the wheel.

Weekend! Only two hours' drive down to the cottage on Friday evenings: three hours' drive back on Sunday nights. The pleasures of greenery and guests in between. They reckoned themselves fortunate, how fortunate!

On Fridays Martha would get home on the bus at six-twelve and prepare tea and sandwiches for the family: then she would strip four beds and put the sheets and quilt covers in the washing machine for Monday: take the country bedding from the airing basket, plus the books and the games, plus the weekend food – acquired at intervals throughout the week, to lessen the load – plus her own folder of work from the office, plus Martin's drawing materials (she was a market researcher in an advertising agency, he a freelance designer) plus hairbrushes, jeans, spare T-shirts, Jolyon's antibiotics (he suffered from sore throats), Jenny's recorder, Jasper's cassette player and so on – ah, the so on! – and would pack them all, skilfully and quickly, into the boot. Very little could be left in the cottage during the week. ("An open invitation to burglars": Martin.) Then Martha would run round the house tidying and wiping, doing this and that, finding the cat at one neighbour's and delivering it to another, while the others ate their tea; and would usually, proudly, have everything finished by the time they had eaten their fill. Martin would just catch the BBC2 news, while Martha cleared away the tea table, and the children tossed up for the best positions in the car. "Martha," said Martin, tonight, "you ought to get Mrs Hodder to do more. She takes advantage of you."

Mrs Hodder came in twice a week to clean. She was over seventy. She charged two pounds an hour. Martha paid her out of her own wages: well, the running of the house was Martha's concern. If Martha chose to go out to work – as was her perfect right, Martin allowed, even though it wasn't the best thing for the children, but that must be Martha's moral responsibility – Martha must surely pay her domestic stand-in. An evident truth, heard loud and clear and frequent in Martin's mouth and Martha's heart.

"I expect you're right," said Martha. She did not want to argue. Martin had had a long hard week, and now had to drive. Martha couldn't. Martha's licence had been suspended four months back for drunken driving. Everyone agreed that the suspension was unfair: Martha seldom drank to excess: she was for one thing usually too busy pouring drinks for other people or washing other people's glasses to get much inside herself. But Martin had taken her out to dinner on her birthday, as was his custom, and exhaustion and excitement mixed had made her imprudent, and before she knew where she was, why there she was, in the dock, with a distorted lamp-post to pay for and a new bonnet for the car and six months' suspension.

So now Martin had to drive her car down to the cottage, and he was always tired on Fridays, and hot and sleepy on Sundays, and every rattle and clank and bump in the engine she felt to be somehow her fault.

Martin had a little sports car for London and work: it could nip in and out of the traffic nicely: Martha's was an old estate car, with room for the children, picnic baskets, bedding, food, games, plants, drink, portable television and all the things required by the middle classes for weekends in the country. It lumbered rather than zipped and made Martin angry. He seldom spoke a harsh word, but Martha, after the fashion of wives, could detect his mood from what he did not say rather than what he did, and from the tilt of his head, and the way his crinkly, merry eyes seemed crinklier and merrier still – and of course from the way he addressed Martha's car.

"Come along, you old banger you! Can't you do better than that? You're too old, that's your trouble. Stop complaining. Always complaining, it's only a hill. You're too wide about the hips. You'll never get through there."

Martha worried about her age, her tendency to complain, and the width of her hips. She took the remarks personally. Was she right to do so? The children noticed nothing: it was just funny lively laughing Daddy being witty about Mummy's car. Mummy, done for drunken driving. Mummy, with the roots of melancholy somewhere deep beneath the bustling, busy, everyday self. Busy: ah so busy!

Martin would only laugh if she said anything about the way he spoke to her car and warn her against paranoia. "Don't get like your mother, darling." Martha's mother had, towards the end, thought that people were plotting against her.

Martha's mother had led a secluded, suspicious life, and made Martha's childhood a chilly and a lonely time. Life now, by comparison, was wonderful for Martha. People, children, houses, conversations, food, drink, theatres – even, now, a career. Martin standing between her and the hostility of the world – popular, easy, funny Martin, beckoning the rest of the world into earshot.

Ah, she was grateful: little earnest Martha, with her shy ways and her penchant for passing boring exams – how her life had blossomed out! Three children too – Jasper, Jenny and Jolyon – all with Martin's broad brow and open looks, and the confidence born of her love and care, and the work she had put into them since the dawning of their days.

Martin drives. Martha, for once, drowses.

The right food, the right words, the right play. Doctors for the tonsils: dentists for the molars. Confiscate guns: censor television: encourage creativity. Paints and paper to hand: books on the shelves: meetings with teachers. Music teachers. Dancing lessons. Parties. Friends to tea. School plays. Open days. Junior orchestra.

Martha is jolted awake. Traffic lights. Martin doesn't like Martha to sleep while he drives.

Clothes. Oh, clothes! Can't wear this: must wear that. Dress shops. Piles of clothes in corners: duly washed, but waiting to be ironed, waiting to be put away.

Get the piles off the floor, into the laundry baskets. Martin doesn't like a mess.

Creativity arises out of order, not chaos. Five years off work while the children were small: back to work with seniority lost. What, did you think something was for nothing? If you have children, mother, that is your reward. It lies not in the world.

Have you taken enough food? Always hard to judge.

Food. Oh, food! Shop in the lunch-hour. Lug it all home. Cook for the freezer on Wednesday evenings while Martin is at his car-maintenance evening class, and isn't there to notice you being unrestful. Martin likes you to sit down in the evenings. Fruit, meat, vegetables, flour for home-made bread. Well, shop bread is full of pollutants. Frozen food, even your own, loses flavour. Martin often remarks on it.

Condiments. Everyone loves mango chutney. But the expense!

London Airport to the left. Look, look, children! Concorde? No, idiot, of course it isn't Concorde.

Ah, to be all things to all people: children, husband, employer, friends! It can be done: yes, it can: super woman.

Drink. Home-made wine. Why not? Elderberries grow thick and rich in London: and at least you know what's in it. Store it in high cupboards: lots of room: up and down the step-ladder. Careful! Don't slip. Don't break anything.

No such thing as an accident. Accidents are Freudian slips: they are wilful, bad-tempered things.

Martin can't bear bad temper. Martin likes slim ladies. Diet. Martin rather likes his secretary. Diet. Martin admires slim legs and big bosoms. How to achieve them both? Impossible. But try, oh try, to be what you ought to be, not what you are. Inside and out.

Martin brings back flowers and chocolates: whisks Martha off for holiday weekends. Wonderful! The best husband in the world: look into his crinkly, merry, gentle eyes; see it there. So the mouth slopes away into something of a pout. Never mind. Gaze into the eyes. Love. It must be love. You married him. *You.* Surely *you* deserve true love?

Salisbury Plain. Stonehenge. Look, children, look! Mother, we've seen Stonehenge a hundred times. Go back to sleep.

Cook! Ah, cook. People love to come to Martin and Martha's dinners. Work it out in your head in the lunch-hour. If you get in at six-twelve, you can seal the meat while you beat the egg white while you feed the cat while you lay the table while you string the beans while you set out the cheese, goat's cheese, Martin loves goat's cheese, Martha tries to like goat's cheese – oh, bed, sleep, peace, quiet.

Sex! Ah sex. Orgasm, please. Martin requires it. Well, so do you. And you don't want his secretary providing a passion you neglected to develop. Do you? Quick, quick, the cosmic bond. Love. Married love.

Secretary! Probably a vulgar suspicion: nothing more. Probably a fit of paranoics, à la mother, now dead and gone.

At peace.

R.I.P.

Chilly, lonely mother, following her suspicions where they led.

Nearly there, children. Nearly in paradise, nearly at the cottage. Have another biscuit.

Real roses round the door.

Roses. Prune, weed, spray, feed, pick. Avoid thorns. One of Martin's few

harsh words.

"Martha, you can't not want roses! What kind of person am I married to? An anti-rose personality?"

Green grass. Oh, God, grass. Grass must be mown. Restful lawns, daisies bobbing, buttercups glowing. Roses and grass and books. Books.

Please, Martin, do we have to have the two hundred books, mostly twenties' first editions, bought at Christie's book sale on one of your afternoons off? Books need dusting.

Roars of laughter from Martin, Jasper, Jenny and Jolyon. Mummy says we shouldn't have the books: books need dusting!

Roses, green grass, books and peace.

Martha woke up with a start when they got to the cottage, and gave a little shriek which made them all laugh. Mummy's waking shriek, they called it.

Then there was the car to unpack and the beds to make up, and the electricity to connect, and the supper to make, and the cobwebs to remove, while Martin made the fire. Then supper – pork chops in sweet and sour sauce ("Pork is such a *dull* meat if you don't cook it properly": Martin), green salad from the garden, or such green salad as the rabbits had left ("Martha, did you really net them properly? Be honest, now!": Martin) and sauté potatoes. Mash is so stodgy and ordinary, and instant mash unthinkable. The children studied the night sky with the aid of their star map. Wonderful, rewarding children!

Then clear up the supper: set the dough to prove for the bread: Martin already in bed: exhausted by the drive and lighting the fire. ("Martha, we really ought to get the logs stacked properly. Get the children to do it, will you?": Martin.) Sweep and tidy: get the TV aerial right. Turn up Jasper's jeans where he has trodden the hem undone. ("He can't go around like *that*, Martha. Not even Jasper": Martin.)

Midnight. Good night. Weekend guests arriving in the morning. Seven for lunch and dinner on Saturday. Seven for Sunday breakfast, nine for Sunday lunch. ("Don't fuss, darling. You always make such a fuss": Martin.) Oh, God, forgotten the garlic squeezer. That means ten minutes with the back of a spoon and salt. Well, who wants *lumps* of garlic? No one. Not Martin's guests. Martin said so. Sleep.

Colin and Katie. Colin is Martin's oldest friend. Katie is his new young wife. Janet, Colin's other, earlier wife, was Martha's friend. Janet was rather like Martha, quieter and duller than her husband. A nag and a drag, Martin rather thought, and said, and of course she'd let herself go, everyone agreed. No one exactly excused Colin for walking out, but you could see the temptation.

Katie versus Janet.

Katie was languid, beautiful and elegant. She drawled when she spoke. Her hands were expressive: her feet were little and female. She had no children.

Janet plodded round on very flat, rather large feet. There was something wrong with them. They turned out slightly when she walked. She had two children. She was, frankly, boring. But Martha liked her: when Janet came down to the cottage she would wash up. Not in the way that most guests washed up – washing dutifully and setting everything out on the draining board, but actually drying and putting away too. And Janet would wash the bath and get the children all sat down, with chairs for everyone, even the littlest, and keep them quiet and satisfied so the grown-ups – well, the men – could get on with their conversation and their jokes and their love of country weekends, while Janet stared into space, as if grateful for the rest, quite happy.

Janet would garden, too. Weed the strawberries, while the men went for their walk; her great feet standing firm and square and sometimes crushing a plant or so, but never mind, oh never mind. Lovely Janet; who understood.

Now Janet was gone and here was Katie.

Katie talked with the men and went for walks with the men, and moved her ashtray rather impatiently when Martha tried to clear the drinks round it.

Dishes were boring, Katie implied by her manner, and domesticity was boring, and anyone who bothered with that kind of thing was a fool. Like Martha. Ash should be allowed to stay where it was, even if it was in the butter, and conversations should never be interrupted.

Knock, knock. Katie and Colin arrived at one-fifteen on Saturday morning, just after Martha had got to bed. "You don't mind? It was the moonlight. We couldn't resist it. You should have seen Stonehenge! We didn't disturb you? Such early birds!"

Martha rustled up a quick meal of omelettes. Saturday nights' eggs. ("Martha makes a lovely omelette": Martin.) ("Honey, make one of your mushroom omelettes: cook the mushrooms separately, remember, with lemon. Otherwise the water from the mushrooms gets into the egg, and spoils everything.") Sunday supper mushrooms. But ungracious to say anything.

Martin had revived wonderfully at the sight of Colin and Katie. He brought out the whisky bottle. Glasses. Ice. Jug for water. Wait. Wash up another sinkful, when they're finished. 2 a.m.

"Don't do it tonight, darling."

"It'll only take a sec." Bright smile, not a hint of self-pity. Self-pity can spoil everyone's weekend.

Martha knows that if breakfast for seven is to be manageable the sink must be cleared of dishes. A tricky meal, breakfast. Especially if bacon, eggs, and tomatoes must all be cooked in separate pans. ("Separate pans mean separate flavours!": Martin.)

She is running around in her nightie. Now if that had been Katie – but there's something so *practical* about Martha. Reassuring, mind; but the skimpy nightie and the broad rump and the thirty-eight years are all rather embarrassing. Martha can see it in Colin and Katie's eyes. Martin's too. Martha wishes she did not see so much in other people's eyes. Her mother did, too. Dear, dead mother. Did I misjudge you?

This was the second weekend Katie had been down with Colin but without Janet. Colin was a photographer: Katie had been his accessorizer. First Colin and Janet: then Colin, Janet and Katie: now Colin and Katie!

Katie weeded with rubber gloves on and pulled out pansies in mistake for weeds and laughed and laughed along with everyone when her mistake was pointed out to her, but the pansies died. Well, Colin had become with the years fairly rich and fairly famous, and what does a fairly rich and famous man want with a wife like Janet when Katie is at hand?

On the first of the Colin/Katie weekends Katie had appeared out of the bathroom. "I say," said Katie, holding out a damp towel with evident distaste, "I can only find this. No hope of a dry one?" And Martha had run to fetch a dry towel and amazingly found one, and handed it to Katie who flashed her a brilliant smile and said, "I can't bear damp towels. Anything in the world but damp towels," as if speaking to a servant in a time of shortage of staff, and took all the water so there was none left for Martha to wash up.

The trouble, of course, was drying anything at all in the cottage. There were no facilities for doing so, and Martin had a horror of clothes lines which might spoil the view. He toiled and moiled all week in the city simply to get a country view at the weekend. Ridiculous to spoil it by draping it with wet towels! But now Martha had bought more towels, so perhaps everyone could be satisfied. She would take nine damp towels back on Sunday evenings in a plastic bag and see to them in London.

On this Saturday morning, straight after breakfast, Katie went out to the car – she and Colin had a new Lamborghini; hard to imagine Katie in anything duller – and came back waving a new Yves St Laurent towel. "See! I brought my own, darlings."

They'd brought nothing else. No fruit, no meat, no vegetables, not even bread, certainly not a box of chocolates. They'd gone off to bed with alacrity, the night before, and the spare room rocked and heaved: well, who'd want to do washing-up when you could do that, but what about the children? Would they get confused? First Colin and Janet, now Colin and Katie?

Martha murmured something of her thoughts to Martin, who looked quite shocked. "Colin's my best friend. I don't expect him to bring anything," and Martha felt mean. "And good heavens, you can't protect the kids from sex for ever; don't be so prudish," so that Martha felt stupid as well. Mean, complaining, and stupid.

Janet had rung Martha during the week. The house had been sold over her head, and she and the children had been moved into a small flat. Katie was trying to persuade Colin to cut down on her allowance, Janet said.

"It does one no good to be materialistic," Katie confided. "I have nothing. No home, no family, no ties, no possessions. Look at me! Only me and a suitcase of clothes." But Katie seemed highly satisfied with the me, and the clothes were stupendous. Katie drank a great deal and became funny. Everyone laughed, including Martha. Katie had been married twice. Martha marvelled at how someone could arrive in their mid-thirties with nothing at all to their name, neither husband, nor children, nor property and not mind.

Mind you, Martha could see the power of such helplessness. If Colin was all Katie had in the world, how could Colin abandon her? And to what? Where would she go? How would she live? Oh, clever Katie.

"My teacup's dirty," said Katie, and Martha ran to clean it, apologizing, and Martin raised his eyebrows, at Martha not Katie.

"I wish *you'd* wear scent," said Martin to Martha, reproachfully. Katie wore lots. Martha never seemed to have time to put any on, though Martin bought her bottle after bottle. Martha leapt out of bed each morning to meet some emergency – miaowing cat, coughing child, faulty alarm clock, postman's knock – when was Martha to put on scent? It annoyed Martin all the same. She ought to do more to charm him.

Colin looked handsome and harrowed and younger than Martin, though

they were much the same age. "Youth's catching," said Martin in bed that night. "It's since he found Katie." Found, like some treasure. Discovered; something exciting and wonderful, in the dreary world of established spouses.

On Saturday morning Jasper trod on a piece of wood ("Martha, why isn't he wearing shoes? It's too bad.": Martin) and Martha took him into the hospital to have a nasty splinter removed. She left the cottage at ten and arrived back at one and they were still sitting in the sun drinking, empty bottles glinting in the long grass. The grass hadn't been cut. Don't forget the bottles. Broken glass means more mornings at the hospital. Oh, don't fuss. Enjoy yourself. Like other people. Try.

But no potatoes peeled, no breakfast cleared, nothing. Cigarette ends still amongst old toast, bacon rind and marmalade. "You could have done the potatoes," Martha burst out. Oh, bad temper! Prime sin. They looked at her in amazement and dislike. Martin too.

"Goodness," said Katie. "Are we doing the whole Sunday lunch bit on Saturday? Potatoes? Ages since I've eaten potatoes. Wonderful!"

"The children expect it," said Martha.

So they did. Saturday and Sunday lunch shone like reassuring beacons in their lives. Saturday lunch: family lunch: fish and chips. ("So much better cooked at home than bought": Martin.) Sunday. Usually roast beef, potatoes, peas, apple pie. Oh, of course. Yorkshire pudding. Always a problem with oven temperatures. When the beef's going slowly, the Yorkshire should be going fast. How to achieve that? Like big bosom and little hips.

"Just relax," said Martin. "I'll cook dinner, all in good time. Splinters always work their own way out: no need to have taken him to hospital. Let life drift over you, my love. Flow with the waves, that's the way."

And Martin flashed Martha a distant, spiritual smile. His hand lay on Katie's slim brown arm, with its many gold bands.

"Anyway, you do too much for the children," said Martin. "It isn't good for them. Have a drink."

So Martha perched uneasily on the step and had a glass of cider, and wondered how, if lunch was going to be late, she would get cleared up and the meat out of the marinade for the rather formal dinner that would be expected that evening. The marinaded lamb ought to cook for at least four hours in a low oven; and the cottage oven was very small, and you couldn't use that and the grill at the same time and Martin like his fish grilled, not fried. Less cholesterol.

She didn't say as much. Domestic details like this were very boring, and any mild complaint was registered by Martin as a scene. And to make a scene was so ungrateful.

This was the life. Well, wasn't it? Smart friends in large cars and country living and drinks before lunch and roses and bird song – "Don't drink *too* much," said Martin, and told them about Martha's suspended driving licence.

The children were hungry so Martha opened them a can of beans and sausages and heated that up. ("Martha, do they have to eat that crap? Can't they wait?": Martin.)

Katie was hungry: she said so, to keep the children in face. She was lovely with children – most children. She did not particularly like Colin and Janet's children. She said so, and he accepted it. He only saw them once a month now, not once a week.

"Let me make lunch," Katie said to Martha. "You do so much, poor thing!"

And she pulled out of the fridge all the things Martha had put away for the next day's picnic lunch party – Camembert cheese and salad and salami and made a wonderful tomato salad in two minutes and opened the white wine – "Not very cold, darling. Shouldn't it be chilling?" – and had it all on the table in five amazing competent minutes. "That's all we need, darling," said Martin. "You are funny with your fish-and-chip Saturdays! What could be nicer than this? Or simpler?"

Nothing, except there was Sunday's buffet lunch for nine gone, in place of Saturday's fish for six, and would the fish stretch? No. Katie had had quite a lot to drink. She pecked Martha on the forehead. "Funny little Martha," she said. "She reminds me of Janet. I really do like Janet." Colin did not want to be reminded of Janet, and said so. "Darling Janet's a fact of life," said Katie. "If you'd only think about her more, you might manage to pay her less." And she yawned and stretched her lean, childless body and smiled at Colin with her inviting, naughty little girl eyes, and Martin watched her in admiration.

Martha got up and left them and took a paint pot and put a coat of white gloss on the bathroom wall. The white surface pleased her. She was good at painting. She produced a smooth, even surface. Her legs throbbed. She feared she might be getting varicose veins.

Outside in the garden the children played badminton. They were bad-tempered, but relieved to be able to look up and see their mother working, as usual: making their lives for ever better and nicer: organizing, planning, thinking ahead, side-stepping disaster, making preparations, like a mother hen, fussing and irritating: part of the natural boring scenery of the world.

On Saturday night Katie went to bed early: she rose from her chair and stretched and yawned and poked her head into the kitchen where Martha was washing saucepans. Colin had cleared the table and Katie had folded the napkins into pretty creases, while Martin blew at the fire, to make it bright. "Good night," said Katie.

Katie appeared three minutes later, reproachfully holding out her Yves St Laurent towel, sopping wet. "Oh dear," cried Martha. "Jenny must have washed her hair!" And Martha was obliged to rout Jenny out of bed to rebuke her, publicly, if only to demonstrate that she knew what was right and proper. That meant Jenny would sulk all weekend, and that meant a treat or an outing mid-week, or else by the following week she'd be having an asthma attack. "You fuss the children too much," said Martin. "That's why Jenny has asthma." Jenny was pleasant enough to look at, but not stunning. Perhaps she was a disappointment to her father? Martin would never say so, but Martha feared he thought so.

An egg and an orange each child, each day. Then nothing too bad would go wrong. And it hadn't. The asthma was very mild. A calm, tranquil environment, the doctor said. Ah, smile, Martha smile. Domestic happiness depends on you. 21×52 oranges a year. Each one to be purchased, carried, peeled and washed up after. And what about potatoes. 12×52 pounds a year? Martin liked his potatoes carefully peeled. He couldn't bear to find little cores of black in the mouthful. ("Well, it isn't very nice, is it?": Martin.)

Martha dreamt she was eating coal, by handfuls, and liking it.

Saturday night. Martin made love to Martha three times. Three times? How virile he was, and clearly turned on by the sounds from the spare room. Martin said he loved her. Martin always did. He was a courteous lover; he knew the importance of foreplay. So did Martha. Three times.

Ah, sleep. Jolyon had a nightmare. Jenny was woken by a moth. Martin slept through everything. Martha pottered about the house in the night. There was a moon. She sat at the window and stared out into the summer night for five minutes, and was at peace, and then went back to bed because she ought to be fresh for the morning.

But she wasn't. She slept late. The others went out for a walk. They'd left a note, a considerate note: "Didn't wake you. You looked tired. Had a cold break-fast so as not to make too much mess. Leave everything 'til we get back." But it was ten o'clock, and guests were coming at noon, so she cleared away the bread, the butter, the crumbs, the smears, the jam, the spoons, the spilt sugar, the cereal, the milk (sour by now) and the dirty plates, and swept the floors, and tidied up quickly, and grabbed a cup of coffee, and prepared to make a rice and fish dish, and a chocolate mousse and sat down in the middle to eat a lot of bread and jam herself. Broad hips. She remembered the office work in her file and knew she wouldn't be able to do it. Martin anyway thought it was ridiculous for her to bring work back at the weekends. "It's your holiday," he'd say. "Why should they impose?" Martha loved her work. She didn't have to smile at it. She just did it.

Katie came back upset and crying. She sat in the kitchen while Martha worked and drank glass after glass of gin and bitter lemon. Katie liked ice and lemon in gin. Martha paid for all the drink out of her wages. It was part of the deal between her and Martin – the contract by which she went out to work. All things to cheer the spirit, otherwise depressed by a working wife and mother, were to be paid for by Martha. Drink, holidays, petrol, outings, puddings, electricity, heating: it was quite a joke between them. It didn't really make any difference: it was their joint money, after all. Amazing how Martha's wages were creeping up, almost to the level of Martin's. One day they would overtake. Then what?

Work, honestly, was a piece of cake.

Anyway, poor Katie was crying. Colin, she'd discovered, kept a photograph of Janet and the children in his wallet. "He's not free of her. He pretends he is, but he isn't. She has him by a stranglehold. It's the kids. His bloody kids. Moaning Mary and that little creep Joanna. It's all he thinks about. I'm nobody."

But Katie didn't believe it. She knew she was somebody all right. Colin came in, in a fury. He took out the photograph and set fire to it, bitterly, with a match. Up in smoke they went. Mary and Joanna and Janet. The ashes fell on the floor. (Martha swept them up when Colin and Katie had gone. It hardly seemed polite to do so when they were still there.) "Go back to her," Katie said. "Go back to her. I don't care. Honestly, I'd rather be on my own. You're a nice old fashioned thing. Run along then. Do your thing, I'll do mine. Who cares?"

"Christ, Katie, the fuss! She only just happens to be in the photograph. She's not there on purpose to annoy. And I do feel bad about her. She's been having a hard time."

"And haven't you, Colin? She twists a pretty knife, I can tell you. Don't you have rights too? Not to mention me. Is a little loyalty too much to expect?"

They were reconciled before lunch, up in the spare room. Harry and Beryl Elder arrived at twelve-thirty. Harry didn't like to hurry on Sundays; Beryl was flustered with apologies for their lateness. They'd brought artichokes from their garden. "Wonderful," cried Martin. "Fruits of the earth? Let's have a wonderful soup! Don't fret, Martha. I'll do it."

"Don't fret." Martha clearly hadn't been smiling enough. She was in danger, Martin implied, of ruining everyone's weekend. There was an emergency in the garden very shortly – an elm tree which had probably got Dutch elm disease – and Martha finished the artichokes. The lid flew off the blender and there was artichoke purée everywhere. "Let's have lunch outside," said Colin. "Less work for Martha."

Martin frowned at Martha; he thought the appearance of martyrdom in the face of guests to be an unforgivable offence.

Everyone happily joined in taking the furniture out, but it was Martha's experience that nobody ever helped to bring it in again. Jolyon was stung by a wasp. Jasper sneezed and sneezed from hay fever and couldn't find the tissues and he wouldn't use loo paper. ("Surely you remembered the tissues, darling?": Martin.)

Beryl Elder was nice. "Wonderful to eat out," she said, fetching the cream for her pudding, while Martha fished a fly from the liquefying Brie ("You shouldn't have bought it so ripe, Martha": Martin) – "except it's just some other woman has to do it. But at least it isn't *me*." Beryl worked too, as a secretary, to send the boys to boarding school, where she'd rather they weren't. But her husband was from a rather grand family, and she'd been only a typist when he married her, so her life was a mass of amends, one way or another. Harry had lately opted out of the stockbroking rat race and become an artist, choosing integrity rather than money, but that choice was his alone and couldn't of course be inflicted on the boys.

Katie found the fish and rice dish rather strange, toyed at it with her fork, and talked about Italian restaurants she knew. Martin lay back soaking in the sun: crying, "Oh, this is the life." He made coffee, nobly, and the lid flew off the grinder and there were coffee beans all over the kitchen especially in amongst the row of cookery books which Martin gave Martha Christmas by Christmas. At least they didn't have to be brought back every weekend. ("The burglars won't have the sense to steal those": Martin.)

Beryl fell asleep and Katie watched her, quizzically. Beryl's mouth was open and she had a lot of fillings, and her ankles were thick and her waist was going, and she didn't look after herself. "I love women," sighed Katie. "They look so wonderful asleep. I wish I could be an earth mother."

Beryl woke with a start and nagged her husband into going home, which he clearly didn't want to do, so didn't. Beryl thought she had to get back because his mother was coming round later. Nonsense! Then Beryl tried to stop Harry drinking more home-made wine and was laughed at by everyone. He was driving, Beryl couldn't, and he did have a nasty scar on his temple from a previous road accident. Never mind.

"She does come on strong, poor soul," laughed Katie when they'd finally gone. "I'm never going to get married," – and Colin looked at her yearningly because he wanted to marry her more than anything in the world, and Martha cleared the coffee cups.

"Oh don't *do* that," said Katie, "do just sit *down*, Martha, you make us all feel bad," and Martin glared at Martha who sat down and Jenny called out for her and Martha went upstairs and Jenny had started her first period and Martha cried and cried and knew she must stop because this must be a joyous occasion for Jenny or her whole future would be blighted, but for once, Martha couldn't.

Her daughter Jenny: wife, mother, friend.

• Close study of character: Martha's 'documents'

It is obvious that Martha needs to be a very well organised person. She probably makes lists to help her through the many tasks she has to perform, and she may even make use of an appointments diary to plan ahead.

Using the story, reconstruct the following 'documents' belonging to Martha:
  (a) shopping list for the week leading up to the 'Weekend',
  (b) list of jobs to be done during the week,
  (c) timetable for the week, set out under the following headings: day, time, activity, comments/remarks.

• Close study of character: Martha's feelings

One of the key aspects of any piece of writing is the points of view which the reader experiences. In this story we share Martha's point of view for much of the time.

Discuss and make notes on the following paragraphs to help you understand
what Martha feels about Martin, the children, herself and her life.

'Martha worried about her age, her tendency to complain, and the
width of her hips. She took the remarks personally. Was she right to
do so? The children noticed nothing: it was just funny lively Daddy
being witty about Mummy's car. Mummy, done for drunken driving.
Mummy, with roots of melancholy somewhere deep beneath the
bustling, busy everyday self. Busy: ah so busy!'

'Katie appeared three minutes later, reproachfully holding out her
Yves St Laurent towel, sopping wet. "Oh dear," cried Martha. "Jenny
must have washed her hair!" And Martha was obliged to rout Jenny
out of bed to rebuke her, publicly, if only to demonstrate that she
knew what was right and proper. That meant Jenny would sulk all
weekend, and that meant a treat or an outing mid-week, or else by
the following week she'd be having an asthma attack. "You fuss the
children too much," said Martin. "That's why Jenny has asthma."
Jenny was pleasant enough to look at, but not stunning. Perhaps she
was a disappointment to her father? Martin would never say so, but
Martha feared he thought so.'

'An egg and an orange each child, each day. Then nothing bad would
go wrong. And it hadn't. The asthma was very mild. A calm, tranquil
environment, the doctor said. Ah, smile, Martha smile. Domestic
happiness depends on you. 21×52 oranges a year. Each one to be
purchased, carried, peeled and washed up after. And what about
potatoes. 12×52 pounds a year? Martin liked his potatoes carefully
peeled. He couldn't bear to find little cores of black in the mouthful.
("Well, it isn't very nice, is it?": Martin.)
Martha dreamed she was eating coal, by handfuls, and liking it.'

- ## Close study of character: Martha's childhood

An aspect of personality which is very important is childhood experience. Use
this extract to note down and compare ideas you have about the sort of
person Martha's mother was, and how this has affected Martha.

'Martin would only laugh if she said anything about the way he spoke to her car and warn her against paranoia. "Don't get like your mother, darling." Martha's mother had, towards the end, thought that people were plotting against her. Martha's mother had led a secluded, suspicious life, and made Martha's childhood a chilly and lonely time. Life now, by comparison, was wonderful for Martha. People, children, houses, conversations, food, drink, theatres – even, now, a career. Martin standing between her and the hostility of the world – popular, easy, funny Martin, beckoning the rest of the world into earshot.

Ah, she was grateful: little earnest Martha, with her shy ways and her penchant for passing boring exams – how her life had blossomed out! Three children too – Jasper, Jenny and Jolyon – all with Martin's broad brow and open looks, and the confidence born of her love and care, and the work she had put into them since the dawning of their days.'

In Martha's life many things are done because they 'must be', or because they are 'right' or because she is ordered to. Collect a list of examples.

● **Written assignment (literature): dossier and report writing**
Increasingly Martha finds herself secretly weeping, secretly eating, and often working through the night to achieve perfection in the house. She gets in touch with Janet who insists she must see a psychiatrist, for the sake of Martin, the children and, of course, herself.

You are the psychiatrist. Drawing on the notes you have made and on the story, compile a dossier on Martha. The dossier contains some of the following:

> interviews with acquaintances: Janet, Kate, the Elders,
> Jolyon's account of the weekend of the story, written for his English teacher in school on Monday,
> information collected from relatives about her childhood,
> an unposted letter to Janet,
> a transcript of a conversation with Martha,
> a memo about her from her employer,
> pages from her appointments diary in which she wrote her lists.

From the dossier you should write up your report on Martha and your recommendations.

- ## Written assignment (literature): letter writing

Write a letter to Martha explaining what you think of her situation and her marriage.

- ## Close study of character: Martin's 'sayings'

In China some years ago it was expected that people should always carry and read a little red book. This contained the thoughts and sayings of Chairman Mao Tse Tung, the leader of China at the time. His ideas were thought to be important for all.

Martin has a fund of sayings that contain his thoughts and ideas on life. Imagine you are going to publish a little red book, with the title 'The Thoughts and Sayings of Martin, Twentieth-Century Man'.

Make a list of his sayings from the story, reconstructing them from reported speech where necessary. Here are two to start with:

> 'Goods in empty cottages are an open invitation to burglars.'
> 'Separate pans mean separate flavours!'

When you have completed your list, divide the sayings into categories. Put those referring to similar things together. Study your list for the next activity.

- ## Spoken activity: 'verbal tennis'

In pairs, from memory, and without the help of your written lists, play verbal tennis, using the thoughts of Martin, Twentieth-Century Man.

This is how it is done. The first person quotes one of Martin's sayings, for example, 'Separate pans mean separate flavours!' The other person replies with another, for example, 'Goods in empty cottages are an open invitation to burglars'. The winner is the one who keeps going longest.

- ## Spoken assignment: role play in pairs

Martin goes to his car-maintenance class and tells a friend about the weekend. Try to use Martin's style, attitudes and feelings.

Do this assignment in pairs, the second person taking an appropriate role as sympathetic listener and questioner.

● Written assignment (language): play writing

The material used in your work on Martin could be written up as a play, with an introduction setting the scene and some instructions for the actor. You might want to add an explanatory introduction about how you see the characters.

● Written assignment (language or literature): narrative

Martha is indisposed the following weekend but urges Martin to go down to the cottage with the children: there are guests expected who cannot be put off.

Write a story about the weekend, remembering to include Martin's point of view, and to reveal his character. The story may well be humorous.

● Narrative technique: subtext

A writer selects setting, incidents and characters to create a particular vision of life. Below the surface of the story are other messages – the 'subtext'.
One of the ways Fay Weldon shapes our vision is to use three married couples who share certain patterns of behaviour: Janet and Colin; Martha and Martin; Beryl and Harry.

Discuss what you think the relationships have in common. Note down the similarities you see and compare your ideas with your partner's.
Writers also create expectations in the reader by using certain patterns of behaviour within the world of the story. This is one of a writer's ways of shaping life.
Look at the following examples from the story of when Martha is upset. How does she deal with her emotions in (a) and (b)? What happens to this pattern of expectation in (c)? Can you suggest reasons why the author breaks the reader's expectations? Discuss this with your partner.

> (a) 'And she yawned and stretched her lean, childless body and
> smiled at Colin with her inviting, naughty little girl eyes, and Martin
> watched her in admiration.

Martha got up and left them and took a paint pot and put a coat of white gloss on the bathroom wall. The white surface pleased her. She was good at painting. She produced a smooth, even surface. Her legs throbbed. She feared she might be getting varicose veins.'

(b) 'But she wasn't. She slept late. The others went out for a walk. They'd left a note, a considerate note: "Didn't wake you. You looked tired. Had a cold breakfast so as not to make too much mess. Leave everything 'til we get back." But it was ten o'clock, and guests were coming at noon, so she cleared away the bread, the butter, the crumbs, the smears, the jam, the spoons, the spilt sugar, the cereal, the milk (sour by now) and the dirty plates, and swept the floors, and tidied up quickly, and grabbed a cup of coffee, and prepared to make a rice and fish dish, and a chocolate mousse and sat down in the middle to eat a lot of bread and jam herself. Broad hips. She remembered the office work in her file and knew she wouldn't be able to do it. Martin anyway thought it ridiculous for her to bring work back at the weekends.'

(c) '"She does come on strong, poor soul," laughed Katie when they'd finally gone. "I'm never going to get married," – and Colin looked at her yearningly because he wanted to marry her more than anything in the world, and Martha cleared the coffee cups.

"Oh don't *do* that," said Katie, "do just sit *down*, Martha, you make us all feel bad," and Martin glared at Martha who sat down and Jenny called out for her and Martha went upstairs and Jenny had started her first period and Martha cried and cried and knew she must stop because this must be a joyous occasion for Jenny or her whole future would be blighted, but for once, Martha couldn't.

Her daughter Jenny: wife, mother, friend.'

The story ends like this:

'Her daughter Jenny: wife, mother, friend.'

Within the experience of the story, what does this sentence mean?

Behind the words, beneath them, are meanings we often call the subtext. For example:

Text: 'Her daughter'

Subtext: 'loved, looked after, given all the right things, to be always made happy, to be given the fulfilment Martha lacked when young...' and so on.

Now, working with your partner, construct similar subtexts for the other words: 'wife', 'mother', 'friend'.

● **Written assignment (language): discursive essay**

What picture of marriage does Fay Weldon present us with, and what do you think of it? You may use the preliminary work you did before reading the story and any of the notes made during subsequent work to help you.

Your title is: 'A Writer's View of Marriage'.

● **Written assignment (literature): appreciation**

1. Discuss what you have appreciated and enjoyed in this story.

2. What have you found interesting about the way Fay Weldon writes? With examples to show what you mean, focus on how she has affected your reactions to characters, events and ideas.

13

The Test

This is intended to be a *controlled conditions assignment*, done without discussion.

Read the story and answer the following questions as fully and as carefully as possible. Remember the work you have done on other short stories.

1. What words and phrases indicate that the story is set in America? Answer as fully as you can.

2. Write about the relationship between Marian and Mrs Ericson. Back up what you say by evidence from the story.

3. What impression do you get of the inspector? Give evidence for your opinion from his actions and speech. What do you think of him? Defend your ideas.

4. What impression do you get of Marian's character? In your answer include discussion of some phrases from the story you consider to be important.

5. There are three main characters – Mrs Ericson, Marian and the inspector. Using the ideas you have collected about the characters, write the diary of *one* character, looking back on the events of the day. Bring out your character's feelings and attitudes in what you write. Use the story as a basis, but feel free to add to it without distorting the characters concerned.
6. This story explores some problems in society. What problems do you think it raises, and what ideas does the story communicate about those problems? You will find it helpful to organise your ideas before you begin writing.

The Test

Angelica Gibbs

On the afternoon Marian took her second driver's test, Mrs Ericson went with her. "It's probably better to have someone a little older with you," Mrs Ericson said as Marian slipped into the driver's seat beside her. "Perhaps the last time your Cousin Bill made you nervous, talking too much on the way."

"Yes, Ma'am," Marian said in her soft unaccented voice. "They probably do like it better if a white person shows up with you."

"Oh, I don't think it's *that*," Mrs Ericson began, and subsided after a glance at the girl's set profile. Marian drove the car slowly through the shady suburban streets. It was one of the first hot days in June, and when they reached the boulevard they found it crowded with cars headed for the beaches.

"Do you want me to drive?" Mrs Ericson asked. "I'll be glad to if you're feeling jumpy." Marian shook her head. Mrs Ericson watched her dark, competent hands and wondered for the thousandth time how the house had ever managed to get along without her, or how she had lived through those earlier years when her household had been presided over by a series of slatternly white girls who had considered housework demeaning and the care of children an added insult. "You drive beautifully, Marian," she said. "Now, don't think of the last time. Anybody would slide on a steep hill on a wet day like that."

"It takes four mistakes to flunk you," Marian said. "I don't remember doing all the things the inspector marked down on my blank."

"People say that they only want you to slip them a little something," Mrs Ericson said doubtfully.

"*No*," Marian said. "That would only make it worse, Mrs Ericson, I know."

The car turned right, at a traffic signal, into a side road and slid up to the curb at the rear of a short line of parked cars. The inspectors had not arrived yet.

"You have the papers?" Mrs Ericson asked. Marian took them out of her bag: her learner's permit, the car registration, and her birth certificate. They settled down to the dreary business of waiting.

"It will be marvellous to have someone dependable to drive the children to school every day," Mrs Ericson said.

Marian looked up from the list of driving requirements she had been studying. "It'll make things simpler at the house, won't it?" she said.

"Oh, Marian," Mrs Ericson exclaimed, "if I could only pay you half of what you're worth!"

"Now, Mrs Ericson," Marian said firmly. They looked at each other and smiled with affection.

Two cars with official insignia on their doors stopped across the street. The inspectors leaped out, very brisk and military in their neat uniforms. Marian's hands tightened on the wheel. "There's the one who flunked me last time," she whispered, pointing to a stocky, self-important man who had begun to shout directions at the driver at the head of the line. "Oh, Mrs Ericson."

"Now, Marian," Mrs Ericson said. They smiled at each other again, rather weakly.

The inspector who finally reached their car was not the stocky one but a genial, middle-aged man who grinned broadly as he thumbed over their papers. Mrs Ericson started to get out of the car. "Don't you want to come along?" the inspector asked. "Mandy and I don't mind company."

Mrs Ericson was bewildered for a moment. "No," she said, and stepped to the curb. "I might make Marian self-conscious. She's a fine driver, Inspector."

"Sure thing," the inspector said, winking at Mrs Ericson. He slid into the seat beside Marian. "Turn right at the corner, Mandy-Lou."

From the curb, Mrs Ericson watched the car move smoothly up the street.

The inspector made notations in a small black book. "Age?" he inquired presently, as they drove along.

"Twenty-seven."

He looked at Marian out of the corner of his eye. "Old enough to have quite a flock of pickaninnies, eh?"

Marian did not answer.

"Left at this corner," the inspector said, "and park between that truck and the green Buick."

The two cars were very close together, but Marian squeezed in between them without too much manoeuvering. "Driven before, Mandy-Lou?" the inspector asked.

"Yes, sir. I had a license for three years in Pennsylvania."

"Why do you want to drive a car?"

"My employer needs me to take her children to and from school."

"Sure you don't really want to sneak out nights to meet some young blood?" the inspector asked. He laughed as Marian shook her head.

"Let's see you take a left at the corner and then turn around in the middle of the next block," the inspector said. He began to whistle 'Swanee River'. "Make you homesick?" he asked.

Marian put out her hand, swung around neatly in the street, and headed back in the direction from which they had come. "No," she said. "I was born in Scranton, Pennsylvania."

The inspector feigned astonishment. "You-all ain't Southern?" he said. "Well, dog my cats if I didn't think you-all came from down yondah."

"No, sir," Marian said.

"Turn onto Main Street and let's see how you-all does in heavier traffic."

They followed a line of cars along Main Street for several blocks until they came in sight of a concrete bridge which arched high over the railroad tracks.

"Read that sign at the end of the bridge," the inspector said.

"'Proceed with caution. Dangerous in slippery weather,'" Marian said.

"You-all sho can read fine," the inspector exclaimed. "Where d'you learn to do that, Mandy?"

"I got my college degree last year," Marian said. Her voice was not quite steady.

As the car crept up the slope of the bridge the inspector burst out laughing. He laughed so hard he could scarcely give his next direction. "Stop here," he said, wiping his eyes, "then start 'er up again. Mandy got her degree, did she? Dog my cats!"

Marian pulled up beside the curb. She put the car in neutral, pulled on the emergency, waited a moment, and then put the car into gear again. Her face was set. As she released the brake her foot slipped off the clutch pedal and the engine stalled.

"Now, Mistress Mandy," the inspector said, "remember your degree."

"*Damn* you!" Marian cried. She started the car with a jerk.

The inspector lost his joviality in an instant. "Return to the starting place, please," he said, and made four very black crosses at random in the squares on Marian's application blank.

Mrs Ericson was waiting at the curb where they had left her. As Marian stopped the car, the inspector jumped out and brushed past her, his face purple. "What happened?" Mrs Ericson asked, looking after him with alarm.

Marian stared down at the wheel and her lip trembled.

"Oh, Marian, *again?*" Mrs Ericson said.

Marian nodded. "In a sort of different way," she said, and slid over to the right-hand side of the car.

14

Country Lovers

● **Group discussion: vocabulary**

Before reading the story, discuss in groups the meanings of the words given below. Write a definition or give an example for each, and decide whether the words can be arranged in pairs or groups:

apartheid	integration
privilege	taboo
deprivation	prejudice
segregation	tolerance

Now read the story. When you have finished it, look again at the list of words and discuss their application to the events in the story. Do any not have a place?

Country Lovers

Nadine Gordimer

The farm children play together when they are small; but once the white children go away to school they soon don't play together any more, even in the holidays. Although most of the black children get some sort of schooling, they drop every year farther behind the grades passed by the white children; the childish vocabulary, the child's exploration of the adventurous possibilities of dam, koppies, mealie lands and veld – there comes a time when the white children have surpassed these with the vocabulary of boarding-school and the possibilities of inter-school sports matches and the kind of adventures seen at the cinema. This usefully coincides with the age of twelve or thirteen; so that by the time early adolescence is reached, the black children are making, along with the bodily changes common to all, an easy transition to adult forms of address, beginning to call their old playmates *missus* and *baasie* – little master.

The trouble was Paulus Eysendyck did not seem to realize that Thebedi was now simply one of the crowd of farm children down at the kraal, recognizable in his sisters' old clothes. The first Christmas holidays after he had gone to boarding-school he brought home for Thebedi a painted box he had made in his wood-work class. He had to give it to her secretly because he had nothing for the other children at the kraal. And she gave him, before he went back to school, a bracelet she had made of thin brass wire and the grey-and-white beans of the castor-oil crop his father cultivated. (When they used to play together, she was the one who had taught Paulus how to make clay oxen for their toy spans.) There was a craze, even in the *platteland* towns like the one where he was at school, for boys to wear elephant-hair and other bracelets beside their watch-straps; his was admired, friends asked him to get similar ones for them. He said the natives made them on his father's farm and he would try.

When he was fifteen, six feet tall, and tramping round at school dances with the girls from the 'sister' school in the same town; when he had learnt how to tease and flirt and fondle quite intimately these girls who were the daughters of prosperous farmers like his father; when he had even met one who, at a wedding he had attended with his parents on a nearby farm, had let him do with her in a locked storeroom what people did when they made love – when he was as far from his childhood as all this, he still brought home from a shop in town a red plastic belt and gilt hoop ear-rings for the black girl, Thebedi. She told her father the missus had given these to her as a reward for some work she had done – it was true she sometimes was called to help out in the farmhouse. She told the girls in the kraal that she had a sweetheart nobody knew about, far away, away on another farm, and they giggled, and teased, and admired her. There was a boy in the kraal called Njabulo who said he wished he could have bought her a belt and ear-rings.

When the farmer's son was home for the holidays she wandered far from the kraal and her companions. He went for walks alone. They had not arranged this; it was an urge each followed independently. He knew it was she, from a long way off. She knew that his dog would not bark at her. Down at the dried-up river-bed where five or six years ago the children had caught a leguaan one great day – a creature that combined ideally the size and ferocious aspect of the croco-dile with the harmlessness of the lizard – they squatted side by side on the earth bank. He told her traveller's tales: about school, about the punishments at school, particularly, exaggerating both their nature and his indifference to them. He told

her about the town of Middleburg, which she had never seen. She had nothing to tell but she prompted with many questions, like any good listener. While he talked he twisted and tugged at the roots of white stinkwood and Cape willow trees that looped out of the eroded earth around them. It had always been a good spot for children's games, down there hidden by the mesh of old, ant-eaten trees held in place by vigorous ones, wild asparagus bushing up between the trunks, and here and there prickly-pear cactus sunken-skinned and bristly, like an old man's face, keeping alive sapless until the next rainy season. She punctured the dry hide of a prickly-pear again and again with a sharp stick while she listened. She laughed a lot at what he told her, sometimes dropping her face on her knees, sharing amusement with the cool shady earth beneath her bare feet. She put on her pair of shoes – white sandals, thickly Blanco-ed against the farm dust – when he was on the farm, but these were taken off and laid aside, at the river-bed.

One summer afternoon when there was water flowing there and it was very hot she waded in as they used to do when they were children, her dress bunched modestly and tucked into the legs of her pants. The schoolgirls he went swimming with at dams or pools on neighbouring farms wore bikinis but the sight of their dazzling bellies and thighs in the sunlight had never made him feel what he felt now, when the girl came up the bank and sat beside him, the drops of water beading off her dark legs the only points of light in the earth-smelling, deep shade. They were not afraid of one another, they had known one another always; he did with her what he had done that time in the storeroom at the wedding, and this time it was so lovely, so lovely, he was surprised . . . and she was surprised by it, too – he could see in her dark face that was part of the shade, with her big dark eyes, shiny as soft water, watching him attentively: as she had when they used to huddle over their teams of mud oxen, as she had when he told her about detention weekends at school.

They went to the river-bed often through those summer holidays. They met just before the light went, as it does quite quickly, and each returned home with the dark – she to her mother's hut, he to the farmhouse – in time for the evening meal. He did not tell her about school or town any more. She did not ask questions any longer. He told her, each time, when they would meet again. Once or twice it was very early in the morning; the lowing of the cows being driven to graze came to them where they lay, dividing them with unspoken recognition of the sound read in their two pairs of eyes, opening so close to each other.

He was a popular boy at school. He was in the second, then the first soccer team. The head girl of the 'sister' school was said to have a crush on him; he didn't particularly like her, but there was a pretty blonde who put up her long hair into a kind of doughnut with a black ribbon round it, whom he took to see films when the schoolboys and girls had a free Saturday afternoon. He had been driving tractors and other farm vehicles since he was ten years old, and as soon as he was eighteen he got a driver's licence and in the holidays, this last year of his school life, he took neighbours' daughters to dances and to the drive-in cinema that had just opened twenty kilometres from the farm. His sisters were married, by then; his parents often left him in charge of the farm over the weekend while they visited the young wives and grandchildren.

When Thebedi saw the farmer and his wife drive away on a Saturday afternoon, the boot of their Mercedes filled with fresh-killed poultry and vegetables from the garden that it was part of her father's work to tend, she knew that she must come not to the river-bed but up to the house. The house was an old one, thick-walled, dark against the heat. The kitchen was its lively thoroughfare, with servants, food supplies, begging cats and dogs, pots boiling over, washing being damped for ironing, and the big deep-freeze the missus had ordered from town, bearing a crocheted mat and a vase of plastic irises. But the dining-room with the bulging-legged heavy table was shut up in its rich, old smell of soup and tomato sauce. The sitting-room curtains were drawn and the TV set silent. The door of the parents' bedroom was locked and the empty rooms where the girls had slept had sheets of plastic spread over the beds. It was in one of these that she and the farmer's son stayed together whole nights – almost: she had to get away before the house servants, who knew her, came in at dawn. There was a risk someone would discover her or traces of her presence if he took her to his own bedroom, although she had looked into it many times when she was helping out in the house and knew well, there, the row of silver cups he had won at school.

When she was eighteen and the farmer's son nineteen and working with his father on the farm before entering a veterinary college, the young man Njabulo asked her father for her. Njabulo's parents met with hers and the money he was to pay in place of the cows it is customary to give a prospective bride's parents was settled upon. He had no cows to offer; he was a labourer on the Eysendyck farm, like her father. A bright youngster; old Eysendyck had taught him brick-laying and was using him for odd jobs in construction, around the place. She did not tell the farmer's son that her parents had arranged for her to marry. She did not tell him, either, before he left for his first term at the veterinary college, that she thought she was going to have a baby. Two months after her marriage to Njabulo, she gave birth to a daughter. There was no disgrace in that; among her people it is customary for a young man to make sure, before marriage, that the chosen girl is not barren, and Njabulo had made love to her then. But the infant was very light and did not quickly grow darker as most African babies do. Already at birth there was on its head a quantity of straight, fine floss, like that which carries the seeds of certain weeds in the veld. The unfocused eyes it opened were grey flecked with yellow. Njabulo was the matt, opaque coffee-grounds colour that has always been called black; the colour of Thebedi's legs on which beaded water looked oyster-shell blue, the same colour as Thebedi's face, where the black eyes, with their interested gaze and clear whites, were so dominant.

Njabulo made no complaint. Out of his farm labourer's earnings he bought from the Indian store a cellophane-windowed pack containing a pink plastic bath, six napkins, a card of safety pins, a knitted jacket, cap and bootees, a dress, and a tin of Johnson's Baby Powder, for Thebedi's baby.

When it was two weeks old Paulus Eysendyck arrived home from the veterinary college for the holidays. He drank a glass of fresh, still-warm milk in the childhood familiarity of his mother's kitchen and heard her discussing with the old house-servant where they could get a reliable substitute to help out now that the girl Thebedi had had a baby. For the first time since he was a boy he came right into the kraal. It was eleven o'clock in the morning. The men were at work in the lands. He looked about him, urgently; the women turned away, each not wanting to be the one approached to point out where Thebedi lived. Thebedi appeared, coming slowly from the hut Njabulo had built in white-man's style, with a tin chimney, and a proper window with glass panes set in straight as walls made of unfired bricks would allow. She greeted him with hands brought together and a token movement representing the respectful bob with which she was accustomed to acknowledge she was in the presence of his father or mother. He lowered his head under the doorway of her home and went in. He said, "I want to see. Show me."

She had taken the bundle off her back before she came out into the light to face him. She moved between the iron bedstead made up with Njabulo's checked blankets and the small wooden table where the pink plastic bath stood among food and kitchen pots, and picked up the bundle from the snugly-blanketed grocer's box where it lay. The infant was asleep; she revealed the closed, pale, plump tiny face, with a bubble of spit at the corner of the mouth, the spidery pink hands stirring. She took off the woollen cap and the straight fine hair flew up after it in static electricity, showing gilded strands here and there. He said nothing. She was watching him as she had done when they were little, and the gang of children had trodden down a crop in their games or transgressed in some other way for which he, as the farmer's son, the white one among them, must intercede with the farmer. She disturbed the sleeping face by scratching or tickling gently at a cheek with one finger, and slowly the eyes opened, saw nothing, were still asleep, and then, awake, no longer narrowed, looked out at them, grey with yellowish flecks, his own hazel eyes.

He struggled for a moment with a grimace of tears, anger and self-pity. She could not put out her hand to him. He said, "You haven't been near the house with it?"

She shook her head.

"Never?"

Again she shook her head.

"Don't take it out. Stay inside. Can't you take it away somewhere. You must give it to someone ..."

She moved to the door with him.

He said, "I'll see what I will do. I don't know." And then he said, "I feel like killing myself."

Her eyes began to glow, to thicken with tears. For a moment there was the feeling between them that used to come when they were alone down at the river-bed.

He walked out.

Two days later, when his mother and father had left the farm for the day, he appeared again. The women were away on the lands, weeding, as they were employed to do as casual labour in summer; only the very old remained, propped up on the ground outside the huts in the flies and the sun. Thebedi did not ask him in. The child had not been well; it had diarrhoea. He asked where its food was. She said, "The milk comes from me." He went into Njabulo's house, where the child lay; she did not follow but stayed outside the door and watched without seeing an old crone who had lost her mind, talking to herself, talking to the fowls who ignored her.

She thought she heard small grunts from the hut, the kind of infant grunt that indicates a full stomach, a deep sleep. After a time, long or short she did not know, he came out and walked away with plodding stride (his father's gait) out of sight, towards his father's house.

The baby was not fed during the night and although she kept telling Njabulo it was sleeping, he saw for himself in the morning that it was dead. He comforted her with words and caresses. She did not cry but simply sat, staring at the door. Her hands were cold as dead chickens' feet to his touch.

Njabulo buried the little baby where farm workers were buried, in the place in the veld the farmer had given them. Some of the mounds had been left to weather away unmarked, others were covered with stones and a few had fallen wooden crosses. He was going to make a cross but before it was finished the police came and dug up the grave and took away the dead baby: someone – one of the other labourers? their women? – had reported that the baby was almost white, that, strong and healthy, it had died suddenly after a visit by the farmer's son. Pathological tests on the infant corpse showed intestinal damage not always consistent with death by natural causes.

Thebedi went for the first time to the country town where Paulus had been to school, to give evidence at the preparatory examination into the charge of murder brought against him. She cried hysterically in the witness box, saying yes, yes (the gilt hoop ear-rings swung in her ears), she saw the accused pouring liquid into the baby's mouth. She said he had threatened to shoot her if she told anyone.

More than a year went by before, in the same town, the case was brought to trial. She came to Court with a new-born baby on her back. She wore gilt hoop ear-rings; she was calm; she said she had not seen what the white man did in the house.

Paulus Eysendyck said he had visited the hut but had not poisoned the child.

The Defence did not contest that there had been a love relationship between the accused and the girl, or that intercourse had taken place, but submitted there was no proof that the child was the accused's.

The judge told the accused there was strong suspicion against him but not enough proof that he had committed the crime. The Court could not accept the girl's evidence because it was clear she had committed perjury either at this trial or at the preparatory examination. There was a suggestion in the mind of the Court that she might be an accomplice in the crime; but, again, insufficient proof.

The judge commended the honourable behaviour of the husband (sitting in court in a brown-and-yellow-quartered golf cap bought for Sundays) who had not rejected his wife and had 'even provided clothes for the unfortunate infant out of his slender means'.

The verdict on the accused was 'not guilty'.

The young white man refused to accept the congratulations of press and public and left the Court with his mother's raincoat shielding his face from photographers. His father said to the press, "I will try and carry on as best I can to hold up my head in the district."

Interviewed by the Sunday papers, who spelled her name in a variety of ways, the black girl, speaking in her own language, was quoted beneath her photograph: "It was a thing of our childhood, we don't see each other any more."

● Written activity: differences and similarities in lifestyle

Make two columns, one headed *black*, the other *white*.
List what we learn about the contrasting lives of black and white people in this story. For example, you might describe Thebedi's hut in one column, the farmhouse in the other.

Although there are significant differences in the way of life of Thebedi and Paulus, the two also have a shared background which is very important. Underneath the two columns you have made above, write down as much information as you can about the life they shared in South Africa.

● Written assignment (language): essay

Imagine that you are Paulus. When you go away to school you are asked to write about your country childhood. Write the essay, using information you have collected from the story.
Your title is: 'Country Life'.

● Discussion and note-making: characters and relationships

There are three main characters in the story: Thebedi, Paulus and Njabulo. We learn a number of factual things about these three. Discuss and write down all the information we have about their appearance, their aptitudes and how they spend their time.

The author gives us very little direct insight into how they feel, but she does give us hints which help us piece together their feelings for each other throughout the story. Write down one thing each of them does which you think reveals something significant about their character. Compare what you have chosen with what others have decided upon.

● **Close study of the relationship between Thebedi and Paulus**

Here is a list of statements about the relationship between Thebedi and Paulus at different points in the story. Find and list evidence in the story to back up each statement.

1. Both of them recognise the need to hide their affection for each other from other people.

2. They both feel a strong sexual attraction towards each other.

3. Paulus feels the need to impress Thebedi at first.

4. After they begin to make love he no longer feels this need.

5. Paulus can only think of himself when he hears of the baby.

6. Thebedi accepts that she must not let anyone know that the baby is his.

7. When she first goes to court, Thebedi is bitter and angry about what Paulus did.

8. When she goes to court the second time, Thebedi no longer cares about Paulus.

● **Written assignment (literature): diary entries/conversation**

Either

1. Imagine that Paulus keeps a diary. Write the diary entries he makes at six different parts of the story.

    (a)   When he receives the bracelet from Thebedi.

    (b)   When he first starts making love to her.

    (c)   When he starts at Veterinary College and goes out with other girls.

    (d)   When he discovers the baby has been born.

    (e)   When he decides to kill the baby.

    (f)   After the trial.

Or

2. Thebedi talks to Njabulo about her love affair with Paulus. Write the conversation they have.

● **Spoken and written activity: 'Consequences'**

You have probably at some time played the game 'Consequences'. In this game you develop a story by means of certain stock situations. Here is a modified version of the game, designed to highlight the structure of the story. Copy this out and fill in the gaps. Discuss what you write with your partner or group.

The story is set in ....

The boy's name is ....

The girl's name is..

The problem is..

He gave her ....

She gave him..

They met at ....

He told her about ....

She responded by..

They made love..

The consequences were:

    1. ....

    2. ....

The result of this was ....

Her world said..

His world said..

The flaw in this version is that it takes no account of Njabulo. Write another version which includes his part in the story.

- **Group discussion: the trial**

In groups, discuss the following:

    1. On which occasion was Thebedi lying about what she saw Paulus do? Why did she lie, and why did she later contradict herself?

    2. What is the significance of the gilt ear-rings?

    3. What do you make of the last paragraph? Look particularly at the possible meanings of:

        'speaking in her own language'

        'it was a thing of our childhood'

        '"We don't see each other any more."'

- ## Class discussion: a 'black' trial

The trial which took place was conducted by a white judge, with a white jury and lawyers. Reconstruct the trial scene, but this time imagine that the judge, jury and lawyers are black. How might the conclusions they come to differ?

- ## Written assignment (language): newspaper reports

Write two newspaper reports of the trial – one for an establishment newspaper, the other for a black underground paper. Make use of the information you have gleaned from the story as a whole. You can interview the parents, the policeman who exhumed the body, and Njabulo and Thebedi.

- ## Written assignment (literature): character comparison

After being married to Njabulo for a year or two, Thebedi gradually grows to appreciate him more and more and starts to see Paulus as selfish and immature. Write a detailed comparison of the two boys from Thebedi's point of view.

15
Beyond the Pale

This is a long and difficult story, but one worth reading.

First, the title is important. The phrase 'beyond the pale' is part of our language. The phrase is used to refer to behaviour that is unacceptable. However, the origins of the phrase are such that as far as this story is concerned, the use of the term says as much about the people who use it as it does about those they consider to be beyond the pale. As we see in this story, there are those who do not want to understand or meet those who are different from themselves.

Second, the setting of the story, Northern Ireland, is also important. Events there feature frequently in the news programmes we ourselves watch. Like the people in the story, we are involved. We cannot say that events there do not concern us. The roots and seeds of violence are in us, too.

Beyond the Pale

William Trevor

We always went to Ireland in June.

Ever since the four of us began to go on holidays together, in 1965 it must have been, we had spent the first fortnight of the month at Glencorn Lodge in Co. Antrim. Perfection, as Dekko put it once, and none of us disagreed. It's a Georgian house by the sea, not far from the village of Ardbeag. It's quite majestic in its rather elegant way, a garden running to the very edge of a cliff, its long rhododendron drive – or avenue, as they say in Ireland. The English couple who bought the house in the early sixties, the Malseeds, have had to build on quite a bit but it's all been discreetly done, the Georgian style preserved throughout. Figs grow in the sheltered gardens, and apricots, and peaches in the greenhouses which old Mr Saxton presides over. He's Mrs Malseed's father actually. They brought him with them from Surrey, and their Dalmatians, Charger and Snooze.

It was Strafe who found Glencorn for us. He'd come across an advertisement in the *Lady* in the days when the Malseeds still felt the need to advertise. "How about this?" he said one evening at the end of the second rubber, and then read out the details. We had gone away together the summer before, to a hotel that had been recommended on the Costa Del Sol, but it hadn't been a success because the food was so appalling. "We could try this Irish one," Dekko suggested cautiously, which is what eventually we did.

The four of us have been playing bridge together for ages, Dekko, Strafe, Cynthia and myself. They call me Milly, though strictly speaking my name is Dorothy Milson. Dekko picked up his nickname at school, Dekko Deakin sounding rather good, I dare say. He and Strafe were in fact at school together, which must be why we all call Strafe by his surname: Major R. B. Strafe he is, the initials standing for Robert Buchanan. We're of an age, the four of us, all in the early fifties: the prime of life, so Dekko insists. We live quite close to Leatherhead, where the Malseeds were before they decided to make the change from Surrey to Co. Antrim. Quite a coincidence, we always think.

"How *very* nice," Mrs Malseed said, smiling her welcome again this year. Some instinct seems to tell her when guests are about to arrive, for she's rarely not waiting in the large low-ceilinged hall that always smells of flowers. She dresses beautifully, differently every day, and changing of course in the evening. Her blouse on this occasion was scarlet and silver, in stripes, her skirt black. This choice gave her a brisk look, which was fitting because being so busy she often has to be a little on the brisk side. She has smooth grey hair which she once told me she entirely looks after herself, and she almost always wears a black velvet band in it. Her face is well made up, and for one who arranges so many vases of flowers and otherwise has to use her hands she manages to keep them marvellously in condition. Her fingernails are varnished a soft pink, and a small gold bangle always adorns her right wrist, a wedding present from her husband.

"Arthur, take the party's luggage," she commanded the old porter, who doubles as odd-job man. "Rose, Geranium, Hydrangea, Fuchsia." She referred to the titles of the rooms reserved for us: in winter, when no one much comes to Glencorn Lodge, pleasant little details like that are seen to. Mrs Malseed herself painted the flower-plaques that are attached to the doors of the hotel instead of numbers; her husband sees to redecoration and repairs.

"Well, well, well," Mr Malseed said now, entering the hall through the door that leads to the kitchen regions. "A hundred thousand welcomes," he greeted us in the Irish manner. He's rather shorter than Mrs Malseed, who's handsomely tall. He wears Donegal tweed suits and is brown as a berry, including his head, which is bald. His dark brown eyes twinkle at you, making you feel rather more than just another hotel guest. They run the place like a country house, really.

"Good trip?" Mr Malseed enquired.

"Super," Dekko said. "Not a worry all the way."

"Splendid."

"The wretched boat sailed an hour early one day last week," Mrs Malseed said. "Quite a little band were left stranded at Stranraer."

Strafe laughed. "Typical of that steamship company," he said. "Catching the tide, I dare say?"

"They caught a rocket from me," Mrs Malseed replied good-humouredly. "A couple of old dears were due with us on Tuesday and had to spend the night in some awful Scottish lodging-house. It nearly finished them."

Everyone laughed, and I could feel the others thinking that our holiday had truly begun. Nothing had changed at Glencorn Lodge, all was well with its Irish world. Kitty from the dining-room came out to greet us, spotless in her uniform. "Ach, you're looking younger," she said, paying the compliment to all four of us, causing everyone in the hall to laugh again. Kitty's a bit of a card.

Arthur led the way to the rooms called Rose, Geranium, Hydrangea and Fuchsia, carrying as much of our luggage as he could manage and returning for the remainder. Arthur has a beaten, fisherman's face and short grey hair. He wears a green baize apron, and a white shirt with an imitation-silk scarf tucked into it at the neck. The scarf, in different swirling greens which blend nicely with the green of his apron, is an idea of Mrs Malseed's and one appreciates the effort, if not at a uniform, at least at tidiness.

"Thank you very much," I said to Arthur in my room, smiling and finding him a coin.

We played a couple of rubbers after dinner as usual, but not of course going on for as long as we might have because we were still quite tired after the journey. In the lounge there was a French family, two girls and their parents, and a honeymoon couple – or so we had speculated during dinner – and a man on his own. There had been other people at dinner of course, because in June Glencorn Lodge is always full: from where we sat in the window we could see some of them strolling about the lawns, a few taking the cliff path down to the seashore. In the morning we'd do the same: we'd walk along the sands to Ardbeag and have coffee in the hotel there, back in time for lunch. In the afternoon we'd drive somewhere.

I knew all that because over the years this kind of pattern had developed. We had our walks and our drives, tweed to buy in Cushendall, Strafe's and Dekko's fishing day when Cynthia and I just sat on the beach, our visit to the Giant's Causeway and one to Donegal perhaps, though that meant an early start and taking pot-luck for dinner somewhere. We'd come to adore Co. Antrim, its glens and coastline, Rathlin Island and Tievebulliagh. Since first we got to know it, in 1965, we'd all four fallen hopelessly in love with every variation of this remarkable landscape. People in England thought us mad of course: they see so much of the troubles on television that it's naturally difficult for them to realise that most places are just as they've always been. Yet coming as we did, taking the road along the coast, dawdling through Ballygally, it was impossible to believe that somewhere else the unpleasantness was going on. We'd never seen a thing, nor even heard people talking about incidents that might have taken place. It's true that after a particularly nasty carry-on a few winters ago we did consider finding somewhere else, in Scotland perhaps, or Wales. But as Strafe put it at the time, we felt we owed a certain loyalty to the Malseeds and indeed to everyone we'd come to know round about, people who'd always been glad to welcome us back. It seemed silly to lose our heads, and when we returned the following summer we knew immediately we'd been right. Dekko said that nothing could be further away from all the violence than Glencorn Lodge, and though his remark could hardly be taken literally I think we all knew what he meant.

"Cynthia's tired," I said because she'd been stifling yawns. "I think we should call it a day."

"Oh, not at all," Cynthia protested. "No, please."

But Dekko agreed with me that she was tired, and Strafe said he didn't mind stopping now. He suggested a nightcap, as he always does, and as we always do also, Cynthia and I declined. Dekko said he'd like a Cointreau.

The conversation drifted about. Dekko told us an Irish joke about a drunk who couldn't find his way out of a telephone box, and then Strafe remembered an incident at school concerning his and Dekko's housemaster, A. D. Cowley-Stubbs, and the house wag, Thrive Major. A. D. Cowley-Stubbs had been known as Cows and often featured in our after-bridge reminiscing. So did Thrive Major.

"Perhaps I *am* sleepy," Cynthia said. "I don't think I closed my eyes once last night."

She never does on a sea crossing. Personally I'm out like a light the moment my head touches the pillow; I often think it must be the salt in the air because normally I'm an uneasy sleeper at the best of times.

"You run along, old girl," Strafe advised.

"Brekky at nine," Dekko said.

Cynthia said good-night and went, and we didn't remark on her tiredness because as a kind of unwritten rule we never comment on one another. We're four people who play bridge. The companionship it offers, and the holidays we have together, are all part of that. We share everything: the cost of petrol, the cups of coffee or drinks we have; we even each make a contribution towards the use of Strafe's car because it's always his we go on holiday in, a Rover it was on this occasion.

"Funny, being here on your own," Strafe said, glancing across what the Malseeds call the After-Dinner Lounge at the man who didn't have a companion. He was a red-haired man of about thirty, not wearing a tie, his collar open at the neck and folded back over the jacket of his blue serge suit. He was uncouth-looking, though it's a hard thing to say, not at all the kind of person one usually sees at Glencorn Lodge. He sat in the After-Dinner Lounge as he had in the dining-room, lost in some concentration of his own, as if calculating sums in his mind. There had been a folded newspaper on his table in the dining room. It now reposed tidily on the arm of his chair, still unopened.

"Commercial gent," Dekko said. "Fertilisers."

"Good heavens, never. You wouldn't get a rep in here."

I took no part in the argument. The lone man didn't much interest me, but I felt that Strafe was probably right: if there was anything dubious about the man's credentials he might have found it difficult to secure a room. In the hall of Glencorn Lodge there's a notice which reads: *We prefer not to feature in hotel guides, and we would be grateful to our guests if they did not seek to include Glencorn Lodge in the* Good Food Guide, *the* Good Hotel Guide, *the* Michelin, Egon Ronay *or any others. We have not advertised Glencorn since our early days, and prefer our recommendations to be by word of mouth.*

"Ah, thank you," Strafe said when Kitty brought his whisky and Dekko's Cointreau. "Sure you won't have something?" he said to me, although he knew I never did.

Strafe is on the stout side, I suppose you could say, with a gingery moustache and gingery hair, hardly touched at all by grey. He left the Army years ago, I suppose because of me in a sense, because he didn't want to be posted abroad again. He's in the Ministry of Defence now.

I'm still quite pretty in my way, though nothing like as striking as Mrs Malseed, for I've never been that kind of woman. I've put on weight, and wouldn't have allowed myself to do so if Strafe hadn't kept saying he can't stand a bag of bones. I'm careful about my hair and, unlike Mrs Malseed, I have it very regularly seen to because if I don't it gets a salt and pepper look, which I hate. My husband, Ralph, who died of food-poisoning when we were still quite young, used to say I wouldn't lose a single look in middle age, and to some extent that's true. We were still putting off having children when he died, which is why I haven't any. Then I met Strafe, which meant I didn't marry again.

Strafe is married himself, to Cynthia. She's small and ineffectual, I suppose you'd say without being untruthful or unkind. Not that Cynthia and I don't get on or anything like that, in fact we get on extremely well. It's Strafe and Cynthia who don't seem quite to hit it off, and I often think how much happier all round it would have been if Cynthia had married someone completely different, someone like Dekko in a way, except that that mightn't quite have worked out either. The Strafes have two sons, both very like their father, both of them in the Army. And the very sad thing is they think nothing of poor Cynthia.

"Who's that chap?" Dekko asked Mr Malseed, who'd come over to wish us good-night.

"Awfully sorry about that, Mr Deakin. My fault entirely, a booking that came over the phone."

"Good heavens, not at all," Strafe protested, and Dekko looked horrified in case it should be thought he was objecting to the locals. "Splendid-looking fellow," he said, overdoing it.

Mr Malseed murmured that the man had only booked in for a single night, and I smiled the whole thing away, reassuring him with a nod. It's one of the pleasantest of the traditions at Glencorn Lodge that every evening Mr Malseed makes the rounds of his guests just to say good-night. It's because of little touches like that that I, too, wished Dekko hadn't questioned Mr Malseed about the man because it's the kind of thing one doesn't do at Glencorn Lodge. But Dekko is a law unto himself, very tall and gangling, always immaculately suited, a beaky face beneath mousy hair in which flecks of grey add a certain distinction.

Dekko had money of his own and though he takes out girls who are half his age he has never managed to get around to marriage. The uncharitable might say he has a rather gormless laugh; certainly it's sometimes on the loud side.

We watched while Mr Malseed bade the lone man good-night. The man didn't respond, but just sat gazing. It was ill-mannered, but this lack of courtesy didn't appear to be intentional: the man was clearly in a mood of some kind, miles away.

"Well, I'll go up," I said. "Good-night, you two."

"Cheery-bye, Milly," Dekko said. "Brekky at nine, remember."

"Good-night, Milly," Strafe said.

The Strafes always occupy different rooms on holidays, and at home also. This time he was in Geranium and she in Fuchsia. I was in Rose, and in a little while Strafe would come to see me. He stays with her out of kindness, because he fears for her on her own. He's a sentimental, good-hearted man, easily moved to tears: he simply cannot bear the thought of Cynthia with no one to talk to in the evenings, with no one to make her life around. "And besides," he often says when he's being jocular, "it would break up our bridge four." Naturally we never discuss her shortcomings or in any way analyse the marriage. The unwritten rule that exists among the four of us seems to extend as far as that.

He slipped into my room after he'd had another drink or two, and I was waiting for him as he likes me to wait, in bed but not quite undressed. He has never said so, but I know that that is something Cynthia would not understand in him, or ever attempt to comply with. Ralph, of course, would not have understood either; poor old Ralph would have been shocked. Actually it's all rather sweet, Strafe and his little ways.

"I love you, dear," I whispered to him in the darkness, but just then he didn't wish to speak of love and referred instead to my body.

If Cynthia hadn't decided to remain in the hotel the next morning instead of accompanying us on our walk to Ardbeag everything might have been different. As it happened, when she said at breakfast she thought she'd just potter about the garden and sit with her book out of the wind somewhere, I can't say I was displeased. For a moment I hoped Dekko might say he'd stay with her, allowing Strafe and myself to go off on our own, but Dekko – who doesn't go in for saying what you want him to say – didn't. "Poor old sausage," he said instead, examining Cynthia with a solicitude that suggested she was close to the grave, rather than just a little lowered by the change of life or whatever it was.

"I'll be perfectly all right," Cynthia assured him. "Honestly."

"Cynthia likes to mooch, you know,' Strafe pointed out, which of course is only the truth. She reads too much, I always think. You often see her putting down a book with the most melancholy look in her eyes, which can't be good for her. She's an imaginative woman, I suppose you would say, and of course her habit of reading so much is often useful on our holidays: over the years she has read her way through dozens of Irish guide-books. "That's where the garrison pushed the natives over the cliffs," she once remarked on a drive. "Those rocks are known as the Maidens," she remarked on another occasion. She has led us to places of interest which we had no idea existed: Garron Tower on Garron Point, the mausoleum at Bonamargy, the Devil's Backbone. As well as which, Cynthia is extremely knowledgeable about all matters relating to Irish history. Again she has read endlessly: biographies and autobiographies, long accounts of the centuries of battling and politics there've been. There's hardly a town or village we ever pass through that hasn't some significance for Cynthia, although I'm afraid her impressive fund of information doesn't always receive the attention it deserves. Not that Cynthia ever minds; it doesn't seem to worry her when no one listens. My own opinion is that she'd have made a much better job of her relationship with Strafe and her sons if she could have somehow developed a bit more character.

We left her in the garden and proceeded down the cliff path to the shingle beneath. I was wearing slacks and a blouse, with the arms of a cardigan looped round my neck in case it turned chilly: the outfit was new, specially bought for the holiday, in shades of tangerine. Strafe never cares how he dresses and of course she doesn't keep him up to the mark: that morning, as far as I remember, he wore rather shapeless corduroy trousers, the kind men sometimes garden in, and a navy-blue fisherman's jersey. Dekko as usual was a fashion plate: a pale green linen suit with pleated jacket pockets, a maroon shirt open at the neck, revealing a medallion on a fine gold chain. We didn't converse as we crossed the rather difficult shingle, but when we reached the sand Dekko began to talk about some girl or other, someone called Juliet who had apparently proposed marriage to him just before we'd left Surrey. He'd told her, so he said, that he'd think about it while on holiday and he wondered now about dispatching a telegram from Ardbeag saying, *Still thinking*. Strafe, who has a simple sense of humour, considered this hugely funny and spent most of the walk persuading Dekko that the telegram must certainly be sent, and other telegrams later on, all with the same message. Dekko kept laughing, throwing his head back in a way that always reminds me of an Australian bird I once saw in a nature film on television. I could see this was going to become one of those jokes that would accompany us all through the holiday, a man's thing really, but of course I didn't mind. The girl called Juliet was nearly thirty years younger than Dekko. I supposed she knew what she was doing.

Since the subject of telegrams had come up, Strafe recalled the occasion when Thrive Major had sent one to A. D. Cowley-Stubbs: *Darling regret three months gone love Rowena.* Carefully timed, it had arrived during one of Cows' Thursday evening coffee sessions. Rowena was a maid, known as the Bicycle, who had been sacked the previous term, and old Cows had something of a reputation as a misogynist. When he read the message he apparently went white and collapsed into an armchair. Warrington P. J. managed to read it too, and after that the fat was in the fire. The consequences went on rather, but I never minded listening when Strafe and Dekko drifted back to their schooldays. I just wish I'd known Strafe then, before either of us had gone and got married.

We had our coffee at Ardbeag, the telegram was sent off, and then Strafe and Dekko wanted to see a man called Henry O'Reilly whom we'd met on previous holidays, who organises mackerel-fishing trips. I waited on my own, picking out postcards in the village shop that sells almost everything, and then I wandered down towards the shore. I knew that they would be having a drink with the boatman because a year had passed since they'd seen him last. They joined me after about twenty minutes, Dekko apologising but Strafe not seeming to be aware that I'd had to wait because Strafe is not a man who notices little things. It was almost one o'clock when we reached Glencorn Lodge and were told by Mr Malseed that Cynthia needed looking after.

The hotel, in fact, was in a turmoil. I have never seen anyone as ashen-faced as Mr Malseed; his wife, in a forget-me-not dress, was limp. It wasn't explained to us immediately what had happened, because in the middle of telling us that Cynthia needed looking after Mr Malseed was summoned to the telephone. I could see through the half-open door of their little office a glass of whisky or brandy on the desk and Mrs Malseed's bangled arm reaching out for it. Not for ages did we realise that it all had to do with the lone man whom we'd speculated about the night before.

"He just wanted to talk to me," Cynthia kept repeating hysterically in the hall. "He sat with me by the magnolias."

I made her lie down. Strafe and I stood on either side of her bed as she lay there with her shoes off, her rather unattractively cut plain pink dress crumpled and actually damp from her tears. I wanted to make her take it off and to slip under the bed-clothes in her petticoat but somehow it seemed all wrong, in the circumstances, for Strafe's wife to do anything so intimate in my presence.

"I couldn't stop him," Cynthia said, the rims of her eyes crimson by now, her nose beginning to run again. "From half past ten till well after twelve. He had to talk to someone, he said."

I could sense that Strafe was thinking precisely the same as I was: that the red-haired man had insinuated himself into Cynthia's company by talking about himself and had then put a hand on her knee. Instead of simply standing up and going away Cynthia would have stayed where she was, embarrassed or tongue-tied, at any rate unable to cope. And when the moment came she would have turned hysterical. I could picture her screaming in the garden, running across the lawn to the hotel, and then the pandemonium in the hall. I could sense Strafe picturing that also.

"My God, it's terrible,' Cynthia said.

"I think she should sleep," I said quietly to Strafe. "Try to sleep, dear," I said to her, but she shook her head, tossing her jumble of hair about on the pillow.

"Milly's right,' Strafe urged. "You'll feel much better after a little rest. We'll bring you a cup of tea later on."

"My God!" she cried again. "My God, how could I sleep?"

I went away to borrow a couple of mild sleeping pills from Dekko, who is never without them, relying on the things too much in my opinion. He was tidying himself in his room, but found the pills immediately. Strangely enough, Dekko's always sound in a crisis.

I gave them to her with water and she took them without asking what they were. She was in a kind of daze, one moment making a fuss and weeping, the next just peering ahead of her, as if frightened. In a way she was like someone who'd just had a bad nightmare and hadn't yet completely returned to reality. I remarked as much to Strafe while we made our way down to lunch, and he said he quite agreed.

"Poor old Cynth!" Dekko said when we'd all ordered lobster bisque and entrecôte béarnaise. "Poor old sausage."

You could see that the little waitress, a new girl this year, was bubbling over with excitement; but Kitty, serving the other half of the dining-room, was grim, which was most unusual. Everyone was talking in hushed tones and when Dekko said, "Poor old Cynth!" a couple of heads were turned in our direction because he can never keep his voice down. The little vases of roses with which Mrs Malseed must have decorated each table before the fracas had occurred seemed strangely out of place in the atmosphere which had developed.

The waitress had just taken away our soup-plates when Mr Malseed hurried into the dining-room and came straight to our table. The lobster bisque surprisingly hadn't been quite up to scratch, and in passing I couldn't help wondering if the fuss had caused the kitchen to go to pieces also.

"I wonder if I might have a word, Major Strafe," Mr Malseed said, and Strafe rose at once and accompanied him from the dining-room. A total silence had fallen, everyone in the dining-room pretending to be intent on eating. I had an odd feeling that we had perhaps got it all wrong, that because we'd been out for our walk when it had happened all the other guests knew more of the details than Strafe and Dekko and I did. I began to wonder if poor Cynthia had been raped.

Afterwards Strafe told us what occurred in the Malseeds' office, how Mrs Malseed had been sitting there, slumped, as he put it, and how two policemen had questioned him . "Look, what on earth's all this about?" he had demanded rather sharply.

"It concerns this incident that's taken place, sir," one of the policemen explained in an unhurried voice. "On account of your wife ..."

"My wife's lying down. She must not be questioned or in any way disturbed."

"Ach, we'd never do that, sir."

Strafe does a good Co. Antrim brogue and in relating all this to us he couldn't resist making full use of it. The two policemen were in uniform and their natural slowness of intellect was rendered more noticeable by the lugubrious air the tragedy had inspired in the hotel. For tragedy was what it was: after talking to Cynthia for nearly two hours the lone man had walked down to the rocks and been drowned.

When Strafe finished speaking I placed my knife and fork together on my plate, unable to eat another mouthful. The facts appeared to be that the man, having left Cynthia by the magnolias, had clambered down the cliff to a place no one ever went to, on the other side of the hotel from the sands we had walked along to Ardbeag. No one had seen him except Cynthia, who from the cliff-top had apparently witnessed his battering by the treacherous waves. The tide had been coming in, but by the time old Arthur and Mr Malseed reached the rocks it had begun to turn, leaving behind it the fully dressed corpse. Mr Malseed's impression was that the man had lost his footing on the seaweed and accidentally stumbled into the depths, for the rocks were so slippery it was difficult to carry the corpse more than a matter of yards. But at least it had been placed out of view, while Mr Malseed hurried back to the hotel to telephone for assistance. He told Strafe that Cynthia had been most confused, insisting that the man had walked out among the rocks and then into the sea, knowing what he was doing.

Listening to it all, I no longer felt sorry for Cynthia. It was typical of her that she should so sillily have involved us in all this. Why on earth had she sat in the garden with a man of that kind instead of standing up and making a fuss the moment he'd begun to paw her? If she'd acted intelligently the whole unfortunate episode could clearly have been avoided. Since it hadn't, there was no point whatsoever in insisting that the man had committed suicide when at that distance no one could possibly be sure.

"It really does astonish me," I said at the lunch table, unable to prevent myself from breaking our unwritten rule. "Whatever came over her?"

"It can't be good for the hotel," Dekko commented, and I was glad to see Strafe giving him a little glance of irritation.

"It's hardly the point," I said coolly.

"What I meant was, hotels occasionally hush things like this up."

"Well, they haven't this time." It seemed an age since I had waited for them in Ardbeag, since we had been so happily laughing over the effect of Dekko's telegram. He'd included his address in it so that the girl could send a message back, and as we'd returned to the hotel along the seashore there'd been much speculation between the two men about the form this would take.

"I suppose what Cynthia's thinking," Strafe said, "is that after he'd tried something on with her he became depressed."

"Oh, but he could just as easily have lost his footing. He'd have been on edge anyway, worried in case she reported him."

"Dreadful kind of death," Dekko said. His tone suggested that that was that, that the subject should now be closed, and so it was.

After lunch we went to our rooms, as we always do at Glencorn Lodge, to rest for an hour. I took my slacks and blouse off, hoping that Strafe would knock on my door, but he didn't and of course that was understandable. Oddly enough I found myself thinking of Dekko, picturing his long form stretched out in the room called Hydrangea, his beaky face in profile on his pillow. The precise nature of Dekko's relationship with these girls he picks up has always privately intrigued me: was it really possible that somewhere in London there was a girl called Juliet who was prepared to marry him for his not inconsiderable money?

I slept and briefly dreamed. Thrive Major and Warrington P. J. were running the post office in Ardbeag, sending telegrams to everyone they could think of, including Dekko's friend Juliet. Cynthia had been found dead beside the magnolias and people were waiting for Hercule Poirot to arrive. "Promise me you didn't do it," I whispered to Strafe, but when Strafe replied it was to say that Cynthia's body reminded him of a bag of old chicken bones.

Strafe and Dekko and I met for tea in the tea-lounge. Strafe had looked in to see if Cynthia had woken, but apparently she hadn't. The police officers had left the hotel, Dekko said, because he'd noticed their car wasn't parked at the front any more. None of the three of us said, but I think we presumed, that the man's body had been removed from the rocks during the quietness of the afternoon. From where we sat I caught a glimpse of Mrs Malseed passing quite briskly through the hall, seeming almost herself again. Certainly our holiday would be affected, but it might not be totally ruined. All that remained to hope for was Cynthia's recovery, and then everyone could set about forgetting the unpleasantness. The nicest thing would be if a jolly young couple turned up and occupied the man's room, exorcising the incident, as newcomers would.

The family from France – the two little girls and their parents – were chattering away in the tea-lounge, and an elderly trio who'd arrived that morning were speaking in American accents. The honeymoon couple appeared, looking rather shy, and began to whisper and giggle in a corner. People who occupied the table next to ours in the dining-room, a Wing-Commander Orfell and his wife, from Guildford, nodded and smiled as they passed. Everyone was making an effort, and I knew it would help matters further if Cynthia felt up to a rubber or two before dinner. That life should continue as normally as possible was essential for Glencorn Lodge, the example already set by Mrs Malseed.

Because of our interrupted lunch I felt quite hungry, and the Malseeds pride themselves on their teas. The chef, Mr McBride, whom of course we've met, has the lightest touch I know with sponge cakes and little curranty scones. I was, in fact, buttering a scone when Strafe said, "Here she is."

And there indeed she was. By the look of her she had simply pushed herself off her bed and come straight down. Her pink dress was even more crumpled than it had been. She hadn't so much as run a comb through her hair, her face was puffy and unpowdered. For a moment I really thought she was walking in her sleep.

Strafe and Dekko stood up. "Feeling better, dear?" Strafe said, but she didn't answer.

"Sit down, Cynth," Dekko urged, pushing back a chair to make room for her.

"He told me a story I can never forget. I've dreamed about it all over again." Cynthia swayed in front of us, not even attempting to sit down. To tell the truth, she sounded inane.

"Story, dear?" Strafe enquired, humouring her.

She said it was the story of two children who had apparently ridden bicycles through the streets of Belfast, out into Co. Antrim. The bicycles were dilapidated, she said; she didn't know if they were stolen or not. She didn't know about the children's homes because the man hadn't spoken of them, but she claimed to know instinctively that they had ridden away from poverty and unhappiness. "From the clatter and the quarrelling," Cynthia said. "Two children who later fell in love."

"Horrid old dream," Strafe said. "Horrid for you, dear."

She shook her head, and then sat down. I poured another cup of tea. "I had the oddest dream myself," I said. "Thrive Major was running the post office in Ardbeag."

Strafe smiled and Dekko gave his laugh, but Cynthia didn't in any way acknowledge what I'd said.

"A fragile thing the girl was, with depths of mystery in her wide brown eyes. Red-haired of course he was himself, thin as a rake in those days. Glencorn Lodge was derelict then."

"You've had a bit of a shock, old thing," Dekko said.

Strafe agreed, kindly adding, "Look, dear, if the chap actually interfered with you ..."

"Why on earth should he do that?" Her voice was shrill in the tea-lounge, edged with a note of hysteria. I glanced at Strafe, who was frowning into his tea-cup. Dekko began to say something, but broke off before his meaning emerged. Rather more calmly Cynthia said, "It was summer when they came here. Honeysuckle he described. And mother of thyme. He didn't know the name of either."

No one attempted any kind of reply, not that it was necessary, for Cynthia just continued.

"At school there were the facts of geography and arithmetic. And the legends of scholars and of heroes, of Queen Maeve and Finn MacCool. There was the coming of St Patrick to a heathen people. History was full of kings and high-kings, and Silken Thomas and Wolfe Tone, the Flight of the Earls, the Siege of Limerick."

When Cynthia said that, it was impossible not to believe that the unfortunate events of the morning had touched her with some kind of madness. It seemed astonishing that she had walked into the tea-lounge without having combed her hair, and that she'd stood there swaying before sitting down, that out of the blue she had started on about two children. None of it made an iota of sense, and surely she could see that the nasty experience she'd suffered should not be dwelt upon? I offered her the plate of scones, hoping that if she began to eat she would stop talking, but she took no notice of my gesture.

"Look, dear," Strafe said, "there's not one of us who knows what you're talking about."

"I'm talking about a children's story, I'm talking about a girl and a boy who visited this place we visit also. He hadn't been here for years, but he returned last night, making one final effort to understand. And then he walked out into the sea."

She had taken a piece of her dress and was agitatedly crumpling it between the finger and thumb of her left hand. It was dreadful really, having her so grubby-looking. For some odd reason I suddenly thought of her cooking, how she wasn't in the least interested in it or in anything about the house. She certainly hadn't succeeded in making a home for Strafe.

"They rode those worn-out bicycles through a hot afternoon. Can you feel all that? A newly surfaced road, the snap of chippings beneath their tyres, the smell of tar? Dust from a passing car, the city they left behind?"

"Cynthia dear," I said, "drink your tea, and why not have a scone?"

"They swam and sunbathed on the beach you walked along today. They went to a spring for water. There were no magnolias then. There was no garden, no neat little cliff paths to the beach. Surely you can see it clearly?"

"No," Strafe said. "No, we really cannot, dear."

"This place that is an idyll for us was an idyll for them too: the trees, the ferns, the wild roses near the water spring, the very sea and sun they shared. There was a cottage lost in the middle of the woods: they sometimes looked for that. They played a game, a kind of hide and seek. People in a white farmhouse gave them milk."

For the second time I offered Cynthia the plate of scones and for the second time she pointedly ignored me. Her cup of tea hadn't been touched. Dekko took a scone and cheerfully said, "All's well that's over."

But Cynthia appeared to have drifted back into a daze, and I wondered again if it could really be possible that the experience had unhinged her. Unable to help myself, I saw her being led away from the hotel, helped into the back of a blue van, something like an ambulance. She was talking about the children again, how they had planned to marry and keep a sweetshop.

"Take it easy, dear,' Strafe said, which I followed up by suggesting for the second time that she should make an effort to drink her tea.

"Has it to do with the streets they came from? Or the history they learnt, he from his Christian Brothers, she from her nuns? History is unfinished in this island; long since it has come to a stop in Surrey."

Dekko said, and I really had to hand it to him, "Cynth, we have to put it behind us."

It didn't do any good. Cynthia just went rambling on, speaking again of the girl being taught by nuns, and the boy by Christian Brothers. She began to recite the history they might have learnt, the way she sometimes did when we were driving through an area that had historical connections. "Can you imagine," she embarrassingly asked, "our very favourite places bitter with disaffection, with plotting and revenge? Can you imagine the treacherous murder of Shane O'Neill the Proud?"

Dekko made a little sideways gesture of his head, politely marvelling. Strafe seemed about to say something, but changed his mind. Confusion ran through Irish history, Cynthia said, like convolvulus in a hedgerow. On May 24th, 1487, a boy of ten called Lambert Simnel, brought to Dublin by a priest from Oxford, was declared Edward VI of all England and Ireland, crowned with a golden circlet taken from a statue of the Virgin Mary. On May 24th, 1798, here in Antrim, Presbyterian farmers fought for a common cause with their Catholic labourers. She paused and looked at Strafe. Chaos and contradiction, she informed him, were hidden everywhere beneath nice-sounding names. "The Battle of the Yellow Ford," she suddenly chanted in a sing-song way that sounded thoroughly peculiar, "the Statutes of Kilkenny. The Battle of Glenmama, the Convention of Drumceat. The Act of Settlement, the Renunciation Act. The Act of Union, the Toleration Act. Just so much history it sounds like now, yet people starved or died while other people watched. A language was lost, a faith forbidden. Famine followed revolt, plantation followed that. But it was people who were struck into the soil of other people's land, not forests of new trees; and it was greed and treachery that spread as a disease among them all. No wonder unease clings to these shreds of history and shots ring out in answer to the mockery of drums. No wonder the air is nervy with suspicion."

There was an extremely awkward silence when she ceased to speak. Dekko nodded, doing his best to be companionable. Strafe nodded also. I simply examined the pattern of roses on our tea-time china, not knowing what else to do. Eventually Dekko said, "What an awful lot, you know, Cynth!"

"Cynthia's always been interested," Strafe said. "Always had a first-rate memory."

"Those children of the streets are part of the battles and the Acts," she went on, seeming quite unaware that her talk was literally almost crazy. "They're part of the blood that flowed around those nice-sounding names." She paused, and for a moment seemed disinclined to continue. Then she said, "The second time they came here the house was being rebuilt. There were concrete-mixers, and lorries drawn up on the grass, noise and scaffolding everywhere. They watched all through another afternoon and then they went their different ways: their childhood was over, lost with their idyll. He became a dockyard clerk. She went to London, to work in a betting shop."

"My dear," Strafe said very gently, "it's interesting, everything you say, but it really hardly concerns us."

"No, of course not." Quite emphatically Cynthia shook her head, appearing wholly to agree. "They were degenerate, awful creatures. They must have been."

"No one's saying that, my dear."

"Their story should have ended there, he in the docklands of Belfast, she recording bets. Their complicated childhood love should just have dissipated, as such love often does. But somehow nothing was as neat as that."

Dekko, in an effort to lighten the conversation, mentioned a boy called Gollsol who'd been at school with Strafe and himself, who'd formed a romantic attachment for the daughter of one of the groundsmen and had later actually married her. There was a silence for a moment, then Cynthia, without emotion, said, "You none of you care. You sit there not caring that two people are dead."

"Two people, Cynthia?" I said.

"For God's sake, I'm telling you!" she cried. "That girl was murdered in a room in Maida Vale."

Although there is something between Strafe and myself, I do try my best to be at peace about it. I go to church and take communion, and I know Strafe occasionally does too, though not as often as perhaps he might. Cynthia has no interest in that side of life, and it rankled with me now to hear her blaspheming so casually, and so casually speaking about death in Maida Vale on top of all this stuff about history and children. Strafe was shaking his head, clearly believing that Cynthia didn't know what she was talking about.

"Cynthia dear," I began, "are you sure you're not muddling something up here? You've been upset, you've had a nightmare: don't you think your imagination, or something you've been reading . . ."

"Bombs don't go off on their own. Death doesn't just happen to occur in Derry and Belfast, in London and Amsterdam and Dublin, in Berlin and Jerusalem. There are people who are murderers: that is what this children's story is about."

A silence fell, no one knowing what to say. It didn't matter of course because without any prompting Cynthia continued.

"We drink our gin with Angostura bitters, there's lamb or chicken Kiev. Old Kitty's kind to us in the dining-room and old Arthur in the hall. Flowers are everywhere, we have our special table."

"Please let us take you to your room now," Strafe begged, and as he spoke I reached out a hand in friendship and placed it on her arm. "Come on, old thing," Dekko said.

"The limbless are left on the streets, blood spatters the car-parks. *Brits Out* it says on a rockface, but we know it doesn't mean us."

I spoke quietly then, measuring my words, measuring the pause between each so that its effect might be registered. I felt the statement had to be made, whether it was my place to make it or not. I said, "You are very confused,

Cynthia."

The French family left the tea-lounge. The two Dalmatians, Charger and Snooze, ambled in and sniffed and went away again. Kitty came to clear the French family's tea things. I could hear her speaking to the honeymoon couple, saying the weather forecast was good.

"Cynthia," Strafe said, standing up, "we've been very patient with you but this is now becoming silly."

I nodded just a little. "I really think," I softly said, but Cynthia didn't permit me to go on.

"Someone told him about her. Someone mentioned her name, and he couldn't believe it. She sat alone in Maida Vale, putting together the mechanisms of her bombs: this girl who had laughed on the seashore, whom he had loved."

"Cynthia," Strafe began, but he wasn't permitted to continue either. Hopelessly, he just sat down again.

"Whenever he heard of bombs exploding he thought of her, and couldn't understand. He wept when he said that; her violence haunted him, he said. He couldn't work, he couldn't sleep at night. His mind filled up with images of her, their awkward childhood kisses, her fingers working neatly now. He saw her with a carrier-bag, hurrying it through a crowd, leaving it where it could cause most death. In front of the mouldering old house that had once been Glencorn Lodge they'd made a fire and cooked their food. They'd lain for ages on the grass. They'd cycled home to their city streets."

It suddenly dawned on me that Cynthia was knitting this whole fantasy out of nothing. It all worked backwards from the moment when she'd had the misfortune to witness the man's death in the sea. A few minutes before he'd been chatting quite normally to her, he'd probably even mentioned a holiday in his childhood and some girl there'd been: all of it would have been natural in the circumstances, possibly even the holiday had taken place at Glencorn. He'd said good-bye and then unfortunately he'd had his accident. Watching from the cliff edge, something had cracked in poor Cynthia's brain, she having always been a prey to melancholy. I suppose it must be hard having two sons who don't think much of you, and a marriage not offering you a great deal, bridge and holidays probably the best part of it. For some odd reason of her own she'd created her fantasy about a child turning into a terrorist. The violence of the man's death had clearly filled her imagination with Irish violence, so regularly seen on television. If we'd been on holiday in Suffolk I wondered how it would have seemed to the poor creature.

I could feel Strafe and Dekko beginning to put all that together also, beginning to realise that the whole story of the red-haired man and the girl was clearly Cynthia's invention. "Poor creature," I wanted to say, but did not do so.

"For months he searched for her, pushing his way among the people of London, the people who were her victims. When he found her she just looked at him, as if the past hadn't even existed. She didn't smile, as if incapable of smiling. He wanted to take her away, back to where they came from, but she didn't reply when he suggested that. Bitterness was like a disease in her, and when he left her he felt the bitterness in himself."

Again Strafe and Dekko nodded, and I could feel Strafe thinking that there really was no point in protesting further. All we could hope for was that the end of the saga was in sight.

"He remained in London, working on the railways. But in the same way as before he was haunted by the person she'd become, and the haunting was more awful now. He bought a gun from a man he'd been told about and kept it hidden in a shoe-box in his rented room. Now and again he took it out and looked at it, then put it back. He hated the violence that possessed her, yet he was full of it himself: he knew he couldn't betray her with anything but death. Humanity had left both of them when he visited her again in Maida Vale."

To my enormous relief and, I could feel, to Strafe's and Dekko's too, Mr and Mrs Malseed appeared beside us. Like his wife, Mr Malseed had considerably recovered. He spoke in an even voice, clearly wishing to dispose of the matter. It was just the diversion we needed.

"I must apologise, Mrs Strafe,' he said. "I cannot say how sorry we are that you were bothered by that man."

"My wife is still a little dicky," Strafe explained, "but after a decent night's rest I think we can say she'll be as right as rain again."

"I only wish, Mrs Strafe, you had made contact with my wife or myself when he first approached you." There was a spark of irritation in Mr Malseed's eyes, but his voice was still controlled. "I mean, the unpleasantness you suffered might just have been averted."

"Nothing would have been averted, Mr Malseed, and certainly not the horror we are left with. Can you see her as the girl she became, seated at a chipped white table, her wires and fuses spread around her? What were her thoughts in that room, Mr Malseed? What happens in the mind of anyone who wishes to destroy? In a back street he bought his gun for too much money. When did it first occur to him to kill her?"

"We really are a bit at sea," Mr Malseed replied without the slightest hesitation. He humoured Cynthia by displaying no surprise, by speaking very quietly.

"All I am saying, Mr Malseed, is that we should root our heads out of the sand and wonder about two people who are beyond the pale."

"My dear," Strafe said, "Mr Malseed is a busy man."

Still quietly, still perfectly in control of every intonation, without a single glance around the tea-lounge to ascertain where his guests' attention was, Mr Malseed said, "There is unrest here, Mrs Strafe, but we do our best to live with it."

"All I am saying is that perhaps there can be regret when two children end like this."

Mr Malseed did not reply. His wife did her best to smile away the awkwardness. Strafe murmured privately to Cynthia, no doubt beseeching her to come to her senses. Again I imagined a blue van drawn up in front of Glencorn Lodge, for it was quite understandable now that an imaginative woman should go mad, affected by the ugliness of death. The garbled speculation about the man and the girl, the jumble in the poor thing's mind – a children's story as she called it – all somehow hung together when you realised they didn't have to make any sense whatsoever.

"Murderers are beyond the pale, Mr Malseed, and England has always had its pales. The one in Ireland began in 1395."

"Dear," I said, "what has happened has nothing whatsoever to do with calling people murderers and placing them beyond some pale or other. You witnessed a most unpleasant accident, dear, and it's only to be expected that you've become just a little lost. The man had a chat with you when you were sitting by the magnolias and then the shock of seeing him slip on the seaweed …"

"He didn't slip on the seaweed," she suddenly screamed. "My God, he didn't slip on the seaweed."

Strafe closed his eyes. The other guests in the tea-lounge had fallen silent ages ago, openly listening. Arthur was standing near the door and was listening also. Kitty was waiting to clear away our tea things, but didn't like to because of what was happening.

"I must request you to take Mrs Strafe to her room, Major," Mr Malseed said. "And I must make it clear that we cannot tolerate further upset in Glencorn Lodge."

Strafe reached for her arm, but Cynthia took no notice.

"An Irish joke," she said, and then she stared at Mr and Mrs Malseed, her eyes passing over each feature of their faces. She stared at Dekko and Strafe, and last of all at me. She said eventually, "An Irish joke, an unbecoming tale: of course it can't be true. Ridiculous, that a man returned here. Ridiculous, that he walked again by the seashore and through the woods, hoping to understand where a woman's cruelty had come from."

"This talk is most offensive," Mr Malseed protested, his calmness slipping just a little. The ashen look that had earlier been in his face returned. I could see he was beside himself with rage. "You are trying to bring something to our doorstep which most certainly does not belong there."

"On your doorstep they talked about a sweetshop: Cadbury's bars and different-flavoured creams, nut-milk toffee, Aero and Crunchie."

"For God's sake pull yourself together," I clearly heard Strafe whispering, and Mrs Malseed attempted to smile. "Come along now, Mrs Strafe," she said, making a gesture. "Just to please us, dear. Kitty wants to clear away the dishes. Kitty!" she called out, endeavouring to bring matters down to earth.

Kitty crossed the lounge with her tray and gathered up the cups and saucers. The Malseeds, naturally still anxious, hovered. No one was surprised when Cynthia began all over again, by crazily asking Kitty what she thought of us.

"I think, dear," Mrs Malseed began, "Kitty's quite busy really."

"Stop this at once," Strafe quietly ordered.

"For fourteen years, Kitty, you've served us with food and cleared away the tea-cups we've drunk from. For fourteen years we've played our bridge and walked about the garden. We've gone for drives, we've bought our tweed, we've bathed as those children did."

"Stop it," Strafe said again, a little louder. Bewildered and getting red in the face, Kitty hastily bundled china on to her tray. I made a sign at Strafe because for some reason I felt that the end was really in sight. I wanted him to retain his patience, but what Cynthia said next was almost unbelievable.

"In Surrey we while away the time, we clip our hedges. On a bridge night there's coffee at nine o'clock, with macaroons or *petits fours*. Last thing of all we watch the late-night News, packing away our cards and scoring-pads, our sharpened pencils. There's been an incident in Armagh, one soldier's had his head shot off, another's run amok. Our lovely Glens of Antrim, we all four think, our coastal drives: we hope that nothing disturbs the peace. We think of Mr Malseed, still busy in Glencorn Lodge, and Mrs Malseed finishing her flower-plaques for the rooms of the completed annexe."

"Will you for God's sake shut up?" Strafe suddenly shouted. I could see him struggling with himself, but it didn't do any good. He called Cynthia a bloody spectacle, sitting there talking rubbish. I don't believe she even heard him.

"Through honey-tinted glasses we love you and we love your island, Kitty. We love the lilt of your racy history, we love your earls and heroes. Yet we made a sensible pale here once, as civilised people create a garden, pretty as a picture."

Strafe's outburst had been quite noisy and I could sense him being ashamed of it. He muttered that he was sorry, but Cynthia simply took advantage of his generosity, continuing about a pale.

"Beyond it lie the bleak untouchables, best kept as dots on the horizon, too terrible to contemplate. How can we be blamed if we make neither head nor tail of anything, Kitty, your past and your present, those battles and Acts of Parliament? We people of Surrey: how can we know? Yet I stupidly thought, you see, that the tragedy of two children could at least be understood. He didn't discover where her cruelty had come from because perhaps you never can: evil breeds evil in a mysterious way. That's the story the red-haired stranger passed on to me, the story you huddle away from."

Poor Strafe was pulling at Cynthia, pleading with her, still saying he was sorry.

"Mrs Strafe," Mr Malseed tried to say, but got no further. To my horror Cynthia abruptly pointed at me.

"That woman," she said, "is my husband's mistress, a fact I am supposed to be unaware of, Kitty."

"My God!" Strafe said.

"My husband is perverted in his sexual desires. His friend, who shared his schooldays, has never quite recovered from that time. I myself am a pathetic creature who has closed her eyes to a husband's infidelity and his mistress's viciousness. I am dragged into the days of Thrive Major and A. D. Cowley-Stubbs: mechanically I smile. I hardly exist, Kitty."

There was a most unpleasant silence, and then Strafe said, "None of that's true. For God's sake, Cynthia," he suddenly shouted, "go and rest yourself."

Cynthia shook her head and continued to address the waitress. She'd had a rest, she told her. "But it didn't do any good, Kitty, because hell has invaded the paradise of Glencorn, as so often it has invaded your island. And we, who have so often brought it, pretend it isn't there. Who cares about children made into murderers?"

Strafe shouted again. "You fleshless ugly bitch!" he cried. "You bloody old fool!" He was on his feet, trying to get her on to hers. The blood was thumping in his bronzed face, his eyes had a fury in them I'd never seen before. "Fleshless!" he shouted at her, not caring that so many people were listening. He closed his eyes in misery and in shame again, and I wanted to reach out and take his hand but of course I could not. You could see the Malseeds didn't blame him, you could see them thinking that everything was ruined for us. I wanted to shout at Cynthia too, to batter the silliness out of her, but of course I could not do that. I could feel the tears behind my eyes, and I couldn't help noticing that Dekko's hands were shaking. He's quite sensitive behind his joky manner, and had quite obviously taken to heart her statement that he had never recovered from his schooldays. Nor had it been pleasant, hearing myself described as vicious.

"No one cares," Cynthia said in the same unbalanced way, as if she hadn't just been called ugly and a bitch. "No one cares, and on our journey home we shall all four be silent. Yet is the truth about ourselves at least a beginning? Will we wonder in the end about the hell that frightens us?"

Strafe still looked wretched, his face deliberately turned away from us. Mrs Malseed gave a little sigh and raised the fingers of her left hand to her cheek, as if something tickled it. Her husband breathed heavily. Dekko seemed on the point of tears.

Cynthia stumbled off, leaving a silence behind her. Before it was broken I knew she was right when she said we would just go home, away from this country we had come to love. And I knew as well that neither here nor at home would she be led to a blue van that was not quite an ambulance. Strafe would stay with her because Strafe is made like that, honourable in his own particular way. I felt a pain where perhaps my heart is, and again I wanted to cry. Why couldn't it have been she who had gone down to the rocks and slipped on the seaweed or just walked into the sea, it didn't matter which? Her awful rigmarole hung about us as the last of the tea things were gathered up – the earls who'd fled, the famine and the people planted. The children were there too, grown up into murdering riff-raff.

● Discussion: background to the story

Read and discuss the following extracts from Robert Kee's *Ireland, a History*. It is unfortunate that most of us have some knowledge of tragic events in Ireland from TV, radio and newspapers, but little from history books.

'One thing a look at Irish history will not do is to provide a 'solution' to the problem of Northern Ireland. Only the people who live in Britain and Ireland can do that. History simply shows how the problem came to be what it is, and how the people came to be what they are. Other disciplines such as psychology, sociology, economics and even plain common sense may help but in the end human beings in society, as in their private lives, have to work things out for themselves. They have some choice in whether they change their lives or not.

Who in this case are 'they'? They are people to whom history has given different identities. Since the problem for them is how to live in harmony it may be useful in conclusion to sum up where their history has left them.

There are five principle categories involved. Firstly, and central to the problem, there are the Northern Protestants, a term which itself covers internal differences but who are generally united in this: that they do not want to share an Irish nationality with the rest of Ireland.

Secondly, there are the inhabitants of the rest of Ireland, predominantly Catholic, who live in a separate sovereign state within it.

Thirdly, there are the Catholic inhabitants of Ireland who do not live in that separate sovereign state but among the Northern Protestants in a society which these Protestants dominate.

Fourthly, there are those both there and in the rest of the island who wish to merge the Protestant-dominated society with the Irish sovereign state by violent, military means – the IRA.

Finally – a strange left-over of history – there is the British government.

The nature and extent of each group's involvement in the problem is different.' (p. 241)

● The significance of the title

Beyond the pale: intolerable, unacceptable. (*Chambers English Dictionary*)

English Pale: the district in Ireland within which alone the English had power for centuries after the invasion in 1172. (*Chambers English Dictionary*)

Pale: the name given to the part of Ireland colonised by the English and comprising portions of the counties of Louth, Dublin, Meath and Kildare. (*Pears Cyclopaedia*)

'Royal government shrank increasingly to a beleaguered, ineffectual thing, enclosed within a self-isolating defensive frontier of a few hundred square miles round Dublin known as "the Pale".

... The term "beyond the Pale" is still used to describe people whose behaviour cannot be coped with or controlled.' (Kee, *Ireland, a History*, p. 30)

● Spoken assignment: discussion

List the references in the story to 'the Pale' and discuss who is 'beyond the pale' in this story.

● Close study of the main characters

It is important to understand the main characters in this story, not because they are all very different, but because they are all very much alike. They are quite capable of deceiving themselves and others and just because one of them, Milly, acts as narrator does not mean that she is necessarily any more reliable than the others.

As you read the story a second time, compile a dossier on each of the four main visitors to the Glencorn Lodge Hotel. List the facts on each of them, as you discover them from the text.

For example, these are the main things we find out about Dekko:

real name Ralph Deakin
at school with Strafe,
has money,
enjoys bridge and fishing,

not married, but takes out younger women,

tall, gangling, always immaculately dressed, beaky face, mousy hair

with flecks of grey, rather a gormless laugh, often loud,

doesn't go in for saying what you want him to say,

always has mild sleeping pills with him,

sound in a crisis,

has never quite recovered from his schooldays.

However, it must be remembered that we only have this information from the narrator, Milly. Because she is a character in the story she may be unreliable and may not be the voice of William Trevor, the author. Discuss her contribution to the story in the light of this fact.

Milly says a number of important things – she is a commentator, and as narrator breaks the first rule she says exists in the group: 'as a kind of unwritten rule we never comment on one another'.

Here are some other things she says:

'Naturally we never discuss her [Cynthia's] shortcomings or in any way analyse the marriage. The unwritten rule that exists among the four of us seems to extend as far as that.'

'"I love you, dear," I whispered to him [Strafe] in the darkness, but just then he didn't wish to speak of love and referred instead to my body.'

'[Dekko] doesn't go in for saying what you want him to say.'

'[Cynthia] reads too much, I always think... it doesn't seem to worry her when no one listens.'

'"Dreadful kind of death," Dekko said. His tone suggested that that was that, that the subject should now be closed, and so it was.'

'... surely she could see that the nasty experience she'd suffered should not be dwelt upon? I offered her the plate of scones, hoping that if she began to eat she would stop talking, but she took no notice of my gesture.'

'No one cares, and on our journey home we shall all four be silent.'

● **Written assignment (literature): role play**

Choose your own title.

After you have compiled your dossiers on each of the characters and studied the implications of what Milly has said, put yourself in the place of one of the other characters and write your secret, unspoken thoughts about yourself and the others in your group. Remember Cynthia's final comment: 'Yet is the truth about ourselves at least a beginning? Will we wonder in the end about the hell that frightens us?'

● Written assignment (language and literature): newspaper reports

On page 242 is part of the front page of an imaginary newspaper. It refers to articles on other pages of the newspaper.

1. Write the feature article referred to in the news item that appears on the front page under the headline 'Tourists flock to Antrim coast'. Your article will be true to the facts in the story. Illustrate it, if possible, with sketches and facts. Consult hotel and holiday brochures to help you capture the style and language of such articles. Many of the free local newspapers have features written in a similar way, if holiday brochures are not available to you.

2. Create two additional front pages for later editions of *The Pale News*. The first is the one that comes out when the mysterious death at the Glencorn Lodge Hotel occurs. The second is the edition that comes out when the London connection becomes clear after investigation of Cynthia's claims about what the young man told her in his final conversation.

Remember that newspapers have a distinctive style of writing about events such as you have to report. The story as told by Cynthia will be your chief source of information.

Before you begin, discuss the headlines listed below and decide what kind of newspapers they might be found in: tabloid or broadsheet.

    'Suicide shocks seaside'

    'Local cliff death leap mystery'

    'Mysterious drowning at local beauty spot'

    'Drowned for love!'

    'Failed search leads to drowning'

    'Well out of it, we say!'

    'Beyond the pale, beyond the pool!'

THE PALE NEWS

NEWS AND FEATURES OF INTEREST TO ALL LOCALLY AND NATIONALLY

Tourists flock to Antrim coast.
Troubles do not deter, latest figures show.

'Hotels have faithful guests,'
says local hotelier.

Local hoteliers, the Malseeds, formerly of Surrey, report that the summer tourist season is likely to be as busy as ever. Their Glencorn Lodge Hotel near Ardbeag is already welcoming some of the many regulars who year after year return to the comfort of its rooms and the warmth of the traditional greetings extended by its staff.

Reasons for the success of local hotels like the Glencorn Lodge are not hard to find. They offer a security and a standard of service not found everywhere these days. They provide havens of rest for those who wish to relax in style, centres for those who wish to visit the many attractions in the area.

One party already ensconced in luxury at the Glencorn comes, by coincidence, from the Malseeds' own home town of Leatherhead in Surrey. Bridge is the passion of the foursome

who have returned to Antrim for their fourteenth visit. We feature this faithful group and the Glencorn Lodge Hotel in our travel section (pages 5 and 6). Our travel writer questions them and their hosts about their plans for this year.

The Glencorn has no need to advertise nationally for custom, as word of mouth spreads the good news.

Belfast troubles do not deter tourists, official figures show

Impressive figures released today show that over the last five years the so-called 'troubles' have had little effect on tourism. Those who wish to visit the province do so without fear of violence. The peace of the Antrim glens remains unbroken and tourists sleep peacefully in their beds, according to officials of the local tourist board.
Full story, page 7.

● **Written assignment (language and literature): theatre programme**

Imagine someone has turned this story into a stage play.

A theatre programme is required. Design one. It will contain the following information:

> a brief summary of the plot, without giving too much away,
>
> a cast list,
>
> character sketches of each of the main characters; details of their appearance and age,
>
> a cover and a back page appropriate to the story,
>
> details of the setting of the action,
>
> background information on the events in Northern Ireland over the last twenty years.

Artist's impressions of the characters may be used, or faces from magazines may be used where appropriate.

● **Discussion: the implications of statements**

Discuss the following quotations until there is general agreement as to their implications. Most of the statements are from the story; three are from Robert Kee's *Ireland, a History* and one is from *Chambers English Dictionary*.

1. 'We watched while Mr Malseed bade the lone man goodnight. The man didn't respond, but just sat gazing. It was ill-mannered, but this lack of courtesy didn't appear intentional: the man was clearly in a mood of some kind, miles away.'

2. 'The term "beyond the pale" is still used to describe people whose behaviour cannot be coped with or controlled.'

3. '... in the end human beings in society, as in their private lives, have to work things out for themselves. They have some choice in whether they change their lives or not.'

4. '"Cynthia likes to mooch ..." ... She reads too much... You often see her putting down a book with the most melancholy look in her eyes... and of course her habit of reading so much is often useful on our holidays: over the years she has read her way through dozens of Irish guide books. "That's where the garrison pushed the natives over the cliffs," she once remarked on a drive... There's hardly a

town or village we ever pass through that hasn't some significance for Cynthia, although I'm afraid her impressive fund of information doesn't always receive the attention it deserves.'

5. '"If she'd acted intelligently the whole unfortunate episode would clearly have been avoided."'

6. 'The nicest thing would be if a jolly young couple turned up and occupied the man's room, exorcising the incident, as newcomers would."'

7. '... they had ridden away from poverty and unhappiness. "From the clatter and the quarrelling," Cynthia said.'

8. '"A fragile thing the girl was, with depths of mystery in her wide brown eyes..."'

9. '"At school there were the facts of geography and arithmetic. And the legends of scholars and of heroes..."'

10. '"Has it to do with the streets they came from? Or the history they learnt...? History is unfinished in this island; long since it has come to a stop in Surrey."'

11. '"Bombs don't go off on their own. Death doesn't just happen to occur in Derry and Belfast, in London and Amsterdam and Dublin, in Berlin and Jerusalem. There are people who are murderers: that is what this children's story is about."'

12. '"The limbless are left on the streets, blood spatters the car-parks. *Brits Out* it says on a rockface, but we know it doesn't mean us."'

13. '"... we should root our heads out of the sand and wonder about two people who are beyond the pale."'

14. '"Murderers are beyond the pale, Mr Malseed, and England has always had its pales."'

15. 'They are people to whom history has given different identities.'

16. '*pale*, a stake of wood driven into the ground for fencing; anything that encloses or fences in; a limit; the limit of what can be accepted as decent or tolerable (*fig.*); an enclosure; a marked-off district...'

● Written assignment (literature): the author's viewpoint

Having discussed the quotations above and satisfied yourself as to their implications, try to describe William Trevor's viewpoint. What is it that he finds so objectionable in middle-class people like those in the story who visit Ireland?

● For the teacher: suggestions for additional assignments

Background to the story

If pupils have read Joan Lingard's books set in Northern Ireland e.g. *Across the Barricades*, or Peter Carter's book *Under Goliath* they will be in a good position to understand this story and the background.

Pupils could choose material from these works, from newspapers and other sources to create a page of background information to add to that quoted from Robert Kee's book.

The meaning of the title

Having discussed the references to the title, groups of pupils could create situations known to them and mime illustrations of what it means to be 'beyond the pale'. For example, bullying behaviour is unacceptable in schools, so a group could mime an incident, with the spectators deciding who in the group of actors is 'beyond the pale' and why.

Close study of the main characters

The compilation of dossiers on the four main characters could be given to the class split into groups, with each group taking one of the four. After they have finished work, one of the groups could be questioned by the rest of the class on the motivation and thoughts that affected the character's conduct and speech.

After this, pupils complete the written assignment set.

Newspaper reports and theatre programme

Instead of these being solo activities, they could be co-operative, group activities, in which the newspaper or programme is prepared in a format to be displayed for comparison and class discussion, if not for competition. This would make it more difficult to assess for examination purposes, though an additional feature could be a log-book or diary based on the reading of the story and the completion of tasks, solo and group.

Implications of statements

This is a difficult assignment. The quotations could be copied on to cards, shuffled and chosen unseen by members of a group. Each individual should then satisfy the group as to the meaning and implications of the chosen text, until the whole group have a clear idea as to what use can be made of the material in the final written assignment.

Further discussion could take place on the likely behaviour of the main characters on their return to England. In particular, how is Cynthia going to behave?

Flexible Learning and Supported Self-study

Many schools and colleges are developing strategies to provide pupils with different ways of learning, which are flexible and tailored to meet the needs of the National Curriculum.

The material in this book is suitable for the purpose and can be used by groups of pupils working within the classroom or outside it under contract or tutorial systems. Pupils can be briefed by teachers who specify the tasks to be undertaken, the constitution of the group, the time allocated, the tutorial arrangement and the expected outcomes in spoken or written work. Contracts similar to the sample below can be kept with the work produced and used in conjunction with records of achievement.

Name: .... Set: ....

Group Assignment

Task Set: ....
....
....

Place of Work: ....
....
....

Partners: ....
....
....

Start Date: .... Finish Date: ....
Tutorial: ....
....
....
....
....

Comments and Assessment of Work: ....
....
....
....
....
....
....

Pupil Signature: ....
Teacher Signature: ....

High standards of behaviour and responsibility are expected of all pupils undertaking these assignments

Acknowledgements

The authors and publisher would like to thank the following for permission to reproduce from copyright material.

My Sad Face by Heinrich Böll reprinted permission of Martin Secker and Warburg Ltd. **The Sound of Thunder** by Ray Bradbury reprinted by permission of Don Congdon Associates Inc. and Abner Stein. Copyright © 1952, renewed 1980 by Ray Bradbury. **The Landlady** by Roald Dahl reprinted from *Kiss Kiss* published by Michael Joseph and Penguin Books Ltd by permission of Murray Pollinger. **Reunion** by John Cheever, copyright © 1962 by John Cheever. **Great Uncle Crow** by H. E. Bates reprinted from *Seven by Five* (Michael Joseph Ltd) by permission of Laurence Pollinger Ltd. **Taddy the Lamplighter** by Bill Naughton reprinted by permission of the author. **More Than Just the Disease** by Bernard MacLaverty reprinted by permission of Collins Publishers. **War of the Worlds** by Ravinder Radhawa reprinted by permission of the author. **The Destructors** by Graham Greene reprinted from *Collected Stories* (William Heinemann Ltd and The Bodley Head Ltd) by permission of Laurence Pollinger Ltd. **The Personal Touch** by Chet Williamson reprinted by permission of the author and the author's agent, James Allen. **Uncle Ernest** by Alan Sillitoe © 1959, 1987. **Weekend** by Fay Weldon © Fay Weldon, 1981, *Watching Me, Watching You*, reproduced by permission of Hodder and Stoughton Limited. **The Test** by Angelica Gibbs reprinted from *Spectrum Two* by permission of the publisher, Longman Cheshire Pty Limited. **Beyond the Pale** by William Trevor reprinted by permission of the Peters Fraser and Dunlop Group Ltd.

Photo acknowledgements:
p. 7 Associated Press. p. 21 Greater London Photograph Library. p. 26 Chris Plowman: *Fiction City*, The Whitworth Art Gallery, University of Manchester. p. 43 Morris Hirshfield: *Jeune fille avec chat angora* (1944), Sidney Janis Gallery, New York © DACS 1991. p. 63 Norfolk Library and Information Service. p. 70 Sally and Richard Greenhill. p. 86 Michael Andrews: *Family in the Garden*, Colecçao de Centro de Arte Moderna/Fundaço Calouste Gulbenkian, Lisboa. p. 86 Nigel Luckhurst. p. 101 Barnaby's Picture Library. p. 137 Equipo Cronica; *Chronique ruale* (1973), by courtesy of Galerie Stadler, Paris. p. 148 Sally and Richard Greenhill. p. 161 Nevinson: *Returning to the Trenches*; The National Gallery of Canada, Ottawa. Gift of the Massey Foundation, 1946. p. 178 Tim Woodcock. p. 183 Paula Rego: *Polly Put the Kettle On*; The Whitworth Art Gallery, University of Manchester. p. 203 © Link/Orde Eliason. p. 219 Herbie Knott (1989): *The Independent*. p. 219 Courtesy of the Irish Tourist Board.

Every attempt has been made to locate holders of all material in this book. The publishers would be glad to hear from anyone whose copyright has been unwittingly infringed.